# Essential Behaviour Analysis

Also in the *Essential Psychology Series*

*Essential Health Psychology*
Mark Forshaw

*Essential Personality*
Donald C. Pennington

*Essential Biological Psychology*
G. Neil Martin

# Essential Behaviour Analysis

## Julian C. Leslie

University of Ulster, Northern Ireland

A member of the Hodder Headline Group
LONDON

Distributed in the United States of America by
Oxford University Press Inc., New York

First published in Great Britain in 2002 by
Arnold, a member of the Hodder Headline Group
338 Euston Road, London NW1 3BH

www.hodderheadline.co.uk

Distributed in the United States of America by
Oxford University Press Inc.,
198 Madison Avenue, New York, NY 10016

The advice and information in this book are believed to be true and
accurate at the date of going to press, but neither the author nor the publisher
can accept any legal responsibility or liability for any errors or omissions.

*British Library Cataloguing in Publication Data*
A catalogue record for this book is available from the British Library

*Library of Congress Cataloging-in-Publication Data*
A catalog record for this book is available from the Library of Congress

ISBN 0 340 76273 X (pb)

2 3 4 5 6 7 8 9 10

Typeset in 10 on 12 Sabon by Phoenix Photosetting, Chatham, Kent
Printed and bound by Replika Press Pvt. Ltd., India

What do you think about this book? Or any other Arnold title?
Please send your comments to feedback.arnold@hodder.co.uk

*'It is in the shelter of each other that the people live.'*
*(Irish proverb)*

For Rosanne, Eddie and Rowan, with love

# Contents

# Preface

This brief outline of behaviour analysis has been written because the basic ideas of the discipline do not currently seem to be available to many of those who study psychology. Although aimed at students in the broadest sense, this book does not provide a full course. Instead, quite a lot of space is devoted to 'setting the scene'. This is followed by a brief and selective presentation of basic principles and findings, followed by treatment of three areas that are of contemporary interest across psychology and the much wider field in which psychology can be applied.

Behaviour analysis has much to contribute and it is hoped that this book will enable more students of psychology to take advantage of what it offers. That will involve going beyond what is offered here, so this book should be seen as an invitation to begin to understand an exciting and developing field.

I always benefit a great deal from interactions with students, colleagues and friends in behaviour analysis. While working on this book, I have been particularly influenced by Mark O'Reilly, Eugene O'Hare, Dermot Barnes-Holmes and Geraldine Leader. I am grateful to them, but the manuscript is entirely my responsibility.

*Julian Leslie*
*June 2001*

# Acknowledgements

Thanks are due to the following authors and publishers for permission to reprint copyright material.

B.F. Skinner Foundation: Figure 3.6 from Skinner, B.F. (1938) *The Behavior of Organisms*, New York: Appleton-Century-Crofts; Figure 4.6 from Ferster, C.B. and Skinner, B.F. (1957) *Schedules of Reinforcement*, New York: Appleton-Century-Crofts.

Prentice Hall Inc.: Figure 4.2 from Azrin, N.H. and Holz, W.C. (1966) Punishment, in W.K. Honig (ed.), *Operant Behavior: Areas of Research and Application*, New York: Appleton-Century-Crofts.

Society for the Experimental Analysis of Behavior: Figure 4.4 from Azrin, N.H., Hutchinson, R.R. and Hake, D.F. (1966) Extinction-induced aggression, *Journal of the Experimental Analysis of Behavior* 9, 191–204; Figure 6.14 from Vollmer, T.R., Iwata, B.A., Zarcone, J.R., Smith, R.G. and Mazaleski, J.L. (1993) The role of attention in the treatment of attention-maintained self-injurious behavior: noncontingent reinforcement (NCR) and differential reinforcement of other behavior (DRO), *Journal of Applied Behavior Analysis* 26, 9–26; Figure 6.15 from France, K.G. and Hudson, S.M. (1990) Behavior management of infant sleep disturbance, *Journal of Applied Behavior Analysis* 23, 91–8. Figure 6.16 from Goh, H. and Iwata, B.A. (1994) Behavioral persistence and variability during extinction of self-injury maintained by escape, *Journal of Applied Behavior Analysis* 27, 173–4.

American Association for the Advancement of Science: Figure 4.5 from Gormezano, I., Schneiderman, N., Deaux, E.B. and Fuentes, I. (1962) Nictitating membrane: classical conditioning and extinction in the albino rabbit, *Science* 138, 33–4; Figure 6.13 from Neisworth, J.T. and Moore, F. (1972) Operant treatment of asthmatic responding with the parent as therapist, *Behavior Therapy* 3, 95–9.

American Psychological Association: Figure 4.12 from Bandura, A. (1965) Influence of model's reinforcement contingencies on the acquisition of imitative responses, *Journal of Personality and Social Psychology* 1, 589–95.

*Journal of Mental Deficiency Research*: Figure 6.10 from Deitz, S.M., Repp, A.C. and Deitz, D.E.D. (1976) Reducing inappropriate classroom behavior of retarded students through three procedures of differential reinforcement, *Journal of Mental Deficiency Research* 20, 155–70.

Paul H. Brookes Publishing Company: Figure 7.4 from Hart, B. and Risley, T.R. (1995) *Meaningful Differences in the Everyday Experience of Young American Children*, Baltimore: P.H. Brookes.

# 1
# Opening Statement

- The message
- Is this a credible theory of human psychology?
- Is that all there is to it?
- Summary

A man who had only ever read two books was asked which he liked best. 'Well,' he said, 'the story was better in *Robinson Crusoe*, but the dictionary explained all the words as it went along.'

Textbook writers always face the difficulty of interesting the reader in the story, or general message that they wish to convey, while using most of the space, and the reader's time, providing detailed explanations. In this book, the strategy used is to set out the main points of the story, or message, first and then go through more details in the remainder of the book.

The most important part of the story is a simple message, or explanatory principle, which will be stated and developed in this brief opening chapter. The rest of the book will provide the following: some historical background (because young sciences cannot ignore their history); evidence of the capacity of the explanatory principle of behaviour analysis to predict behaviour in experimental procedures; demonstrations of how phenomena of human psychology can be interpreted in its terms; examples of issues to which it can be applied; and discussion of how this message contrasts with those given, on apparently similar issues, by other contemporary approaches to psychology. A certain amount of space will be devoted to making clear what is not part of the message, and which implications it does not have. It is necessary to deal with these issues because, although the explanatory principle of behaviour analysis is simple, it has sometimes proved very hard for people, including some of those who are expert in other approaches to psychology, to grasp its key features.

## 1.1 THE MESSAGE

The message is that human psychology is a *biological science* in which the key process is one of *selection,* as is also the case in evolutionary biology. What is selected in the realm of psychology, however, are behavioural characteristics of the individual person (rather than characteristics within a population of a species). In a lifelong process, there is continual interaction between the current behavioural characteristics (usually called simply *behaviours*) of the individual and the prevailing *environment* of that person. At every stage, those behaviours that have particular *consequences* are selected and tend to become more frequent, or persistent, in the current environment, at the expense of alternative behaviours that become less frequent. This process of selection by consequences is usually called *operant conditioning.*

Because psychology is a biological science, we would expect to find a high degree of similarity between humans and other species in the ways in which operant conditioning works, and this turns out to be the case. While there are also important differences between humans and other species, the most striking finding has been the similarity of the effects of operant conditioning across a huge range of species of animals. This suggests that operant conditioning is an important adaptive mechanism that has been favoured by natural selection.

The behaviours that are affected by operant conditioning are *functionally defined.* This means that those actions of an individual that count as examples of one type (or class) of behaviour are those that have the same function for that individual. Let us consider two examples of classes of behaviour. In simple terms, 'shutting the door' is a class of behaviour. Because this class is functionally defined, different members of the class will not look the same as each other; we say that they have different topographies (this term is explained below). After all, I can shut a door with many different movements on different occasions, and sometimes different movements are required because of the shape and position of the door, or I can shut it by asking someone standing next to it to do that for me. Despite this variation in form of behaviour-class members, it is also true that the class members could be the same for many different individuals, if we were shutting the same doors. For a second class of behaviour, 'meeting a friend', the situation is more complicated again. One person's friends are different from those of another and thus the behaviour class will have different members for each individual. Given this complexity, even with apparently simple examples, how can we be justified in treating functionally defined classes of behaviour as our basic unit of analysis? This is a very important question, and later on I will show how this claim is supported by experimental findings. At this stage, where we are engaged in preliminary discussion and interpretation of behavioural and psychological phenomena, we can only give a verbal argument in its favour.

The key verbal argument is that classes of behaviour are defined by the consequences that they produce in the environment of the individual. This principle is embedded in a lot of the language we use to describe human behaviour and actions. Reverting to the two examples given above, door-shutting behaviour has occurred if the door is now clearly closed (half-hearted shoving, which leaves it ajar, is not an instance of that class of behaviour), and we have only succeeded in meeting a friend (no matter how long we waited at the railway station) if we are now in the presence of one of our favourite people. In both examples, then, we examine possible instances of the behaviour class to see whether they produce a particular consequence, and only include those examples which do produce that consequence or effect. Thus, we are clearly using functionally defined classes of behaviour. These examples are not unusual: we talk mostly of action-outcomes rather than patterns of bodily movements in describing behaviour. We are thus wedded to describing behaviour in terms of its consequences in the environment, and generally do this at the expense of describing bodily movements. Descriptions of bodily movements, which we will refer to as *topographically defined* classes of behaviour, are resorted to for particular reasons. These might include accounts of physical exercises (e.g., 'Lie flat on your back, and then raise both knees to your chest'), or for literary effect (e.g., 'He swung round, and his outstretched fist met his assailant's face'), but they are rare in everyday accounts of human interaction. As we talk to each other in our routine discourse, functionally defined behavioural classes are usually employed.

Our account of psychology is necessarily *interactive*; an account of the person, from a psychological perspective, can never be given without also providing an account of their environment. Along with other approaches to psychology, behaviour analysis uses the term 'environment' to mean those aspects of the physical world that are perceived by the individual and may have an influence on their behaviour (this is a different and more restricted meaning than that used, for example, in the physical sciences). Whether the members of a class of behaviour are the same or different for different individuals, class members can never be defined except with reference to the environment. We must specify *stimulus classes* as part of the process of specifying the behaviour class.

As with classes of behaviour, stimulus classes are also functionally defined. To take our two examples, what are doors and who are my friends? Well, doors are those objects that through being opened provide access to enclosed spaces, and my friends are those people with whom I have a previous history of positive social interactions or, in less formal language, those with whom I have had a good time in the past. These provisional definitions are functional ones, because they refer to the functions that objects or other people, respectively, have in relation to the behaviour class that is being defined. Note also that there are two stimulus classes that generally participate in the definition of each functionally defined class of behaviour. The first of these is the situation, or *context*, in which the behaviour occurs; the second of these is the outcome, or *consequence*, that the behaviour has. In the first example, the context is 'being at a door' and the important consequence, as previously noted, is the successful closure of the door. In the second example, of meeting a friend, possible contexts might be highly diverse but it is clear that they will be functionally rather than topographically defined. That is, there is nothing about the physical location or physical features of a place (these would be topographic features) which make it likely that friends may be met there. Instead, meeting places for friends are either socially and culturally defined (they may meet in places where such meetings are common, perhaps a public space such as a railway station or a restaurant), or they are defined by the history of interaction of those two people (they may meet in places with which they are both familiar). In each case, the context is defined by the function it has for the participants.

The classes of stimuli that act as effective consequences that maintain or change behaviour are also functionally defined. In the case of the door-closing example, the possible functions are familiar but not fixed. That is, we know why we want doors to be closed, but the reason (function) is not always the same. Closing the door may shut out unwanted noise or cold air, it may keep in heat, or it may make the enclosed space more useful for conversation or other social interaction. When we meet a friend, this may have consequences with many different functions. We may receive friendly smiles and gestures or verbal approval, anxiety that arises from loneliness may be reduced, or many subtle but personally important other events may ensue. It is important to recognize that the consequences that are effective in such cases are not only functionally defined, but are also specific to that particular interaction between people. What 'works' in that encounter depends on the *history of interaction* between the people involved. We can say that they have learnt to treat each other in particular ways (although they may not be entirely conscious of how they behave towards each other) and these patterns of behaviour now contribute substantially to maintaining the relationship between them. An important point to note here is that the behaviour of each of them supplies the context and the consequences for the behaviour of the other. This is an important fact about human psychology; many of the important stimuli or environmental events for one person arise from the behaviour of other people. What behaviour analysis adds to this insight is the notion that the particular histories of interactions between people modify the stimulus functions they each have for each other. In other words, what people do for each other, and the reasons why they spend time with each other, depend a great deal on what has happened when they have been together previously.

From this perspective, the psychology of an individual consists primarily of an account of those functionally defined behavioural characteristics that occur in the environments typically encountered by that individual. A person, if you like, is primarily to be understood as 'what he or she does' and that account of their behaviour cannot, as we have already seen, be described without also describing the location or occasion of those behaviours and the important consequences of those behaviours. There are thus three components to our basic unit of analysis – the context, the behaviour and the consequence – and each of these is functionally defined with respect to the other two. This triumvirate is often called the *three-term relationship of operant conditioning*.

From the perspective of behaviour analysis, the key process of psychological change is operant conditioning, whereby *those behaviours that are functionally effective* for the individual *become more frequent* (in the corresponding environment) while *other behaviours decline in frequency*. To return to our two examples, we would speculate (if we had no direct evidence) that we have learnt to shut doors in the following sense. We have varied the action used on many occasions when shutting familiar, and sometimes less familiar, doors, and those actions that have had the effect (or consequence) of actually shutting the doors in question have become more frequent when similar situations have subsequently been encountered. At the same time, failing efforts – actions that were not effective in shutting doors – have become less frequent and are now seldom seen. Thus, our history of interaction with the environment (in this case, an aspect of the physical environment) has selected a functional class of behaviour. In the case of meeting friends, there may have been a history of the following kind. We have, over a period of time, made various sorts of arrangements to meet friends; some of these have been followed by successful encounters, while this has not happened in other cases. When meetings have occurred, we have interacted with the friends involved in a variety of ways. Across this more complex set of contexts, behaviours and consequences, those choices that have led in the past to successful social encounters are likely to determine how we behave currently. That is, we will propose meeting places that have been successful in the past, and when the meetings occur we will behave in the ways that have led to desirable consequences on previous occasions. Again, it is our history of interaction with the environment (in this case, aspects of the social environment) that has selected a functional class of behaviour.

It is important to note that behaviour (either shutting a door or meeting a friend, in the two examples used) is not said to be caused by either the individual or the environment. Rather it is the history of interaction between the behavioural repertoire of the individual (that is, the whole range of behaviours shown by the person) and the environment that selects, and in a sense causes, the behaviour. Another important point is that as the history of interaction changes, so the behaviour will change. If the next few doors encountered are of a different design than those encountered earlier, then the class of door-closing behaviours will change. Similarly, if well-tried strategies for meeting friends become ineffective, then that behaviour class will also change. That is likely to happen, for example, if the person concerned goes to live in a different culture.

## 1.2 IS THIS A CREDIBLE THEORY OF HUMAN PSYCHOLOGY?

Because the behaviour analysis approach is rooted in biological and experimental science, our first steps in providing empirical support for it, beginning in Chapter 3, will be to show how experimental techniques have been developed with non-human animal species, and to present data that show how operant conditioning effectively changes behaviour in those species. Only findings of empirical research – as opposed to the interpretations of the hypothetical examples given above – should be used as evidence in support of a theoretical position in science. As will be explained in Chapter 2, early researchers in psychology were keen to see whether they could devise ways of studying learning in animals under controlled laboratory conditions that might provide pointers to important processes in human psychology. In this aspiration they were following explicit suggestions from Charles Darwin, published in the 1870s.

Darwin's theory of evolution through natural selection revolutionized the science of biology in the nineteenth century, but it also provided a new impetus to the faltering start that had been made in developing a scientific approach to psychology. Darwin asserted that there was continuity between all species, in that all current species were historically linked to common ancestors, and he suggested that similar psychological processes might be thus be found across animal species.

It was in the development of operant conditioning techniques in the mid-twentieth century that this prediction became a scientific and practical reality. These experimental methods have revealed that the interaction between the behavioural repertoire and the environment proceeds in a similar fashion, and thus throws up similar behavioural phenomena, across a remarkably wide range of animal species, including human beings.

Having established that operant conditioning has a role to play in the analysis of behaviour of many species, researchers in behaviour analysis have also addressed issues that are germane to humane psychology *per se*. These include:

- demonstrations that behavioural phenomena seen under the more highly controlled experimental conditions possible with other species can also be replicated in human psychology
- use of experimental techniques, usually with non-human animal species, to investigate behavioural neuroscience, and thus begin to understand the links between behavioural processes and brain processes
- development of intervention techniques, based on behavioural principles established through laboratory experiments, to alleviate human and social problems
- analysis of those aspects of human psychology, namely language and cognition, that seem not to be common to other species.

All these issues will be reviewed in later chapters of this book, to give the reader a flavour of the behavioural approach to the whole of psychology and thus to enable its overall credibility to be assessed. This brief opening chapter highlights the distinctive conceptual framework that behaviour analysis uses because other contemporary approaches to psychology do not share it. While they do attempt a scientific analysis of human psychology, they presume that internal mechanisms (e.g., cognitions) must be used to explain psychological processes. As will be explained in Chapter 7, this has the unintended but unfortunate consequence of blurring the distinction between scientific accounts of human psychology and informal or commonsensical ones. In the latter type of account, the individual is seen as having free will, or personal autonomy, and human behaviour moves out of the realm of those issues that can successfully be analysed scientifically.

Whether approached through behaviour analysis or through the cognitive psychology that is currently popular, it must be recognized that scientific psychology is a young discipline grappling with a complex subject matter. Consequently, the student, scientist or general reader must anticipate that the 'answers' available at the moment can only provide a partial account of the whole field. From the perspective of behaviour analysis, scientific psychology is seen as building out and up from the behavioural phenomena that have been reliably established in the experimental analysis of behaviour, largely with non-human animals in the first instance. While it has sometimes been possible to apply the principles that have been established to complex human behavioural problems with remarkable success (see Chapter 6), there are many areas where the empirical work has yet to be done.

Until recently, not much had been achieved in the behavioural analysis of language and cognition, and this led to scepticism among psychologists that this science-based account had the potential to provide a complete account of human psychology. However, research over the last 20 years has completely transformed the situation. Studies of stimulus equivalence and relational learning (introduced in Chapter 7) have shown how a behavioural account of language and cognition will be provided by an extension of well-established principles of behaviour analysis.

The extension of behaviour analysis, outlined in Chapter 7, begins to include an account of aspects of 'mental life' or 'thinking'. Introductory texts on psychology usually begin by stating that psychology seeks to provide a scientific account of human behaviour and mental life. That is our objective here, too, but from the perspective of behaviour analysis the problem takes on a different shape.

Other contemporary psychological theories, usually called cognitive approaches, retain the common-sense view that there is a causal sequence of perception → thought → action. That is, the individual perceives the environment, this causes some mental processes to occur including 'deciding what to do', and these mental processes in turn cause some action or behaviour.

A number of problems arise from this view, however obvious and attractive it seems. Some of the problems concern the requirements of scientific methods. Science requires that terms or concepts be defined, and that ways be found for measuring them. While we can make measurements of the environment, and we can also observe and measure behaviour, the same cannot be said about the concepts of 'perception' and 'decision-making' (and other mental events) if these are defined as events that occur 'in the head' and cause behaviour. These are necessarily unobservable entities, the existence of which can only be inferred from those data we can observe, namely environmental events and human behaviour. Given this, it is not surprising that cognitive psychology is a discipline with many different theories that compete to explain similar phenomena of human psychology. Given certain 'inputs' (the environmental events) and 'outputs' (aspects of behaviour), it is obvious that many different theoretical systems can be postulated to link the two via a number of intervening, unobservable, entities. While collection of further relevant data (e.g., relations between additional environmental events and behavioural changes) may allow us to eliminate some theories of cognition in favour of others, many possible theories may remain.

Neuroscientists are currently making rapid progress in developing techniques that allow them to observe events occurring in the brain, which occur while the postulated events of perception and decision-making are taking place. These are valuable and very exciting new observations. However, the neural phenomena that take place turn out to be very complex (for example, they involve many aspects of the brain simultaneously) and do not correspond directly to any of the relatively simple cognitive theories that have been proposed. Consequently, they do not help us to distinguish easily between competing cognitive theories; rather, they prompt us to ask what the cognitive theories are for.

From the perspective of behaviour analysis, the theories of cognitive psychology are doomed to fail and are thus a distraction, or a blind alley, arising from a mistaken assumption about necessary features of psychological explanation. The mistake is to assume that behaviour (what someone does) is necessarily caused by cognition (what that person thinks). Behaviour analysis instead states that both overt (visible) behaviour and the other apparently 'private' aspects of human psychology arise from interaction with the environment. As Chapter 7 explains, this provides a perspective on central aspects of human psychology that is very different from the common-sense or cognitive-psychological one.

Among other changes in perspective, the approach of behaviour analysis disposes with the problems that arise from the 'thought must precede behaviour' principle. We are all aware that, on the one hand, we often arrive at a decision then take the corresponding action but, on the other hand, we sometimes arrive at a decision but never take the action or, again, we take an action but have recollection of deliberating over it. All these relationships between the thought and the deed are dealt with readily within behaviour analysis, where both are seen as aspects of behaviour.

Consider a question often studied by social psychologists: 'What is the relationship between attitudes (a type of cognition) and behaviour?' This is an issue with practical implications for politicians who wonder whether those people who have expressed a positive view of their policies will actually vote for them, or will they vote for another party which they supported in the last election? Much social-psychological research has shown that, while attitudes and behaviour are linked, there is not a one-to-one causal relation between them. For example, changes in behaviour may lag behind changes in attitude. This contradicts a simple 'attitudes cause behaviour' theory, but it is easy to incorporate within a behavioural approach which regards 'the behaviour of expressing an attitude' and the 'voting behaviour' of the same person as linked but non-identical aspects of that person. Both these behaviours may change as a result of the person's experience of the world – their interactions with their social environment – but not necessarily at the same rate.

Behaviour analysis has sometimes been said to ignore, or regard as unimportant, the brain and the neural events that occur in parallel with human or animal behaviour. Such statements are completely incorrect. Behaviour analysis and neuroscience come together in the discipline of behavioural neuroscience, and some of the basics of this discipline are outlined in Chapter 5. Incorrect statements have been made about behaviour analysis because it denies that cognitions cause behaviour, as explained above, and has thus questioned the value of postulating or inventing cognitions.

Neural events occur in parallel with behavioural ones. As there is a continual 'stream' of both types of event – complex brain events go on all the time and we are always behaving, even when we are sleeping – thus every action has 'neural correlates' occurring simultaneously with it, and other neural events precede it. However, from the perspective of behaviour analysis these two streams of events do not cause each other in any important sense, and there certainly is not 'one-way causation' of behavioural events by neural ones. Rather, they are both aspects of the activity of the individual, which are changed through interaction with the environment. Because behavioural and neural processes are linked, when behaviour changes – through interaction with the environment – the brain changes as well. Examples of this effect will be given in Chapter 5.

## 1.3 IS THAT ALL THERE IS TO IT?

That is, is an understanding of the process of operant conditioning all that is required to account for human psychology? No. There is certainly more to it than that. As will be outlined in Chapter 7, operant conditioning has been extended through providing an account of relational human learning, and has begun to deal with the issues that have been of central concern to cognitive psychology. None the less, operant conditioning cannot provide a complete account of psychology from a behavioural perspective, even in principle.

The selection process of operant conditioning is the most important part of the account of psychology provided by behaviour analysis, because it encompasses the lifelong interaction between the behavioural repertoire of the individual and his or her environment, but it can only provide part of a complete behavioural account of human psychology. To return to the formal analogy with evolutionary biology, there must be some *variation* in a characteristic if selection is to operate (at the level of populations or of individuals), and there must be means of *retention* of changes. We now know, although Darwin did not, that genetic material provides both the potential for variation in a characteristic in the members of a species and the means by which selected characteristics are transmitted from one generation to the next. Although Darwin did not know what the mechanism was, he realized that variation and retention were essential parts of the system that, together with natural selection, generated adaptation of the population characteristics to the prevailing environment. Along with our account of operant conditioning, we must identify the mechanisms of *variation* in behaviour and *retention* of behavioural changes that are part and parcel of the selection process of operant conditioning.

Operant conditioning is the process by which those behaviours that are effective are selected and become more frequent than other forms of behaviour. This will not happen, however, unless the individual's behaviour in the context of interest shows some variation. While it is easily observed that behaviour, whether human or of another species, always shows at least some variation from occasion to occasion, a further important general task for behaviour analysis is to identify the sources of variation. Some of these are integral to operant conditioning. As will be explained in Chapter 2, there are ways in which operant conditioning generates behavioural variation as well as increasing the frequency of functionally effective responses. There also a number of other ways in which human behaviour is varied, and new or additional behaviour occurs. These include other types of conditioning such as *classical conditioning*, originally investigated by Ivan Pavlov, modelling, and verbal instruction. As will be explained in Chapter 3, Pavlov's study of classical conditioning, a learning process that is different from operant conditioning, was a crucial event in the history of psychology and behaviour analysis. The process identified by Pavlov is one of the ways that behavioural variation occurs, because the outcome of classical conditioning is that new behaviour, or conditioned responses, occur in the presence of stimuli that did not previously produce that behaviour.

A more dramatic source of variation in human behaviour occurs with *modelling*, a type of observational learning. Humans show a very strong tendency to imitate each others' behaviour, and the basics of this behavioural process will be outlined in Chapter 4. This process, which is particularly effective with children, makes a huge contribution to variation in behaviour: showing someone how to do something is frequently the quickest way to get them to do it, particularly if they have never done that particular behaviour before. Finally, *verbal instruction*, discussed in Chapter 7, is another source of behavioural variation: we do many things simply because we are told to, or because the consequences of the action are explained to us. Verbal instruction is, of course, a behavioural process that is not seen in any meaningful way with any other species. (Despite much effort by researchers, little evidence has yet been found of language-like activities in other animals, even primates such as chimpanzees or cetaceans such as dolphins.)

The changes in behavioural repertoire that are brought about through interaction with the environment must be retained. At one level, this simply means that there have been changes to the behavioural repertoire, and the next time the same or a similar environment is encountered the behaviour that is shown will reflect the learning or behaviour change that occurred on previous occasions. General findings in behaviour analysis are that such changes are not readily 'forgotten' over quite long periods of time, and that behaviour learnt in one context generalizes to other contexts to the extent that the contexts are functionally similar for the person concerned. That is, if a person encounters an environment that is similar 'for them', they will tend to show the same behaviour as on the previous occasion. Other questions, however, can be addressed at the interface between behaviour analysis and behavioural neuroscience. What are the neurological processes that are critical if learnt behaviour is to be retained over time, and how are these affected by drugs known to affect psychological processes, or by neuropathological changes such as, for example, those characteristic of Alzheimer's disease? Rapid developments in behavioural neuroscience are enabling us to start to answer these multidisciplinary questions, and some information on these issues is given in Chapter 5.

## 1.4 SUMMARY

The purpose of this chapter is to outline some of the story that is spelt out in the rest of the book, and to emphasize the main message. This message is that in a lifelong process there is continuous interaction between behaviour and the prevailing environment, and this process of selection changes human behaviour over time.

This process of selection by consequences is called operant conditioning, and consists of a three-term relationship between the context, the behaviour and its consequences. All these terms are functionally defined, and this corresponds well to the ways we talk informally about human behaviour. From the perspective of behaviour analysis, human psychology provides an account of what the person does through reference to their history of interaction with the environment. Over a period of time, that interaction causes their behaviour to change, often to a very great degree.

Subsequent chapters will introduce behaviour analysis more systematically, present the basic principles of behaviour analysis, outline some more advanced principles that are required to deal with the richness and complexity of human psychology, and then introduce behavioural neuroscience, the applications of behaviour analysis to human behavioural problems, and the behavioural account of language and cognition. The overall aim of these chapters is to provide a brief introduction to the behavioural account of all of psychology.

It is important to realize that the conceptual framework offered by behaviour analysis differs from the more common-sense one provided by cognitive psychology. From the perspective of behaviour analysis, both overt behaviour and more private behaviour, such as thinking, are influenced by their consequences. This is a radically different view which, while it deals with some philosophical problems attached to the common-sense view, must be justified by its effectiveness in dealing with the subject matter of psychology. The reader can begin to assess that effectiveness by examining the contents of the rest of this book.

Operant conditioning is a process of selection of behaviour of the individual through the interaction of behaviour with the environment. Along with a selection process, there must also be means by which behaviour shows variation, and means for the retention of behavioural changes. These processes are also introduced later in the book. Means of variation of behaviour include classical conditioning, modelling and verbal instruction. Retention of behavioural changes can be analysed both behaviourally and at the level of the correlated neural changes.

## Study questions for Chapter 1

To aid the reader's cumulative understanding of the behavioural approach to psychology, a small number of questions, or exercises for further study and consideration, will be provided at the end of each chapter.

This opening chapter is concerned only with general issues about how to develop a scientific approach to psychology. As indicated, it is important to discuss these issues, but in the end it will be corroboration from empirical findings that determines the success of the behaviour analysis approach. Consequently, the rest of this book is concerned mainly with outlining some of those empirical findings.

A major theme of this opening chapter, which deals with theoretical or philosophical issues, is that *thought does not cause action*. Instead, behaviour analysts believe that these are both aspects of a person's behaviour – of what they do – and are to be understood as arising through their interaction with their environment.

Assuming for the moment that this is true, and that thought does not cause action, consider the following two questions.

1. If thoughts are a type of behaviour, it should be possible to change the frequency of classes of thoughts using operant conditioning techniques. Try to devise a method to alter some of your own thoughts.

2. We are resistant to the idea that thought does not cause action, because subjectively we experience thought causing action! How can this be?

*Now check your answers with my suggestions in the 'Possible answers to study questions' section, see page 219.*

# 2
# An Introduction to Behaviour Analysis

- A scientific approach to behaviour
- Early attempts to explain human behaviour
- The conceptual framework of behaviourism
- 'Selectionism' and B.F. Skinner's account of the experimental analysis of behaviour
- Other aspects of Skinner's approach to psychology
- Applied behavioural analysis and functional analysis
- Analysis of language and cognition
- Summary

This chapter begins with a brief review of how psychology has developed as a science from its origins in philosophy and how various conceptual frameworks have been proposed. The behaviourism proposed by J.B. Watson in the early twentieth century is then outlined, and it is explained that this was a radical and disturbing agenda, but one that found favour because of the lack of progress and inherent subjectivism of early scientific mentalism. The next section explains how Skinner took the approach forward, both conceptually, by using a principle of selection, and methodologically in various ways that led to the studies now called the experimental analysis of behaviour. Skinner's broader views are outlined and some familiar myths about them are disposed of. The overarching notion of functional analysis is introduced (this is a theme that will be returned to several times). Finally, it is indicated how behaviour analysis can embrace those issues in human psychology (language and cognition) that have been seen as problematic in the past.

## 2.1 A SCIENTIFIC APPROACH TO BEHAVIOUR

Acceptance of the view that a scientific account of the world around us is possible and effective is now widespread, but this is a relatively recent development. It is not long, from an historical point of view, since the time when having a view of the universe that did not place 'man' (as human beings were described) at its centre was heretical. The power of the Church made this a dangerous view to hold, and Galileo (1564–1642) was prosecuted in the seventeenth century for publishing the view that the earth may go round the sun. Now, it is widely known that the earth is but one of the smaller planets orbiting a star that is one of around 100 billion ($10^{11}$) in a galaxy, which in turn is one of perhaps $10^{11}$ galaxies in the universe.

Even more recently (about 150 years ago), Charles Darwin's (1809–82) account of the origin of species, including human beings, was received with horror because it appeared to further undermine our uniqueness and importance. He claimed that all species – including the human species – evolve through natural selection rather than being immutable, and that all current species have gradually evolved from a smaller number of common ancestors. Although he was vilified and derided for these views, much evidence in support of them has since been collected and all contemporary biology is placed in the context of Darwinism.

Although we have come to accept that human beings are not at the centre of the universe, and that our creation was not a unique event but part of a process that created all livings things on earth, there is still resistance to the notion that a scientific analysis is possible for psychological processes. Perhaps this is because these are the aspects of ourselves that seem most private and important. None the less, moves towards such scientific analysis began around the time of Galileo and have been gathering pace. Some of the earlier developments are briefly outlined in the next section.

## 2.2 EARLY ATTEMPTS TO EXPLAIN HUMAN BEHAVIOUR

As with many other topics, there were some developments in ideas about psychology well before the seventeenth century, and these occurred in classical philosophy. By 325 BC, in ancient Greece, Aristotle had combined observation and interpretation into a naturalistic, if primitive, account of behaviour. Aristotle was concerned with explaining the various activities of an individual by showing these to be specific instances of general 'qualities', such as appetite, passion, reason and will. The observations and classifications of Aristotle and the Greek investigators who followed him represented a substantial beginning in a naturalistic attempt to understand the causes of human and animal behaviour. However, these steps towards a scientific approach ceased with the demise of Hellenic civilization. In the western world, the early Christian era and the Middle Ages produced an intellectual climate poorly suited to observation and investigation: in the conceptual framework of that period, the causation of human behaviour was entirely attributed to the soul, but the soul was regarded as non-material, in-substantial and super-natural.

The *dualistic* (or two-system) doctrine which developed at that time stated that there was no direct connection between soul and body, and that each inhabited a separate realm. By locating the causes of behaviour in the unobservable realm of the spirit or soul, dualism inhibited a naturalistic study of behaviour, and for a very long time no interest was taken in an empirical or observational approach to behaviour. Not until the seventeenth century was further progress towards the development of a science of behaviour made in the work of René Descartes (1596–1650), the French philosopher and mathematician. Although Descartes produced one of the clearest statements of the dualistic position and asserted that voluntary behaviour was under the control of the soul or mind of the individual, he also advanced behavioural science by suggesting that bodily movement might be the result of mechanical, rather than supernatural, causes.

Descartes imagined that animals and human beings might be a kind of complex machine, perhaps constructed with hydraulic control systems. He suggested that animal spirits – a sort of intangible, invisible, elastic substance – might flow in the nerves in such a way as to enter the muscles, thereby causing them to expand and contract, and in turn make the limbs move. Furthermore, he believed that external events might activate this mechanism and thus cause bodily movements. However, Descartes' willingness to view human behaviour as determined by external events was only partial. He confined his mechanical hypotheses to certain 'involuntary' activities and supposed the rest to be governed by the soul, located in the brain. Indeed, he thought that the soul guided even the mechanisms of those involuntary activities.

In spite of this dualism, and in spite of his choice of a hydraulic principle, Descartes' formulation represented an advance over earlier thinking about behaviour. The theory of the body as a specific kind of machine was one that was *testable by observation and experiment*. This property of 'testability' was conspicuously lacking in the mediaeval explanations that preceded Descartes. In re-establishing the idea that at least some of the causes of animal and human behaviour might be found in the observable environment, Descartes laid the philosophical foundations that would eventually lead to an experimental approach to behaviour.

Between 1750 and 1900 there were many investigations in experimental physiology of reflexes. Physiologists discovered that many specific environmental events, or *stimuli*, produced specific behavioural changes, or *responses*, in the way that Descartes had suggested. At the same time, nerve action became understood as an electrical system, and the older hydraulic or mechanical models were discarded. By the end of the nineteenth century, Sir Charles Sherrington, an English physiologist, could summarize the principles of reflex behaviour in quantitative *stimulus-response laws*. These laws relate the speed, magnitude and probability of the reflex response to the intensity, frequency and other measurable properties of the stimulus.

By 1900 there could be no doubt that reflexive behaviour was a suitable subject for scientific analysis and that analysis was well advanced. However, reflexes accounted for only a small proportion of the behaviour of human beings and so-called 'higher animals', and it had yet to be established that the remainder of behaviour could be subjected to the same sort of analysis. The next important development came just before the beginning of the twentieth century when Ivan Pavlov (1849–1936), a Russian physiologist, was carrying out experiments on the digestive secretions of dogs. He noticed that while the introduction of food or acid into the mouth resulted in a flow of saliva, the mere appearance of the experimenter bringing food would also elicit a similar flow. He called these reactions 'conditional reflexes', because they depended, or were conditional, upon some previous events in the life of the animal. Pavlov's unique contribution was to show experimentally how *conditioned reflexes* (an early translation from the Russian rendered 'conditional' as 'conditioned', and this has become the normal expression) came to be acquired, how they could be removed (or extinguished), and what range of stimuli was effective in their production. Pavlov (1927) devised a general law of conditioning: after repeated presentation of two stimuli at overlapping times, the one that occurs first comes eventually to elicit (that is, produce automatically) the response that is normally elicited by the second stimulus. Pavlov's realization that he was investigating phenomena that might be of general significance, his development of sound experimental techniques and, above all, his careful collection of a body of systematically related experimental findings over a period of more than 30 years, mean that he was a great scientist. We now call the conditioning process he investigated *classical conditioning*, because it was the type of conditioning that was investigated earliest, and research has continued over the 100 years since his original studies.

Pavlov's work showed how 'new' reflexes could be acquired to supplement those 'built in' reflexes that the organism possesses prior to any appreciable experience of the world. As such, it represents the culmination of Descartes' mechanistic view of reflex behaviour. However, it appeared that only those responses that form part of an existing reflex (such as the salivation produced by the stimulus, dry-food-in-the-mouth) can become conditioned reflexes, and thus much non-reflexive behaviour still remained to be scientifically analysed. This behaviour comes into the category traditionally described as voluntary, or under the control of the will, and it is just this category that Descartes assigned to the control of an unobservable soul. Descartes' manoeuvre only postponed a scientific inquiry, however, because we are now faced with the difficult problem of describing the relations between the soul, which we cannot observe, and patterns of behaviour, which we do observe.

The view that voluntary human behaviour was not a suitable subject for scientific study came under attack in 1859. In that year, Charles Darwin proposed his theory of evolution, holding that human beings are members of the animal kingdom, and that differences between humans, and other animals are quantitative and matters of degree. Darwin's theory derived support from the many careful observations that he had made of fossils, and the structure of flora and fauna living in isolated areas of the earth. In addition, he had investigated the behaviour by which animals adapted to their environments. Darwin's interest in behaviour, however, was based on what it could reveal about mind. Thus, the demonstration of complexity and variety in adaptive behaviour of animals in relation to their changing environments seemed to prove that they, like human beings, must also think, have ideas and feel desires. Eventually, Darwin was to be criticized for his anthropomorphism – that is, for trying to explain animal behaviour in terms of mentalistic concepts generally used to account for human behaviour. But few thought at the time to raise the far more radical question, 'Do traditional mentalistic concepts (thoughts, ideas, desires) have explanatory value for human behaviour, or are they part of the behaviour that needs to be explained?'

Darwin did not conduct experiments on animal behaviour, but in 1898 Edward L. Thorndike (1874–1949), of Columbia University in the USA, published the results of a number of laboratory studies of 'problem-solving behaviour' in kittens, dogs and chicks. His methods departed radically from those of the casual observers who had preceded him. The behaviour studied was escape from a confining enclosure, or puzzle box, and the acts – such as pulling a string, moving a latch, pressing a lever or prising open a lock – were chosen for their convenience and reliability of observation. Since any of these responses could be arranged to be instrumental in producing escape from the box, Thorndike (1898) classed them as *instrumental behaviour*. A common feature of all his experiments was that, as a result of experience in the experiment, the behaviour of each animal that took part was systematically changed.

Thorndike noticed that when animals were first put into the puzzle box, they made many diffuse struggling responses. Eventually, one of these responses would happen to operate the escape mechanism and the door would open, permitting the animal to escape from the box and to obtain a small quantity of food. Thorndike observed that the behaviour which first let the animal out was only one of many that the animal made in the situation. Yet, as the animal was repeatedly exposed to the situation, it came to make fewer and fewer superfluous responses before making the 'correct' response. Eventually, it made practically none apart from the successful responses.

Thorndike concluded from his experimental findings that the successful past results, consequences or *effects* of behaviour must be an important influence in determining the animal's present behavioural tendencies. Consequently, Thorndike called this ability of the past effects of behaviour to modify the behaviour patterns of the animal the *law of effect*. It survives today as a fundamental principle of the analysis of adaptive behaviour. In brief modern form, the law of effect states that if a response, or class of behaviour, is reliably followed by an important consequence (such as food for a hungry organism), that response will become more frequent.

The importance of Thorndike's formulation of the law of effect for the development of behavioural analysis lies in its generality. Unlike Pavlov's laws of the conditioned reflex, the law of effect was readily applied to those responses usually regarded as voluntary. Indeed, it is more applicable to that type of behaviour than to reflexive behaviour, which is relatively insensitive to its consequences or effects.

## 2.3 THE CONCEPTUAL FRAMEWORK OF BEHAVIOURISM

Until a scientific discipline is well established, it is not clear what its conceptual framework will be. What happens in the early stages is that the conceptual framework is actively debated, and those 'findings' that are produced are interpreted in different ways by adherents to different conceptual frameworks. The quotation marks are used here because, in the absence of agreement about what is to be investigated and how those investigations may proceed, there are not really any findings in the sense generally understood in science. That is, a scientific finding can only be understood and interpreted once the 'rules' for that particular science are known.

As we have seen, by 1900 systematic investigations of behaviour were being carried out in various fields, although the field called 'psychology' at that time was seen as a science of mental contents, mental processes and mental acts. From the results of the investigations of nineteenth-century psychologists, inferences were made about the mental processes that were presumed to be crucially involved. In some of the studies that were carried out at that time, associations of ideas were inferred from the learning of nonsense syllables, or identical sensations were inferred from observations of behaviour when a human experimental participant matched two different environmental objects in different contexts (for example, two samples of grey paper under different conditions of illumination), or speed of the mental process was inferred from an individual's reaction time. Given these uses of behavioural procedures, and the influence of Darwin discussed earlier, it was perhaps not surprising that when Thorndike – who was trained in nineteenth-century psychology – designed his study of problem-solving, he chose animals to participate in the experiments. If the behaviour of human organisms could lead to inferences about mental processes, why not the behaviour of animals? Furthermore, as Pavlov's and Thorndike's work revealed, the study of animal behaviour may allow specific research questions to be addressed more precisely through the use of carefully controlled experiments.

Despite Thorndike's innovations, the man who did the most to clarify the relationship between behaviour and psychology was John B. Watson (1878–1958). The earliest work of this American psychologist was concerned with the sense-modalities that the rat uses in learning to find its way through a maze. As Watson carried on his animal studies, he came to be more and more disturbed by the prevailing view that behaviour possessed significance only as it shed light on mental or conscious processes. It occurred to Watson that the data of behaviour were valuable in their own right and that the traditional problems of psychology, such as imagery, sensation, feeling and association of ideas, could all be studied by strictly behavioural methods.

In 1913, Watson published a now classic paper defining psychology as the science of behaviour, and naming this new psychology 'behaviourism'. Watson argued in this paper that the study of behaviour could achieve an independent status within science. The goal of such a science could be the prediction and control of the behaviour of all animals, and no special preference need be given to human beings. The *behaviourist*, claimed Watson, need relate his studies of rats and cats to human behaviour no more (nor less) than the zoologist need relate his dissections of frogs and earthworms to human anatomy. With this doctrine, Watson was attacking the 'homocentric' (human-centred) theory of human importance in the behavioural world just as much as Copernicus, a predecessor of Galileo, had attacked the 'geocentric' (earth-centred) theory of the universe, 400 years earlier. Watson's main theme was that psychology must be objective – that is, it must have a subject matter which, like that of the other sciences, remains independent of the observer. Up until that time, psychology had attempted to take as its subject matter self-observation of mental processes, but this strategy lacks an independent observer located outside of the system being considered. Watson realized that this meant that conflicts about the contents of consciousness could not be resolved, even in principle. There were no grounds for preferring one person's report over another's. This, he argued, made that approach inherently unscientific, but the problem could be resolved if behaviour itself was treated as the primary subject matter of psychology. If we take 'behaviour' to include only those human or animal activities that are, in principle, observable, then any statement about behaviour made by one observer or experimenter can be verified by another person repeating the observations.

Watson's programme for the new science of behaviour was far-reaching and, for its time, remarkably sophisticated. It had the following important features.

- There was insistence on behaviour as an independent subject matter of a science aimed at the prediction and control of behaviour itself.
- Relatedly, behaviour was not regarded as only an indication of some other unobservable psychological states.
- There was a stress on a detailed analysis of the environment and behaviour into stimuli and responses.

- Reducing the environment and behaviour to these simple elements was seen to be crucial as the way to eventual understanding of complex patterns of behaviour.

Watson's programme laid the basis for more modern viewpoints that are explained in all the later chapters of this book.

## 2.4 'SELECTIONISM' AND B.F. SKINNER'S ACCOUNT OF THE EXPERIMENTAL ANALYSIS OF BEHAVIOUR

Thorndike's early experiments on animal behaviour and Watson's definition of a science of behaviour established the potential value of experimental research with animals. However, relatively little had been discovered at that early stage. In Pavlov's principle of conditioned reflexes, Watson thought he saw an explanatory mechanism for the many complex and subtle adjustments that adult organisms, including humans, make to their environments. But the attempt to force *all* behaviour into the reflex mould was to prove unsuccessful, and Watson failed to appreciate the significance of Thorndike's law of effect. Further progress was slow until another American, B.F. Skinner (1904–90), made a number of innovations.

In a series of papers beginning in 1930, Skinner proposed an account of how behaviour is changed through interaction with the environment, which arose out of observations made on single organisms responding in a carefully controlled and highly standardized artificial experimental situation (see Skinner, 1938, for the classic statement of his approach). Skinner called his approach the *experimental analysis of behaviour*. Skinner's chosen organism was the white rat, a laboratory animal that had also been studied by Watson and others, but his apparatus consisted of an enclosure or box containing a small metal bar, or lever, which, if depressed by the rat, resulted in the delivery of a small pellet of food to a cup located directly under the lever. This apparatus can be called an operant test chamber, but has come to be known as the 'Skinner box'. A typical version of the apparatus, and details of how it is used, are explained in the next chapter. What is important here is to explain the conceptual scheme that Skinner developed, based on the results obtained with this simple, and in many ways strange, experimental procedure.

One key idea of Skinner's, and one shared with his predecessors Pavlov, Thorndike and Watson, was that the class of behaviour being investigated was arbitrary. That is, a particular action was not being investigated because it was of importance in its itself. Rather, it was being investigated in the hope that it might reveal *behavioural processes* (that is, the ways in which behaviour and the environment characteristically interact) which transcend the specific features of the experiment. Furthermore, Skinner saw the necessity for making available a sensitive and reliable measure; some quantitative aspect of behaviour which could vary over a wide range and enter into consistent and orderly relationships with past and present aspects of the environment. He found that the frequency of occurrence of the lever-press response in a Skinner box during a given interval of time, the *response rate*, satisfied these conditions, and this was a major step towards an analysis of how behaviour is modified by many aspects of the environment.

Skinner's approach to the study of behaviour differed in a number ways from those of both his predecessors and his contemporaries. As a fundamental proposition, he held that a science of behaviour could be what he called descriptive or functional – that is, it could aim to discover relationships or correlations between measurable variables. He maintained that the identification of such *functional relationships* between aspects of behaviour (the dependent variables) and parameters of the environment (the independent variables) should be the goal of a science of behaviour. Skinner also argued that the investigations must be systematic, in that the relationships obtained should be linked by a common thread. By confining his observations to the ways in which a single dependent variable, response rate (the rate, or frequency in time, of an arbitrary piece of behaviour), changed with varied environmental conditions, Skinner kept his own early work highly systematic (Skinner, 1938). However, he and many other subsequent investigators have also found that many aspects of the basic Skinner box experiment can be varied without changing the results of the experimental procedures. We will see in the next chapter that Skinner boxes have been used with many species other than rats, making many different responses, and provided with a variety of consequences. Despite these changes, the same behavioural processes are revealed in the experiments.

What are these behavioural processes? Well, many of them will be introduced in the next chapter, but a number of them are aspects of what Skinner called *operant conditioning*. A more formal account will be given later, but the key feature of operant conditioning is that when it is arranged that occurrences of a particular class of behaviour are followed by certain consequences, then that class of behaviour will increase in frequency. Skinner called such classes of behaviour *operants*, because they generally operate upon the environment to change it, and he gave the name *reinforcing stimuli* to those consequences that will produce operant conditioning. Skinner's principle of operant conditioning in part simply restates Thorndike's law of effect, but in restating it he removed some mentalistic terminology (which was not used in the modern version of Thorndike's law given earlier), and he made it clear that it was a descriptive principle of selection in which the terms are functionally defined. We will briefly consider all aspects of this statement, because they are all crucial to understanding the ways in which the field of behaviour analysis has developed.

# A descriptive principle

Although Skinner devised very simple experimental environments in which to study operant conditioning, this was done in order to isolate *a process that goes on all the time*. Consider an analogy with the principle of gravity. If several objects of known mass are dropped in a vacuum tube, we may observe the time it takes them to fall various distances, note that these times do not vary with the mass of the object, and compute that the objects all accelerate at a fixed rate. Armed with this information about the operation of gravity as an isolated process, we can then interpret the movements of bodies in the real world in terms of the force of gravity upon them. Similarly, in ways that will be explained in the next chapter, we can see the effects of operant conditioning on behaviour under experimental conditions. This leads us to expect to see the operation of this principle in the highly complex social world of humans (and the somewhat simpler environments of non-human animals) outside the laboratory. In both cases, a process (gravity or operant conditioning) that can be studied in the laboratory is believed to be everywhere around us in the natural world. The physicists or psychologists are beginning to describe and explain processes that existed before scientists attempted any investigation of them. The principle of operant conditioning is thus a formal statement which describes a process that can be isolated in the laboratory, but that takes place all the time in the interaction between the behaviour of people and their environments.

# A process of selection

What goes on in operant conditioning is that, over time, certain classes of behaviour become more frequent. This happens because of an interaction with the environment, and we can say that those classes of behaviour have been *selected through* that process of *interaction*. A necessary corollary of this is that other classes of behaviour will have become less frequent over the same period of time. As mentioned in Chapter 1, there is an analogy here with the process of evolution by natural selection. The difference is that in the case of operant conditioning we are describing a process that takes within the lifetime of the individual (and also much shorter periods of time) and has the effect of modifying the repertoire of behaviour shown by the individual, whereas natural selection takes place over many generations of a species and has the effect of modifying the distribution of characteristics across members of a species. A similarity with natural selection is that it is important to remember that the outcome of operant conditioning – the pattern or type of behaviour eventually shown – will entirely depend on the interaction between the behaviour the individuals starts off with (the pre-existing behavioural repertoire) and the environments encountered. It makes no sense to try to attribute the changes in behaviour solely to the environment. Another similarity with natural selection is that the process never ends. Behaviour that is currently frequent, because of the operation of operant conditioning processes up until now, will decline if subsequent interactions with the environment no longer lead to favourable outcomes. Similarly, natural selection means that if there are changes in the environment of the species, characteristics of the species that may have been highly probable for a long time may subsequently decline because they are no longer adaptive. Another similarity between operant conditioning and evolution by natural selection is that the process has no built-in 'goal'. Over the course of a lifetime, the behaviour of an individual is successively modified through interaction with the many environments encountered. This may mean that socially useful behaviour at one stage of the life of an individual (e.g., community service) is eventually replaced by undesirable behaviour (e.g., drug abuse), or the opposite sequence may occur. Similarly, species are not evolving towards any particular end; they are just evolving because of the interaction with the environment.

## Functionally defined terms

Operant conditioning occurs when members of a class of behaviour (lever pressing by a laboratory rat in Skinner's original studies) are followed on occasion by a reinforcing stimulus (small pieces of food when the rat was hungry, in those studies). The phrase 'lever pressing', rather like 'door closing', which was discussed in Chapter 1, is one of many in everyday language in which behaviour is described by the effect it has on the environment of the organism (laboratory rat or person, in our two examples). Furthermore, as mentioned above, Skinner embodied this aspect in the term 'operant': an operant is a class of behaviour defined by the effect it has on the environment, and thus by the function it has for the individual. As we shall see throughout this volume, this way of organizing our account of psychology has huge benefits. When we are describing simple laboratory studies of non-human animal behaviour, using a functional definition of a class of behaviour seems merely to be convenient shorthand, but when we examine complex human behaviour the value is considerable. Thus, in the case of 'lever pressing' we use this term instead of describing a range of forms, or topographies, of behaviour, many of which would be 'paw movements', that might lead to the operation of the lever in the Skinner box. In the case of the human action of 'door closing', however, it is not possible to replace the functional definition with a topographical one. That is, we cannot give even a general statement, or list, of all the topographies that behaviour might take which leads to the door being closed in everyday human environments (to take an extreme example, you may recall from Chapter 1 that one way of closing the door is to ask someone else to do it instead). However, we readily recognize an instance of 'door closing' when it occurs, because the door in question is now shut! Furthermore, we are familiar with many more subtle descriptions of behaviour in which the functional class is modified somewhat, such as 'he slams doors when he is angry', or 'she never shuts that door properly'. Interestingly, the functional nature of ordinary language was recognized by one of Skinner's contemporaries, E.R. Guthrie (1886–1959), who also contributed to the development of the behavioural approach in the mid-twentieth century. Guthrie wrote that:

> Common speech defines acts in terms of their results, not in terms of the movements by which those results are accomplished. We eat a dinner, sail a boat, ride a horse, play a selection on the piano. For each of these acts there may be a thousand different patterns of muscular contraction in the details of the achievement, and the act may still be known by the same name (1940: 127–8).

So far, we have only indicated that functionally defined classes of behaviour are a major and familiar feature of talk about behaviour, but a major goal of the present book is to show *through experiments* how functionally defined classes of behaviour can be useful in providing an account of psychological processes.

In the approach originated by Skinner, stimulus classes are also functionally defined. This is true both of those constituting the context in which the behaviour of interest occurs and those that act as reinforcing stimuli that modify the frequency with which the behaviour occurs in that context. Let us first consider the context. Lever pressing by a laboratory rat in Skinner's original studies occurred in the context of a Skinner box, but we must distinguish carefully between the Skinner box as a physical object and the Skinner box as a member of a functional stimulus class. We could do this, in an experiment, by varying a number of aspects, or dimensions, of the apparatus. Only if this variation produces a change in the lever-pressing behaviour would we conclude that the dimension varied is part of the functional stimulus class for that behaviour. For example, we might vary the size of the box and find that this change tends to disrupt lever pressing, but vary the colour of the interior walls of the box and find that this had no effect on the behaviour. Thus, of two simple physical dimensions of the apparatus one affects behaviour and is a part of the functional stimulus class, and the other does not and thus is not. To take an everyday human example, you may work each day on a computer with a keyboard and a screen. It might turn out to be the case that changing the colour of the keyboard and the screen surround has no effect on your typing speed, but that changing the size of the screen does alter your typing speed. We would similarly conclude that one dimension of the apparatus was important psychologically, and featured in the functional stimulus class, while the other did not.

A similar analysis applies to the definition of reinforcing stimuli. In Skinner's original studies, lever pressing by a hungry laboratory rat was followed by small pieces of food. This had the effect of increasing the frequency of lever pressing in the Skinner box. We could again show, through experiments, that the 'food' is a member of a functionally defined stimulus class. For example, we might substitute one type of food with a physically very different one (we might replace pieces of biscuit with pieces of cheese, for example) and find that this made little difference, and that 'lever-pressing-for-food' continued at much the same rate. This would show that these different objects are both members of a class that will act as reinforcing stimuli in this context. On the other hand, if we changed the conditions so that the rat was no longer hungry, the same object (e.g., a piece of biscuit) would not act as a reinforcing stimulus, or reinforcer. As with functionally defined classes of behaviour, a major goal of the present book is to show through experiments how functionally defined classes of stimuli can also be useful – and are indeed essential – in providing an account of psychological processes.

The value of the approach adopted by contemporary 'behaviourists' as they are often termed, or 'behaviour analysts' as they describe themselves (because this term captures the emphasis on experimental methods), should be assessed in terms of the progress they have made towards establishing a coherent and useful account of human psychology. However, other psychologists make many objections to the strategies adopted by behaviour analysts and it will be useful to review these when the issues come up. In fact, those issues that are the greatest sources of disagreement and confusion have already been outlined twice – in Chapter 1 and again in the last few paragraphs – and some of the objections will be discussed here.

It is often said by cognitive psychologists (but also by specialists in other areas of psychology, and in allied disciplines such as neuroscience or physiology) that behaviour analysts maintain that the environment acts directly upon behaviour, and that this must be a mistaken assumption. They believe that this is mistaken because, in their view, the individual may selectively attend to only certain aspects of the stimulus and will then actively process the information that has been received before deciding what action to take. However, the mistake here lies with the cognitive psychologist who fails to distinguish between two meanings of 'environment'. These are on the one hand the environment as an array of physical events or objects and, on the other, the environment as a set of elements of functional stimulus classes. It is only the latter that, on a behavioural account, enters into direct relationships with behaviour. The behavioural approach deals, albeit in a different way from that of cognitive psychology, with the phenomena of both 'attention' and 'information processing'. Consider, yet again, the example of Skinner's original studies: lever pressing by a hungry laboratory rat was followed by small pieces of food, and this had the effect of increasing the frequency of lever pressing in the Skinner box. When the rat encountered the Skinner box part way through such an experiment, only certain dimensions of that physical environment entered into the functional stimulus class that provided the context for lever pressing (only some features were attended to), and a high rate of lever pressing occurred because of the previous history of this behaviour being followed by reinforcing stimuli in this context. This last statement attributes the current behaviour of the organism to its history in this and related situations, rather than to an invisible information-processing mechanism. It is thus a different type of explanation than that offered by a cognitive psychologist, but it is important to realize that both behavioural and cognitive accounts address a central issue that is often missed by non-psychologists: *the environment is never the same for two different people.* On the behavioural account the environment inevitably differs because each individual has a different history of interactions with their environment and thus has different functional stimulus classes; while, on the cognitive account, each person processes the information differently (presumably because each individual has a different history of interactions with their environment).

## 2.5 OTHER ASPECTS OF SKINNER'S APPROACH TO PSYCHOLOGY

B.F. Skinner wrote about his approach to psychology for around 60 years. The present volume will examine how the approach he devised – now called behaviour analysis[1] – copes with central aspects of psychology. Consequently, subsequent chapters will set out carefully the basic principles of behaviour analysis as established through laboratory experiments, how they can be extended to deal with human language and cognition, how they can be used to help us understand brain functions, and how they can be applied outside the laboratory to psychological and social problems. In his long career, Skinner turned his attention to many other issues as well. In this he emulated his predecessor, J.B. Watson, because both sought to show how they could deal with issues across a broad sphere, as well as those that are central to psychology.

Skinner termed his approach, or philosophy, *radical behaviourism*, to distinguish it from other related approaches. 'Radical' here means 'thorough-going', and is used denote an approach that seeks to explain behavioural phenomena using scientific methods but without recourse to other levels or types of explanation. Throughout the twentieth century, and continuing into the twenty-first, there have been a number of alternative approaches to the explanation of psychological phenomena, all of which do appeal to other levels

---

1. This approach will be given the name 'behaviour analysis' throughout this book. The alternative, 'behavioural analysis', is more correct from a grammatical point of view, but 'behaviour analysis' has become the more widely used term by scientists and practitioners.

or types of explanation. These include medical accounts in which psychological problems are said to be caused by underlying malfunctions of the central nervous system, psychodynamic accounts in which psychological problems are thought to be caused by unconscious psychic conflicts, and traditional mentalism or contemporary cognitive psychology where psychological phenomena are said to be caused by unobserved mental or cognitive events.

Skinner repeatedly pointed out that all these approaches share the potentially fatal flaw of trying to explain the observed with the unobserved. In adopting such a strategy, they risk breaching the rules of scientific method. Indeed, in his view they were generally not scientific in the methods they used, and thus their conclusions need not be taken seriously. He stated this view clearly and often, and thus attracted a continuing hostile response from many practitioners of those other approaches who wished to defend their various disciplines. Rather than reviewing any of those acrimonious debates, we will briefly set out here the main features of the argument.

What behaviour analysis seeks to do is to establish the conditions under which psychological phenomena occur. What experience is necessary, for example, for reading skills to be enhanced, or alternatively for a phobia of dental treatment to develop? Such issues have been investigated mainly through programmes of experiments designed to show when the behaviour in question will and will not occur. Once such a programme is complete, the behaviour has been explained from the perspective of behaviour analysis: we now know 'where the behaviour comes from'. Proponents of various other approaches object that even when such programmes of experiments have been successfully completed, only part of the interesting question has been addressed. For example, a proponent of the medical model would say that we also need to know what changes in the central nervous system underlie the behaviour seen, while a psychoanalyst would want to know what unconscious processes were involved, and a cognitive psychologist would wish to identify the cognitive processes that mediated the behaviour observed.

It is important to realize that any phenomenon can be understood on various levels, and the phenomenon of human behaviour is clearly the concern of political science, economics, sociology, neurology, molecular biology and genetics, as well as of psychology. The question at issue here is: what is the best – that is, the most effective – way of 'doing psychology'? The view developed by Skinner, and characteristic of behaviour analysis today, is: that, if psychology is to be a science, it should seek to explain human psychological phenomena by identifying causal factors that lie *outside the individual*; otherwise there is a serious risk that the intended explanation is no more than a re-statement of that which is to be explained, but now described in different terms.

A point often stressed by Skinner is that we have not explained any aspect of behaviour by appeal to another level if the only evidence we have for the value of that explanation is the behaviour itself. For example, when asked why one person can recite large amounts of poetry, we may assert that the person in question has a good memory. When further asked how we know this, we may point to the large amounts of poetry that they recite. Clearly, this is a circular and thus useless explanation. A cognitive psychologist may retort that this an unfair example, and that they would always seek to establish the validity of the memory process under study by showing, for example, that someone who has a good memory of this type in one context shows similarly superior ability on other, different tasks. Well, even if that safeguard against spurious explanation is in place, the behaviour-analytic view is that at the stage where 'good memory' had been invoked as the explanation of behaviour we have really only *re-described* the behaviour. What determines who has a good memory? The easiest way to answer that question unambiguously is to carry out experiments to establish the conditions under which 'good' or 'bad' memory (that is, variation in the behaviour of reciting poetry) occurs. This will involve identifying the key experiences (that is, interactions between behaviour and the environment) that lead to the behaviour of interest.

We should make a distinction here between criticism of the *hypothetical constructs* proposed by mentalists, cognitivists or psychoanalysts purportedly to explain psychological phenomena, and neurological mechanisms or correlates of behaviour. The various types of hypothetical constructs are inferred from behaviour and then offered as explanations of behaviour. Behavioural neuroscientists, on the other hand, make observations, usually through experiments, of both behavioural and brain processes, and then make suggestions as to the relationships that exist between phenomena on these two different but related levels. This is a field, as we shall see in Chapter 5, to which behaviour analysis makes a large contribution in terms of the methodology used. Behaviour analysts would argue that a full account of behavioural processes is required as a basis for an effective behavioural neuroscience where brain processes are identified. Additionally, there are important questions germane to behaviour analysis that can only be answered through research in neuroscience.

It was noted in Chapter 1 that selection of behaviour, as occurs in operant conditioning, must be part of a system where behaviour varies, is selected through interaction with the environment, and the selected variant of behaviour is retained (and recurs when a similar environment is encountered). In this book we will devote a lot of space to selection and a certain amount to variation of behaviour, but will have less to say about retention. As also noted in Chapter 1, the most striking feature of retention from a behavioural point of view is its effectiveness. That is to say, there can be a very long interval between an occasion on which behaviour has been selected and the next occasion when the same environment is encountered, but the same behaviour will occur. We notice this, for example, when we meet an old friend after a gap of perhaps many years and 'take up where we left off'. While from a behavioural point of view we simply have this ability (and we can show, for example, the importance of context reinstatement in producing the behaviour that has not occurred for a long time), Skinner, and subsequently other behaviour analysts, have also been interested in knowing how these persistent changes in the behavioural repertoire are mediated by the central nervous system. There have been false starts in formulating answers to questions of this type. For example, recent research in brain imaging is revealing that the long-held assumption of so-called localization of function is unfounded. Although it has been believed since the brain was first investigated that certain psychological processes (such as vision, or verbal memory) are located (or 'localized') primarily in restricted areas or 'centres' of the brain, this is not the case. Instead, it turns out that patterns of activity throughout the brain are associated with each of many psychological processes.

Given progress in our understanding of brain processes, long-standing questions as to how psychological processes affect the brain can be reformulated. Behavioural analysis and neuroscience thus always mirror each other, and can be thought of as mapping complementary domains of enquiry. Which is important depends on what question we wish to answer and the details of our state of knowledge. For example, if we wish to deal with sleep problems in infants we may use a purely behavioural strategy (see Chapter 6), even though much is known about the physiology of sleep, but if we wish to counter the intellectually deleterious effects of neurological diseases, such as Alzheimer's or Parkinsonism, we may seek to devise an intervention that modifies brain function directly (see Chapter 5). Even in the latter case, however, we will use techniques of behaviour analysis both to operationalize the intellectual deficit of concern and to monitor the effects of our intervention.

Recent work in neuroscience has also revealed that, in line with Skinner's views, the behavioural and neurological domains interact, rather than there being a one-way causal link from brain to behaviour. It is now widely recognized that both morphological and biochemical indices in the brain undergo alterations in response to environmental influences, and so-called *environmental enrichment* can compensate for damage done to the brain in other ways. Such findings are consistent with the notion that complex interrelationships exist between the many aspects of the brain-behaviour system, and environmental interactions concurrently affect both. To revert to the examples of the previous paragraph, we will expect successful intervention with sleep problems to be reflected in physiological as well as behavioural changes, and, once we have devised experiments which enable us to model Alzheimer's disease, for example, we can go on to see whether environmental manipulations can be used to reverse the behavioural and neurological changes that will lead to deterioration.

As well as being concerned with the nature of behavioural explanation and its relation to the neurosciences, Skinner also sought to apply radical behaviourism to social issues. His primary concerns here were twofold: to point out that conditioning processes always operate in human life, and to suggest ways in which understanding those processes might enable us to improve the human condition. Again, his extensive writings on these topics were the source of much controversy and here we will only review some general features of the debate between behaviour analysts and others.

The first point was introduced earlier in this chapter by noting that operant conditioning is a descriptive principle. This book is not an introduction to novel techniques that may change human behaviour, it is an introduction to the study of processes that change human behaviour all of the time, analogously to the way that gravity acts on all the objects on the earth all of the time. Consequently, a lot of space in this book will be devoted to outlining the scientific evidence for the claim that operant conditioning operates in this general way. The case made here will not 'prove' that behaviour analysts are right about this, because no scientific theory can be proved in that sense, but it is hoped that a strong enough case can be outlined to persuade the reader that it is a sustainable working hypothesis. Skinner recognized – indeed he often pointed out – the fact that this view poses a threat to the notion of 'human autonomy', and this in turn is the reason for much heated debate.

As explained earlier in this chapter, developments in various biological sciences over the last 150 years have greatly encroached on the previously well-entrenched view that science may be able to explain everything *except* human psychology. If that view is abandoned, then notions of autonomy go with it. That is, we are not really 'free' to think and behave as we wish, in the sense that a science is developing that will eventually be able to explain why we think and act as we do. Even in the early days of that science (that is, at present) it may be possible to account for some human behaviour. That is, we may be able to set up procedures with which, on the basis of previous experimental findings, we can successfully predict what people will do.

The type of science developed by behaviour analysts that may account for human behaviour will be explained in this volume, but it is important to realize that the same threat to human autonomy is posed by all scientific accounts of psychology. Contemporary cognitive psychology, for example, is 'determinist' in the same sense. Although the explanatory mechanisms proposed are different, the intention none the less is to provide a scientific account that leaves no room for free will. Despite this similarity of strategies, Skinner was attacked for his determinism far more often than leading proponents of other scientific approaches to psychology.

The alternative view that a scientific account of human psychology is not possible is, of course, sustainable. However, as the twenty-first century begins, the 'non-scientific' view is out of step with a wide range of sources of evidence that indicate continuity between psychology and other sciences. Even those who strongly believe that scientific psychology is not desirable or feasible tend to accept that disordered behaviour – such as the challenging behaviour of those with learning disabilities or the behaviour of extremely depressed people – should be explained in terms that do not attribute 'blame' for the behaviour to the individual who exhibits it. We are increasingly aware that 'stress' seems to produce both medical and psychological problems in people who are otherwise regarded as healthy, responsible adults, and so on. The consensus view, then, is that a scientific explanation of human behaviour is being developed and, as it develops, our view of ourselves as autonomous beings will tend to be eroded.

Given that scientific 'laws' influence human behaviour, Skinner often discussed how the principles of behaviour analysis, derived from experimental research under well-specified conditions, might account for the phenomena of everyday life, and how a knowledge of those principles might inform improvements in human life. Much of what he suggested was speculative, of course, as is always the case when scientific principles are applied in circumstances that are much less well understood than those of the laboratory where they were discovered. We will briefly discuss here two related themes in Skinner's extensive writings on general and social issues. One is that positive reinforcement is highly effective in bringing behavioural change without undesired 'side-effects', and the other is that when people seek 'freedom' what they really seek is the removal of aversive practices in their society.

# Use of positive reinforcement

As will be explained in the next chapter, the basic operant conditioning procedure involves positive reinforcement of behaviour, in the sense that a class of behaviour is increased in frequency because it is arranged that a reinforcing stimulus will occur if the behaviour occurs. Skinner argued that many effective educational strategies were examples of positive reinforcement, while ineffective or counter-productive ones did not involve this process (see, for example, Skinner, 1953). Again, it must be remembered that the reinforcing stimulus in any positive reinforcement procedure is functionally defined, and may well be different – even in the same educational setting – for different students or different tasks. That is to say, if a group of three students work well in a reading class with a particular teacher, the effective reinforcer may differ for each student: the reinforcer for progress in reading for the first student might be praise from the teacher; for the second student it might be the removal of the teacher's criticism, which occurs when she is not attending to her class work; and, for the third, it might be her mother's delight when she goes home with good results. How could we check whether these suggestions are correct? As with an experimental situation, we would do this by changing the relationship between the behaviour and the putative reinforcer; if it really were the reinforcer, the behaviour in the reading class would subsequently change. This could be tested by arranging for the teacher to change her reactions to the student's behaviour in the first two cases, and arranging for the mother to react differently to news of school results in the third case. This hypothetical example shows that because reinforcing stimuli are functionally defined, a teacher saying 'Well done!' is not necessarily an example of positive reinforcement. If this seems counter-intuitive, imagine a situation where every time you completed a work assignment, someone you did not like came up and spoke to you. Would this increase or decrease the amount of work you did?

Skinner's main idea was that, as has been explained earlier, the reinforcement process is ubiquitous – it goes on all the time – and so it is better to use it effectively rather than try to ignore it. It would obviously be a good idea if the teacher saying 'Well done!' always did act as positive reinforcement for appropriate behaviour in class, and it is possible to bring this about if all the students have a history of positive interactions with that teacher. Whereas 'common sense' tells us that teacher praise should always be an effective reinforcer, behaviour analysis teaches us that this will only be the case where the student has had the appropriate previous experience with the teacher in question.

## Removal of aversive control

Like many species of social animals, human beings use aversive methods of changing each others' behaviour. That is, one person may be hit or shouted at by another, usually in order to stop or reduce some class of behaviour. Skinner (e.g., Skinner, 1972) argued that when we talk of 'freedom' we generally mean freedom from this type of aversive or coercive influence. We wish, he said, to live in a social world where there are many sources of positive reinforcement and few occasions where our behaviour is followed by aversive or painful events. He linked this suggestion to re-statements of the view, explained earlier, that human behaviour is never 'free', because it is subject to scientific laws and thus determined.

In summary, Skinner's approach was that of radical behaviourism. He supported his approach by demonstrating how it dealt with the phenomena of psychology, and how this contrasted with other approaches. He was particularly concerned to point out that many – but not all – alternative approaches are prone to posit unobservable entities as proposed explanations of psychological phenomena. These attempts fail because they do not relate human behaviour to measurable events that lie outside the organism. He also applied radical behaviourism methodically to all areas of psychology. He was often able to suggest very simple ways in which an understanding of the principles of behaviour analysis would help to resolve serious problems or illuminate areas of debate. Because the general understanding of psychology could be said to be at a pre-scientific stage, where there is no consensus about the conceptual framework to be used, this often led to debate about the validity of his scientific principles. However, it also led to effective applications to human problems and some of these are introduced in the next section.

## 2.6 APPLIED BEHAVIOUR ANALYSIS AND FUNCTIONAL ANALYSIS

There have been many applications of the principles of behaviour in dealing with serious real-world human problems. These applications have led in turn to the development of further principles that arise primarily in real-world applications, rather than in the laboratory. The move to applications was initially promoted by Skinner, but was then taken up by a large number of other investigators. Many of these were clinical psychologists who saw in *applied behaviour analysis* the possibility of introducing techniques to their work that would be effective in bringing about *behaviour change*. Some early studies involved engaging human participants in procedures that closely resembled Skinner's experimental studies with animals, in that an arbitrary class of behaviour was used in an operant conditioning procedure. More typically, many early studies showed that if an appropriate reinforcing stimulus was arranged to occur following socially acceptable or personally useful behaviour, then that behaviour increased in frequency while other destructive or socially unacceptable behaviour declined. In making these applications to the behaviour of human adults it was often necessary to select reinforcers that were effective for particular individuals because, as we have noted already, reinforcers are functionally defined and depend on the individual's learning history.

The behavioural orientation of applied behaviour analysis distinguishes it from all other approaches to dealing with human psychological problems, most notably from those that derive from either a medical or a psychodynamic model. This behavioural orientation involves an initial *behavioural assessment* of the problem, the specification of *behavioural objectives* (that is, the changes in behaviour that would be desirable), the use of an *intervention strategy* derived from the experimental analysis of behaviour, and an assessment of the *outcome*. That is, have the behavioural objectives been achieved? As applied behaviour analysis developed, most attention was directed to the use of effective intervention strategies and demonstrations that behavioural objectives had been achieved following intervention. This approach is not confined to clinical psychology and applications continue to be developed in an increasing number of areas.

By 1980 there were many areas in which applied behaviour analysis had been shown to be useful in dealing with serious human behavioural problems. It had often been 'the treatment of last resort' in the sense that a 'case' (for example, of a child with moderate intellectual disability who showed a severe level of self-injurious behaviour through gouging at his face with his hand) had been approached using applied behaviour analysis only after more conventional medical and psychological treatments had failed to be effective. When applied behaviour analysis succeeded in producing behavioural improvements in such cases, great impetus was given to its use in similar cases, and it became more likely that it would become the preferred initial treatment for this type of behavioural problem.

In the early days of applied behaviour analysis, when practitioners were mostly concerned with the simple strategy of implementing an operant conditioning procedure, there were successes, but also a considerable 'unevenness' in treatment outcomes. That is, not every person showing a particular problem, such as self-injurious behaviour, was helped by the behavioural intervention methods typically used. A major breakthrough on this issue began with the procedure that has come to be called *functional analysis*. This was first carried out in cases of self-injurious behaviour, rather like the one mentioned above. This type of problem had often been very successfully treated using applied behaviour analysis; however, in any given treatment programme, there always seemed to be at least a significant minority that did not improve. The pioneers in this field (such as Iwata *et al.*, 1982 and 1994) noted that earlier work had focused on specifying behavioural objectives and implementing treatment, but has paid little attention to establishing the environmental determinants of self-injury prior to any intervention. That is, the question as to why the behaviour was occurring was not being properly addressed. They remedied this by devising operant methods for assessing functional relationships between self-injury and the physical and social environment. In their original study, and subsequent ones, they found that self-injury occurs for different reasons in different people. Persons that engage in self-injury may do so because it results in attention from others, because it allows them to escape from other demands (such as doing school work), because it raises the level of sensory stimulation, or for a combination of these reasons. Importantly, behavioural interventions become much more effective when the treatment strategy for each individual is based directly on a prior functional analysis of their behaviour.

Methods of functional analysis have now been developed for many types of behavioural problem, and functional analysis is now seen as the key element in the behavioural assessment that should precede any behavioural intervention. We noted earlier that Skinner (1938) stated that *functional relationships* between aspects of behaviour and parameters of the environment should be the goal of a science of behaviour. With the increasing prominence of functional analysis in behavioural assessment, along with the use of functionally defined behavioural intervention, functional relationships can now be seen as the central feature of applied behaviour analysis, as they are in all behaviour analysis.

## 2.7 ANALYSIS OF LANGUAGE AND COGNITION

Although behaviour analysis began with Skinner's publications in the 1930s, and has even earlier links with Watson's behaviourism and Pavlov's work on conditioned reflexes, it has only recently begun to analyse language and related psychological phenomena effectively. There are a number of ways of looking at this delay. Many from outside behaviour analysis (for example, some of those working in cognitive psychology) have taken the view that these areas are of overwhelming importance and that little has been said about 'real issues' in human psychology until they are addressed. Alternatively, one might say that a science may not 'run before it can walk' and that it is fanciful to expect a fledgling discipline to address complex issues immediately.

In any case, the situation has changed dramatically in the last 20 years, and behaviour analysis has begun to provide an analysis of language and cognition. Importantly, this analysis is an extension of principles established for other types of behaviour. There is thus a prospect of behaviour analysis providing an account of the whole of psychology, based on the same principles throughout.

In all approaches to psychology, there is an intimate relationship between language, which behaviour analysts prefer to call *verbal behaviour*, and cognition. That is, no account of so-called verbal processing is attempted without giving a more general account of cognitive processes. One of the earliest debates, once psychology became a distinct discipline, concerned the relationship between language and thought. It was debated whether there could be only thought without language. The debate has moved on since then because of discoveries that psychologists have made about the 'cognitive' abilities of animals. These will be explained in the next two chapters but, in brief, there is much evidence for cognitive abilities in non-human animals that show no evidence of linguistic abilities. This shows, perhaps, that some 'thought' occurs without language. However, as will be explained in Chapters 4 and 7, recent research in behaviour analysis has shown that there are some *relational learning* abilities readily shown by humans for which there is little or no evidence in other species. These probably underpin our linguistic abilities, and we are thus developing a well-grounded psychological account of how humans differ intellectually from other species.

This developmental and evolutionary account of cognition can be linked to a behavioural account of language, or verbal behaviour. The aspect of the account provided by behaviour analysis that linguists and others have found most surprising is that it is a functional and not a structural account. Talking, the most important type of verbal behaviour, has a structure that can be described in terms of a complex series of sounds, but it also has a function. We talk, most often, because talking has *effects* on other people. As we will see in Chapter 7, the behaviour analysis account of verbal behaviour describes it in terms of various types of operants that have different functions. For example, a person might say something that has the consequence of someone else shutting a door which is letting in a cold draught. That is its function; its form can be quite variable. It might be to say 'Shut the door!', or 'It is draughty in here', or even to gesture at the person standing nearest the door that they should close it. Another type of verbal operant is where a person might say

'What a beautiful day', or 'It has turned out nice again', or the person may simply smile with pleasure as they emerge from a building into the sunshine. Such utterances or actions are often followed by social approval or conversation with other people. Dialogue or conversation is very important to this account of verbal behaviour. In the simple case of a two-person conversation, two people repeatedly swap the roles of speaker and listener, or 'take turns', and thus the behaviour of one is followed by consequences (further speech) provided by the other. This second utterance, then, provides the context for the next statement or utterance by the first person, and so on. (A fuller account of the basics of this approach will be provided in Chapter 7.)

## 2.8 SUMMARY

Although there has been interest in psychology for centuries, the long-standing acceptance of dualism delayed the development of psychology as a scientific discipline. Dualism is the view that while the physical universe can be understood through science the workings of the human mind cannot; Descartes provided the classic statement of this position. Eventually, a range of developments in the biological sciences in the nineteenth century came together to undermine the prevailing view that a scientific approach to psychology was not feasible. The two most important developments were Darwin's work on evolution by natural selection, and the work of many people, including Sherrington, on experimental physiology of the nervous system.

Darwin's evolutionary theory predicts that there will be continuity in all respects between human beings and other species, and that we should expect to find psychological processes that are shared between humans and other species. The success of experimental physiologists in isolating reflexes suggested that a complete account of even the human nervous system and its relation to behaviour might be constructed out of the interaction of these simple units. Pavlov, a Russian experimental physiologist who began work in the late nineteenth century, took all these ideas further by demonstrating the acquisition of conditioned reflexes through classical conditioning. The procedures required to produce changes in behaviour were well specified by Pavlov, and he saw this as a general method that would apply to many species, including humans. Thorndike, an American researcher also working at the turn of the twentieth century, made further progress by devising another method that produced systematic changes in animal behaviour. Again, he saw this as a step towards the explanation of changes in human behaviour through identifying a general law of learning, or behavioural process.

The development of psychology as an independent scientific discipline was advanced by Watson's proclamation of 'behaviourism' as an alternative to the rather unscientific 'mentalism' that had preceded it. Watson promoted the view that psychologists should ensure, above all, that their approach was scientific, and that this could be achieved by focusing exclusively on subject matter that could reliably be observed. On this principle, the focus should be on human and non-human animal behaviour, and also on the careful specification of the environment in which that behaviour occurs.

The approach instituted by Watson was much modified and enhanced by Skinner, whose work had an impact from the time of his early publications in the 1930s. In this period the approach became known as behaviour analysis, and was strongly but not exclusively associated with Skinner. Some of Skinner's contributions were methodological; he developed a simple but widely applicable piece of apparatus, now generally known as the Skinner box, for studying aspects of the behavioural process first investigated by Thorndike, and he identified a measure of behaviour, the rate of response, that could be measured in that apparatus and that also turned out to be useful in a wide range of applications. His conceptual or theoretical contributions were also numerous. The most important of these was the realization that the learning process first studied by Thorndike, and which is now called operant conditioning, is a process of selection. The interaction between the behaviour of the individual and the environment of that individual results in some categories of behaviour being selected, and thus becoming relatively more frequent while others become less frequent in that environment. Since Skinner, both response and stimulus classes have been functionally defined. This means that a response class is defined in terms of its consequences or effects. This corresponds well to most everyday terms used to describe categories of behaviour, which describe the effects of behaviour rather than the movements that make up the behaviour. Similarly, the environment is said in behaviour analysis to be made up of functionally defined stimulus classes. This means, among other things, that every individual's environment is unique, because their own history of interaction with the environment defines their functional stimulus classes.

Skinner's radical behaviourism has been applied to all aspects of psychology and to many issues in related domains. Within psychology, he developed and defended the view that any explanation of psychological or behavioural phenomena must make reference to events outside the individual, rather than appeal to hypothetical events believed to occur inside the individual, as many alternative (e.g., medical, psychodynamic or cognitive) ones do. Even if internal events (e.g., brain changes) are known to exist, the question still arises as to which interactions with the environment produces those changes. Radical behaviourism has also been applied to social issues, where it is particularly associated with the general view that a scientific explanation of human behaviour is possible and, as it advances, our notion of human autonomy will inevitably be undermined. While this is a logical consequence of radical behaviourism and behaviour analysis, it also follows directly from any scientific approach to psychology.

More specifically, Skinner made two particular recommendations in his writings on social issues. He recommended that positive reinforcement be used wherever possible when changes in behaviours are required, and he stated that there is a strong desire for the removal of forms of aversive control in society. These two claims both reflect his view that positive reinforcement should be used effectively, and at the same time methods of aversive control of human behaviour should be removed, to create a better society.

There have been many developments in applied behaviour analysis – an applied field that takes both the principles and the experimental procedures developed in laboratory studies of behaviour analysis and seeks to modify unwanted or inappropriate patterns of human behaviour. This approach to psychological problems offers a scientifically based alternative to medical or psychodynamic strategies. It involves the stages of behavioural assessment, specification of behavioural objectives for change, the use of an intervention strategy and an assessment of the outcome. Since 1980, the effectiveness of this approach has been enhanced through functional analysis. Functional analysis seeks to identify why the problem behaviour is occurring, or what motivates it, at the assessment stage and thus provides a more secure rationale for intervention.

Early work on behaviour analysis was derived from experimental studies with non-human animals, and had little to say about language and cognition. This has changed in recent times, as behaviour analysts have taken further Skinner's idea that verbal behaviour, just as other behaviour, should be conceptualized in functional terms. Other recent research has shown that relational learning, which again is defined in functional terms, may underpin humans' verbal learning ability. Taken together, these developments are taking us towards an account of language and cognition that is rooted in the principles of behaviour analysis.

## Study questions for Chapter 2

The use of functionally defined terms in behaviour analysis may be the most important feature of the approach. The reasons for this claim should become apparent later in the book, but it should already be evident that (i) a lot of everyday language accounts of human behaviour depend on functional terms, but that (ii) these terms seem to raise some scientific or philosophical problems.

In order to reflect on the use of functional terms, try an exercise of the following type. Write out, in a few paragraphs, an account of a familiar social event, such as a family having a meal together, a commentary on a football match, a conversation on a bus, or any other event involving several people. Then try to identify every functionally defined term describing a piece of behaviour (response), or a situation or consequence (stimulus). You will probably find that most of the terms you have used to describe antecedents, behaviour or consequences are functionally defined.

The general scientific or philosophical problem is that using functionally defined terms seems to make all the definitions circular in the sense that each is defined with respect to the other two and there is no external reference. For example, if you say 'I hid in the hiding place, so as not to be found', you have described the antecedent (hiding place), the behaviour (hiding) and the consequence (not being found). However, if we want to define each of these terms we can only do so with respect to the other two. Hiding behaviour, for example, is what occurs in a hiding place and is followed by success in not being found. Reflect on this issue before looking at the suggested answers.

*Now check your answers with my suggestions in the 'Possible answers to study questions' section, see page 220.*

# 3 Basic Principles of Behaviour Analysis

- Classical conditioning
- Operant behaviour and operant conditioning
- An operant conditioning experiment in a Skinner box
- The changes in behaviour that characterize operant conditioning
- Outcomes of operant conditioning
- The definition of response classes
- Response differentiation and response shaping
- Operants and reinforcing stimuli
- Stimulus control
- Perceptual stimulus classes
- Stimulus control in classical conditioning
- The three-term relationship of operant conditioning
- The ABC of behaviour analysis
- Summary

So far, we have been concerned with setting the scene for the scientific approach to psychology that led to the emergence of behaviour analysis. This chapter moves from scene-setting to the important matter of describing the basic principles of behaviour analysis. While these principles will be augmented substantially in the following chapters, the principles presented in this chapter are fundamental to those that come later. Although we will mostly be dealing with aspects of operant conditioning, it was in the field of classical conditioning that some of the most important aspects of the general experimental strategy were developed, and these will be described first. As the account of operant conditioning unfolds, there are various links to classical conditioning and these will be indicated.

## 3.1 CLASSICAL CONDITIONING

There can be no science without effective methods of measurement, and those methods to some extent define the contents of the science. Behaviour analysis developed because innovative scientists found ways of bringing behavioural phenomena under experimental control. The first behavioural process to be identified in this way was what we now call classical conditioning, and some of the initial work done by Pavlov is described in this section.

It is important to realize that *behavioural processes occur over time*, and thus have to be observed over a period of time. Each of the processes we will outline in this chapter involves the interaction of the behaviour of an individual organism with its environment. Over a period of time, this interaction leads to a characteristic outcome. However, the eventual outcome cannot be fully understood unless the process has also been observed. This is why experimental study of the process is crucial.

Around the turn of the twentieth century, Ivan Pavlov, a Russian scientist, carried out Nobel prize-winning research in physiology on the digestive system, using dogs. While carrying out experiments on physiology, he made observations that led to important developments in psychology. He noticed that while the introduction of a stimulus of food or acid into the mouth of the dog resulted in a response of salivation the regular appearance of the experimenter bringing food would also elicit a similar response. Pavlov was by no means the first person to make observations of this sort; but he seems to have been the first to suspect that their detailed study might explain how animal behaviour is able to adapt to circumstances. It was this insight that led him to a systematic study of the phenomenon he had come across accidentally.

We noted in Chapter 2 that nineteenth-century physiologists, of whom Pavlov was one, had developed an extensive knowledge of the built-in reflex relationships whereby specific external stimuli produce specific behavioural and physiological responses. Pavlov used his knowledge of these reflex relationships, such as the fact that food-in-the-mouth (a stimulus) immediately produces salivation (a response), to design his experiments on digestion. As noted in Chapter 2 he called the additional stimulus-response relationships he observed 'conditional reflexes', because they depended or were conditional upon some previous events in the life of the animal: the appearance of the experimenter had not originally elicited saliva, it was only after his appearance had frequently occurred along with food or acid that it had this effect. *Conditioned reflexes* has become the normal expression to describe the change in behaviour. Similarly, the term *conditioning* has come to be used to describe any simple form of learning that arises through some specified history of interaction with the environment of the behaviour of the individual.

After carrying out very many experiments, Pavlov (1927) summarized his findings with a general law of conditioning: after repeated presentation of two stimuli at overlapping times, the one that occurs first comes eventually to elicit (that is, produce automatically) the response that is normally elicited by the second stimulus. A modified version of this law, or behavioural principle, still stands and will be given later in this chapter.

Very often, major advances in a field are the result of, or are accompanied by, methodological innovations. This is certainly true in the case of Pavlov and conditioned reflexes. Pavlov discovered that *controlled environmental conditions* were essential for successful behavioural experimentation. His dogs had to be kept in steady temperatures and in soundproof chambers for the experiments, during which stimuli were presented in a controlled fashion and responses recorded in ways that did not interfere too much with the experimental participant. He also realized that only dogs in good general health made satisfactory participants in experiments. An illustration of the typical experimental arrangements, as used at the end of the nineteenth century by Pavlov and his colleagues at the Institute of Experimental Medicine in St Petersburg, appears in Figure 3.1.

The dog pictured would have been familiarized with the experimental situation until it showed no disturbance when put in the harness and left in the soundproof room. The figure shows that minor surgery has been performed on the dog so that the saliva from one of the cheek glands will run into a recording apparatus and the number of drops of saliva occurring at any stage can be recorded. The experimenter sits in the next room and is in a position to measure the salivary response precisely. He or she is also able to control carefully the presentations of various stimulus events to the organism.

**Figure 3.1** A typical arrangement for studying conditioning in Ivan Pavlov's original nineteenth-century laboratory in St Petersburg, Russia

Because Pavlov's research team made a number of important methodological innovations, we will examine in detail an experiment by one of Pavlov's students (Anrep, 1920), as an example of the Pavlovian method and results. In this experiment, a tone was sounded in the animal's room for five seconds. Then, two or three seconds later, a piece of food was given to the dog. This *pairing* of tone with food presentation was repeated after intervals ranging from 5 to 35 minutes. In order to observe the effect of the tone alone, the experimenter occasionally presented it for 30 seconds, unpaired with (i.e., not followed by) food. Over the course of 16 days, 50 tone-food presentations and six tone-alone tests were made. The principal data of Anrep's experiment were obtained during the six tone-alone tests. During these tests, he carefully measured both the total number of drops of saliva and the time (or latency) between the onset of the 30-second test tone and the first drop of saliva. He found that, after one tone-food pairing, presentation of the tone alone produced no salivation at all. After 10 such pairings, however, six drops appeared in the tone-alone test, and the first of these six drops came 18 seconds after the onset of the test tone. After 20 such pairings, 20 drops were produced, the first drop coming now at only 9 seconds. From 30 pairings onward, approximately 60 drops of saliva were obtained during each test, and they began to appear in the first second or two after the onset of the test tone. The results of the experiment are clear-cut: salivation occurs reliably to an arbitrarily selected stimulus, an auditory tone, after the tone is paired with food 30 times.

Results of behavioural experiments such as these are much more easily understood when presented graphically, and Figure 3.2 presents the data

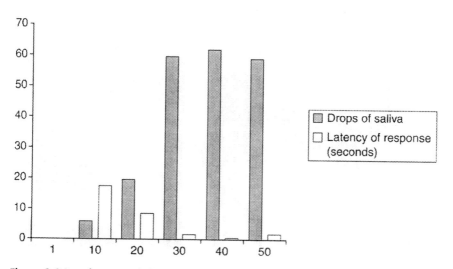

**Figure 3.2** Data from Anrep's (1920) experiment: acquisition of a conditioned salivary response to a tone (see text for details of this experiment)

for the test trials that have just been described. (Each time at which some event is presented in an experiment such as this is called a 'trial' and the events that are tests are thus called 'test trials'.) Figures of this type are often called 'learning curves', because over a period of time the amount of responding increases fairly steadily and then reaches a steady state where it no longer increases. (We will see in the next section that learning in the early stages of operant conditioning often proceeds in a more sudden fashion than this.) Note that conditions in the experiment are sufficiently well controlled that data from each observation with an individual organism are reported. The reliability of these data contrasts with that obtained in many other approaches to experimental psychology, where persistent variability leads to averaging of data across many occasions and for groups of participants.

In the terminology we shall use here, if a *conditioned stimulus* (CS) – such as the ringing of a bell in one of Pavlov's experiments – is reliably followed by an *unconditioned stimulus* (US) – such as food in the mouth – on a number of occasions, then the CS comes to elicit (or automatically produce) a *conditioned response*. Two aspects of this behavioural process – the increasing size and speed of the conditioned response across trials – are shown in Figure 3.2. Pavlov demonstrated this process many times, and gradually varied some features of his experiments to establish the generality of the effect. He also showed that there were a number of related phenomena concerned with *discrimination*, which we will discuss later in this chapter, and *extinction* which we will discuss in the next chapter.

Pavlov believed, and later investigators demonstrated, that he was investigating a process that enabled many species – not just dogs – to adapt to many aspects of their environments. He is thus credited with discovering the first 'general learning process'. It is general because it can affect many response systems, can involve many types of stimuli and is seen in many animal species. It is importantly involved in human behaviour and an understanding of classical conditioning has led to the development of methods of therapy that are used in the alleviation of human behavioural problems, particularly anxiety.

## 3.2 OPERANT BEHAVIOUR AND OPERANT CONDITIONING

As we saw in the previous chapter, the notion that much animal behaviour consists of reflexes was well known to the scientific community by the latter part of the nineteenth century, and Pavlov's ideas about conditioned reflexes as a model for the way in which the behaviour of individual organisms adapted to their environments were also rapidly and widely disseminated. However, there is much behaviour that apparently occurs at the instigation of the individual, rather than being elicited by the onset of an external stimulus as occurs in classical conditioning. This includes those actions of human beings traditionally described as voluntary, purposeful, spontaneous, or wilful, and this class of behaviour was thought to be beyond the scope of a scientific or experimental analysis until the turn of the twentieth century.

The experimental analysis of so-called voluntary or purposive behaviour has proceeded in a fashion typical of the development of scientific explanation and understanding in many other disciplines. Typically, a small number of systematic relationships are established first and repeatedly investigated. As new relationships are added to those previously established, the group of principles, or 'laws', begins to give a partial understanding of the area. Starting with Thorndike's extensive pioneer work on learning in cats and chicks, psychologists have searched for relationships between purposive behaviour and other events.

If a piece of behaviour has a purpose, then that purpose can be described by the usual consequences or effect of that behaviour. Indeed, we could almost say that purposive behaviour is that behaviour which is defined by its consequences. For example, we say that we tie a shoelace to keep our shoe on, but an equivalent statement is that we tie a shoelace, and on previous occasions when we tied it, it did stay on. Furthermore, we identify instances of shoelace tying by their effects: if the shoe stays on, then this counts as an example of 'shoelace tying'; otherwise, it does not. As discussed in Chapters 1 and 2, many other everyday behaviours can be subjected to a similar analysis. As well as those mentioned earlier, these include going to school, making a cup of coffee, playing a musical instrument and so on.

Apparently, we have two ways in our language to account for the same behaviour. These are: (i) the purposive, in which we use the term 'to' (or, 'in order to') and imply the future tense; and (ii) the descriptive, in which we state the present behaviour and conjoin it with what happened in the past. Which is more appropriate for use in a scientific analysis of behaviour? Consider the following example:

> During the war the Russians used dogs to blow up tanks. A dog was trained to hide behind a tree or wall in low brush or other cover. As a tank approached and passed, the dog ran swiftly alongside it, and a small magnetic mine attached to the dog's back was sufficient to cripple the tank or set it afire. The dog, of course, had to be replaced (Skinner, 1956: 228).

In this distressing example, the dog's behaviour can be explained by reference to past events, as it presumably had been rewarded for running to tanks by food, petting and the like, but not by reference to its current purpose.

We can reject the idea that the dog ran to the tank in order to be blown up. This extreme case illustrates the general principle that *the future does not determine behaviour*. When we use 'purposive language', we are drawing on our knowledge of the effects of our behaviour on earlier occasions; it is that 'history' that determines behaviour.

In brief, a very real and important class of behaviour, arising out of situations that seem to involve choice or decision, is called purposive behaviour. Such behaviour falls into Descartes' category of 'voluntary' (see Chapter 2) and constitutes action that is often called 'wilful', or said to be done by 'free choice'. Our present analysis indicates that this behaviour is in some way related to, and thus influenced by, its consequences on previous occasions. For that reason we will replace the older term, purposive, with Skinner's term, 'operant'. Calling behaviour 'operant' (or in Thorndike's term, 'instrumental') suggests that, by operating on the environment the behaviour is instrumental in obtaining consequences: the behaviour 'does something' to the environment. The term 'operant' gets rid of the confusing conceptual scheme implied by 'purposive', and captures the fundamental notion that the past consequences of such behaviour are one of its important determinants.

## 3.3 AN OPERANT CONDITIONING EXPERIMENT IN A SKINNER BOX

As discussed in Chapter 2, B.F. Skinner took further the findings of E.L. Thorndike. He made a number of methodological innovations through using a very simplified environment in which consequences can be arranged for one class of behaviour. This has turned out to be a very useful situation for identifying behavioural processes. Indeed, it has often been described as the 'microscope of behaviour analysis'. Because of its importance, its use will be described in some detail. Although details are given here for the apparatus as used with one species, the laboratory rat, equivalent apparatus has been developed for a number of other species of mammals (including primates), birds, fish and even insects.

A typical experiment can be carried out as follows. A laboratory rat is put into a small enclosure, such as the one shown in Figure 3.3, and certain procedures are carried out. The significant features of the enclosure, called an operant test chamber or *Skinner box*, are: (i) a tray for delivery of a small pellet of food to the rat; and (ii) a lever or bar, protruding from the front wall that, when depressed downward with a force of about 10 grams, closes a switch, permitting the automatic recording of this behaviour. The rat is healthy but somewhat hungry and accustomed to eating one meal each day at about the same hour as it is now in the box, and it has previously been acclimatized to

**Figure 3.3** An operant test chamber, or Skinner box, for a laboratory rat. This version has two levers

this box. During the acclimatization period, food was occasionally delivered into the tray, and it now readily approaches the food tray and eats food whenever it is available.

The rat is left in the box for an observation period of 15 minutes. During this time no food is delivered, but the rat engages in a lot of exploratory behaviour. It noses the corners, noses the food tray, occasionally depresses the lever, rears up against the walls, and so forth. Other activities observed include sniffing and grooming. None of these responses is reflexive. That is, no specific eliciting stimulus can be identified for any of them, and we call them *emitted responses*. Clearly, there are stimuli present that are related to the occurrence of these responses – the general construction of the box obviously determines which responses can occur, for example – but none of the stimuli elicits specific responses at specific times. The term 'emitted' captures the idea that the responses simply occur, or 'come out', from time to time.

The rate and pattern of the emitted responses of an animal in an environment in which no special consequences are being provided for any response defines the *operant level* of those responses. Operant level recordings will provide an important baseline against which we shall later compare the effects of providing special consequences for one or a number of the emitted responses.

After the observation period, the following procedure is begun. Each time the rat presses the lever, a pellet of food is delivered into the tray. As the rat is hungry and has previously learned to retrieve food pellets and eat them as soon as they are delivered, each lever-pressing response is now immediately followed by the rat eating a food pellet. We have introduced an 'if-then' relationship, or *contingency* between the lever-pressing response and the delivery of food pellets. Provided the operant level of lever pressing is above zero (that is, lever presses already occur from time to time), this new contingency will produce a number of behavioural changes. Soon the rat is busily engaged in lever pressing and eating pellets. These marked changes in its behaviour usually occur in a relatively short period of time. In common parlance, the rat is said to have learned to press the lever to get food, but such a statement implies purpose in the rat's behaviour. It is more accurate and informative to say that the rat is pressing the lever frequently now and getting food, and this follows a number of previous occasions on which lever pressing has occurred and been followed by food.

The experiment we have described is a version of one of the original experiments on operant behaviour carried out by B.F. Skinner in the 1930s. The most striking change in behaviour that occurs when food is presented to a hungry rat as a consequence of lever pressing is that lever pressing dramatically increases in rate. This is an example of *operant conditioning*, because the increase in rate is a result of the contingency between the lever-pressing response and the food. If there is a contingency between two events, A and B, this means that B will occur if, and only if, A occurs. We say that B is dependent upon A, or that A predicts B, because when A occurs, B occurs; but if A does not occur, B will not occur. Sequences of events in which B is contingent upon A and when B is independent of A are illustrated in Figure 3.4. In our present example, food (B) is contingent upon lever pressing (A). Another way of saying this is that food (B) is a consequence of lever pressing (A). This is a simple example of a *reinforcement contingency*, a term we will use later for more complex examples.

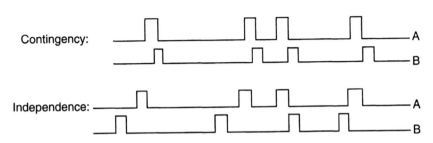

**Figure 3.4** Event records, or 'timelines' indicating a contingency between, or independence of, Event A and Event B; time elapses from left to right and an event occurs when the recording line shifts from the lower ('off') position to the upper ('on') position; in an operant conditioning procedure, Event A might be a lever press and Event B might be food delivery

## 3.4 THE CHANGES IN BEHAVIOUR THAT CHARACTERIZE OPERANT CONDITIONING

Because these outcomes are common features of many operant conditioning procedures, we will describe in detail, and as quantitatively as possible, the changes in behaviour that result from the simple operation of providing a special consequence for only one of an individual's normal ongoing activities in a situation. To do that, we shall consider four complementary ways of viewing the changes in the rat's behaviour when, as here, one of its behaviours is selected out and given a favourable consequence. These are:

- the increase in response frequency
- changes in other behaviour
- sequential changes in responding
- changes in response variability.

*The increase in response frequency* can clearly be seen on the ink recorder developed by Skinner (the Cumulative Recorder illustrated in Figure 3.5). The pen moves continuously across the paper in one direction at fixed speed, and this axis thus records elapsed time. Whenever a

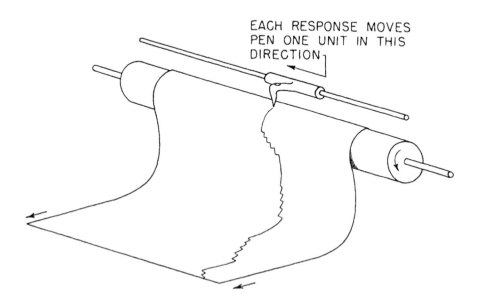

EACH RESPONSE MOVES
PEN ONE UNIT IN THIS
DIRECTION

**Figure 3.5** A cumulative recorder similar in design to the one devised by B.F. Skinner; modern computer software produces printouts organized in the same way

response occurs, the pen moves in a perpendicular direction by a small step of fixed size. The resulting *cumulative record* shows the number of responses and the time during which they occurred, and so illustrates the pattern of behaviour. Examples of actual records from experimental participants exposed to a procedure like the one outlined are shown in Figure 3.6. When a contingency between lever pressing and food was established for these experimental participants, there was a relatively abrupt transition to a high rate of response. It should be noted that the time spent in the experiment before this transition varied could be up to 30 minutes in the examples in Figure 3.6. Once the transition had occurred, the rate of responding was fairly constant; this is shown by the steady slopes of the graphs. The transition, because of its suddenness, can be termed a 'step change' rather than a gradual change. Ink recorders of the type used by Skinner in the 1930s have now been replaced by computer systems, which can be programmed to draw graphs of the progress of an experiment using exactly the same dimensions as those shown in Figure 3.6.

In any case of operant conditioning, there will always be concomitant *changes in other behaviour* as the operant response increases in frequency. If the experimental participant is a laboratory rat, and it begins to spend a large part of its time lever pressing, retrieving and eating food pellets, there must necessarily be a reduction in the frequency of some of the other responses (Rs) that were previously occurring in the Skinner box. For example, in an

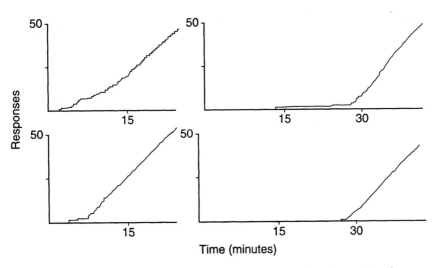

**Figure 3.6** Cumulative records obtained from four hungry rats on their first session of operant conditioning in a Skinner box; each lever press produced an incremental step of the recorder pen (Skinner, 1938)

undergraduate classroom demonstration of lever-press operant conditioning at Carnegie-Mellon University, the following behaviours of a hungry rat were recorded over 15 minutes of operant level, and then over a subsequent 15 minutes of conditioning the lever pressing:

$R_L$ = lever pressing
$R_S$ = sniffing
$R_C$ = pulling of a small chain that dangled into the box from overhead
$R_T$ = nosing the food tray
$R_B$ = extending a paw to a lead block that rested in one of the far corners
$R_I$ = remaining approximately immobile for 10 consecutive seconds.

It was found that while lever pressing and tray nosing increased, the other responses that were not associated with eating declined. Indeed, the operant conditioning process can be seen as one of *selection*. Those responses that are selected increase in relative frequency, while most of the remainder decline. Figure 3.7 illustrates with a histogram how the pattern of behaviour had changed.

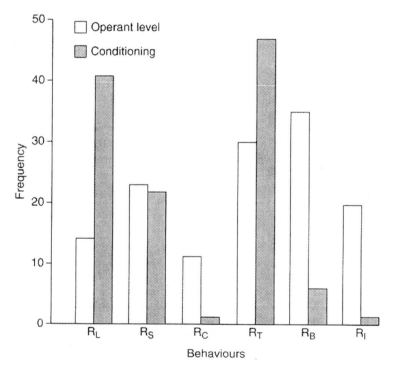

**Figure 3.7** Frequencies of several behaviours occurring in a Skinner box before and after conditioning of lever pressing (see text for details)

*Sequential changes in responding* also occur. When food is made contingent upon a response, other activities involved in food-getting increase in frequency, but this is not the only change that takes place. A sequence of responses is rapidly established and maintained. In the lever pressing example, the sequence might be:

lever press > tray approach > tray entry > eat food > lever approach > lever press ... and so on.

This continuous loop of behaviour is quite different from that seen in operant level. Two members of the established loop will serve to illustrate the point. Let us ignore for the moment all the other possible behaviour in the situation and confine our attention to (i) pressing the lever and (ii) approaching the food tray. Prior to conditioning of the lever press, these two responses occur in such a way that, when the animal performs one of them, it is likely to repeat that one again rather than perform the other. Thus, a fairly typical operant-level sequence of lever press ($R_L$) and tray-approach responses ($R_T$) might be:

$R_L R_L R_T R_L R_L R_L R_T R_T R_T$ ...

During conditioning, this sequence quickly changes to the pattern of strict alternation:

$R_L R_T R_L R_T R_L R_T$ ...

with hardly any other pattern to be seen. This re-organization of behaviour usually takes place as soon as rapid responding begins.

*Changes in response variability* always occur in operant conditioning. 'The rat presses the lever' describes an effect the rat has on the environment, not a particular pattern of movements by the rat. There is a wide range of movements that could have the specified effect. Presses can be made with the right paw, with the left, with nose, shoulder, or even tail. We group all of these instances together and say that the class of responses that we call lever pressing is made up of all the possible ways of pressing a lever. However, not all members of the class are equally likely to occur in an experiment nor, on the other hand, does the same member occur repeatedly. Several processes interact to determine exactly which forms of the response are observed. First, there is a tendency for the topography of the response to become *stereotyped* under certain conditions. By 'topography' we mean the pattern of muscular movements that make up the response; when this becomes stereotyped, the response looks exactly the same on each occasion that it occurs. Stereotyped behaviour develops very quickly when very little effort is required to make the response, and is also seen when an action (for example, operating a machine) has been performed very many times. A second process involved is described by Skinner's (1938) 'law of least effort'. This states that the form of the response made will tend to be that which requires the least effort. In the experiment described above, it is typically found that, while different participants start out by pressing the lever in various ways, as the experiment progresses, they show an increasing tendency to use an economical paw movement to press the lever. Third, the biology of the species influences what can be learnt. Thorndike was the first to realize that not all behaviours can be equally easily changed by certain effects or consequences. Seligman (1970) called this the *preparedness* of certain behaviours to be modified by certain consequences, and related this phenomenon to the evolutionary history of the species.

## 3.5  OUTCOMES OF OPERANT CONDITIONING

In summary, when operant conditioning is implemented in a simple laboratory situation such as a Skinner box, behaviour changes in four ways.

1. The rate of the operant response increases relative to its operant or base level.
2. The rate of the operant response increases relative to the rate of other responses occurring in the situation.
3. The pattern or sequence of behaviour changes to a loop involving the operant response and this loop is repeated again and again.
4. The form or topography of that response becomes stereotyped, while requiring a minimum effort and being influenced by the participant's preparedness to make the response for the consequence arranged for it.

In simple laboratory experiments with a variety of species, lever pressing, string pulling and pole tilting represent convenient acts chosen by experimenters to study the effects of environmental consequences on behaviour. The suitability of these responses for studying operant conditioning depends critically upon their ability to be modified as described. Formally, responses or response classes are defined as *operants* if they can be increased in frequency and strengthened in the four stated ways by making certain consequences contingent upon them. The selection of the operant response for experiments is often said to be 'arbitrary', in that the experimenter is generally not interested in lever pressing *per se*, but only as an example of a response that can be modified by its consequences. In general, lever pressing and other simple pieces of animal behaviour are chosen for experiments because they are easily observed and measured by the experimenter, and can be executed at various rates and in various patterns by the organism. Throughout this book, we will continuously extend the applicability of the principles of operant conditioning and the term 'operant' well beyond lever presses and rats.

## 3.6 THE DEFINITION OF RESPONSE CLASSES

Having identified operant conditioning as a behavioural process and described the typical behavioural changes, we need to define all the terms involved. The definition of a response class was discussed in part in the previous two sections, but there are still some issues that require clarification.

One of the reasons that the science of behaviour has been late in developing lies in the nature of its subject matter. Unlike kidney tissue, salt crystals or rock formations, behaviour cannot easily be held still for observation or removed from its context. Rather, the movements and actions of organisms appear to flow in a steady stream of interactions with the environment, with no clear-cut beginning or end. When a rat moves from the front to the back of its cage, when you drive 100 miles non-stop in your car or when you read a book, it is difficult to identify points at which the continuous 'behaviour stream' can be broken into natural units. A further complication is that no two instances of an organism's actions are ever exactly the same, because no response is ever exactly repeated.

Because of these complications, we speak of response categories or response classes. A *response class* might be defined as a set of behaviours that meet certain requirements and fall within certain limits along specified response dimensions. This would be a *topographically defined* response class, where topography is defined as specific patterns of bodily positions and movements. We can then check whether this response class meets the criterion for an operant response class by implementing operant conditioning in a way similar to that described earlier in this chapter. If the whole class becomes more frequent, then we have successfully defined an operant response class.

Examples of response classes of this type, for a seated person, might be: movement of the left forearm from a straight orientation through an angle of 45 degrees; or raising the right foot off the ground by straightening the leg until the leg is horizontal. These descriptions of behaviour seem awkward or artificial, however. We generally describe behaviours, even simple arm or leg movements, in terms of the function they have. In cases similar to the ones just given, the specified response might then be to move the left hand until the switch is reached, or to raise the right foot until it strikes the footrest. We call these *functionally defined* response classes, where the function is described in terms of the effect it has on the environment.

The use of functionally defined operant response classes greatly facilitates analysis, because not only do such units closely correspond to the way in which we talk about behaviour (as in the expressions 'he missed the train' or 'please shut the door'), but also measurement is made easier. When a rat is placed in a conventional Skinner box, it is easy to measure how many times the lever is depressed by a certain amount; it is much more difficult to record how many paw movements of a certain type occur. Similarly, it is fairly easy to record how often a child gets up from a seat in a classroom, but hard to measure the postural changes involved.

## 3.7  RESPONSE DIFFERENTIATION AND RESPONSE SHAPING

One of the most important features of operant conditioning is that response classes, as defined in the previous section, can change. Formally, this process is called *response differentiation* and its practical application is called *response shaping*. Through response shaping, new response classes can be created.

Operant conditioning always involves response differentiation, because emission of a specified response class is always required. Let us consider a case in which the specification of the operant response class is in terms of a single behavioural dimension: the minimum force required to depress the lever in a Skinner box. Hays and Woodbury (cited in Hull, 1943) conducted such an experiment, using a minimum force of 21 grams weight. That is, to 'count' as a lever press, there had to be a downward pressure on the lever of 21 grams weight or more. As in the experiment described in Section 3.3, these responses by a hungry rat were followed by food presentations. After the conditioning process had stabilized, Hays and Woodbury examined the distribution of response force for a large number of individual responses. While many responses were close to 21 grams in force, there was a roughly symmetrical distribution with a maximum at 29 grams, or 8 grams above the minimum force required. The force requirement was then changed to a minimum of 36 grams. Over a period of time, the rat's behaviour changed correspondingly, and the centre of the distribution of response forces became 41 to 45 grams. Conditioning of this new class of behaviour had thus been successful, but there had been a further important consequence of this conditioning. Novel emitted forces, never before seen in the animal's behavioural repertoire (those over 45 grams), were now occurring with moderate frequency. (The term 'behavioural repertoire' refers to the range of behaviour that typically occurs in the range of environments encountered by the animal.) The results of the experiment are shown in Figure 3.8.

The great power of the response differentiation procedure, when used with a changing series of response classes, lies in its ability to create and then sustain behaviours hitherto unobserved in the person's or animal's repertoire. This power is extended very much further in cases in which progressive differentiations take place over time. We call this method of introducing new behaviour into the repertoire *response shaping by successive approximation*. By such a process of successive approximation on the lever-force dimension, Skinner (1938) was able to train 200-gram rats to perform the Herculean feat of pressing a bar requiring a 100-gram minimal force! A better-known example from human behaviour is the record time for the 100 metres race: a

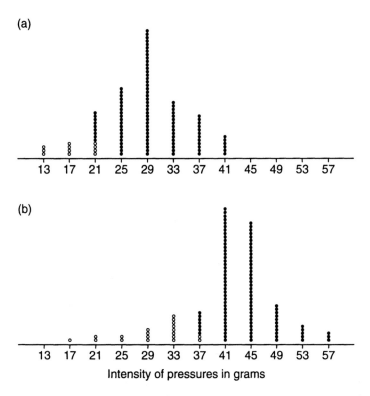

**Figure 3.8** Distribution of response forces of lever presses: in (a), all responses with a force of more than 21g were reinforced; in (b), all responses with a force of more than 36g were reinforced

time that would have been the world record in 1950 is now routinely improved on by athletes in training. We can think of this as a skilled performance that has been shaped within individuals, and passed on by other means between individuals.

Response shaping by successive approximation has a straightforward and very important use in the operant-conditioning laboratory. Suppose an experimenter wishes to increase the pecking of a wall-mounted key or disk by pigeons through operant conditioning. (A key-pecking response is generally used in the Skinner box as the operant for this species, rather than lever pressing.) This response often has an operant level of zero (that is, prior to training it does not occur at all) and thus must be shaped. The experimenter successively approximates the desired form of the behaviour, beginning with a form that may not resemble key pecking at all. For example, all movements in the vicinity of the key may first be followed by food presentations to a hungry pigeon. Once these movements have increased in relative frequency, food presentation is made contingent on head movements directed towards the key. Once such movements are frequent, reinforcement is made contingent upon striking the key with the beak and, finally, upon depressing the key with the beak. The process of introducing a response not previously in the repertoire can be very easy or very difficult. The degree of difficulty experienced reflects both the preparedness of the organism to associate the specified response and reinforcer as well as the stringency of the response differentiation required by the experimenter. (Remember that 'preparedness' refers to a characteristic of the species, not an 'opinion' of the individual in the experiment!)

Response shaping is also a highly important technique in the application of behavioural analysis to human problems. Many such problems can be characterized as *behavioural deficits*: the individual concerned does not succeed in making 'normal' responses and this may have serious consequences for their interactions with other people. This is an important idea, so we will give some detailed examples. From a behaviour analysis perspective, much of our behaviour is 'maintained' through our interactions with other people. If, for example, one person tells a lot of jokes in company with friends, this behaviour will continue at a moderate or high rate (that is, be maintained) if their friends react in a positive way to the jokes. If on the other hand, the jokes are not acceptable to the group, the 'joke rate' of that person will tend to decline. What, though, of the person who 'can't tell jokes'? They will have a zero operant level of this behaviour, and their response rate will not be modified through interactions with others in social settings and thus will remain at zero. This is a trivial example – we do not need to tell jokes – but the same analysis can also be applied to important categories of behaviour. Many people with moderate learning disabilities have virtually no speech; this is a major behavioural deficit and talking in such a person is not maintained by the social consequences that influence the behaviour of others. However, response shaping can be used gradually to work with some of their behaviour, such as inarticulate speech sounds, until 'normal' behaviour occurs, in the form of the sounds of simple words. Once some movement towards a more conventional behavioural repertoire has occurred through explicit training, the person concerned may interact more successfully with other people in informal settings. That is, they will start to talk to other people and those people will now reply to them. It is response shaping that can bring about this important change in their lives. Examples of shaping adaptive responding in applied or clinical settings will discussed in Chapter 6.

## 3.8 OPERANTS AND REINFORCING STIMULI

Which are the consequences of behaviour that will produce operant conditioning? This is a central issue that we have not yet discussed. In his first version of the law of effect, Thorndike stressed the importance of 'satisfiers'. He stated that if a satisfier, or satisfying state of affairs, was the consequence of a response, then that response would be 'stamped in' or increased in frequency. At first sight, Thorndike seems to have provided an answer to the question we posed, but he merely leaves us with another: which events will act as satisfiers? It seems obvious that food may be satisfying to a hungry organism, and further reflection will produce a list of events likely to prove satisfying in general, such as warmth, activity, play, contact, power, novelty and sex. We might also notice that there are some events that become very satisfying once the organism has been appropriately *deprived*. Food comes into this category, along with water when thirsty, air when suffocating and rest when fatigued. Interestingly, it is also evident that when we are *satiated*, these response-increasing effects are clearly removed and may even be reversed. It is usually unpleasant to eat a meal immediately after completing a previous one, or to have to stay in bed when completely rested.

Rather than speculating, how can we firmly establish whether certain events are satisfying? One way is to see whether they have the consequence specified by the law of effect, or, more specifically, produce the four outcomes listed in Section 3.5. However, according to Thorndike's definition, they must have these properties or these events are not satisfiers! A plausible alternative suggestion was made by Hull (1943). He claimed that all such events reduce a basic need or drive of the organism and that this 'drive reduction' is crucial to their response-increasing effect. Subsequent research has failed, however, to support Hull's suggestion, for there are many satisfiers whose ability to reduce a basic need seems questionable. These include 'artificial sweeteners' that have no nutritional value but make soft drinks just as attractive as the sugar they replace.

Thorndike's term, 'satisfier', carries the implication that such events will be pleasurable, or 'things that we like', but this does not help us to identify them in practice. Therefore, we shall replace Thorndike's term, 'satisfier', with Skinner's more neutral term, *reinforcing stimulus*, or, simply, *reinforcer*. The operation of presenting a reinforcer contingent upon a response we will denote as *reinforcement*. A reinforcing stimulus can be defined as an event that, in conjunction with at least some behaviour of an individual, produces the changes in behaviour specified by the law of effect and listed earlier in the chapter. So far, we lack an independent method of identifying reinforcers other than by their effects on behaviour. Moreover, the work of Premack (e.g., 1965) suggests that this represents an inherent limitation, because he established through ingenious experiments that the property of being a reinforcer can be a relative one.

In one experiment, rats making the operant response of turning an activity wheel were reinforced with water. To ensure that water acted as a reinforcer, the rats were made thirsty at the time of the experiment in the normal way. In this very conventional part of the experiment, wheel turning duly increased in frequency. In another part of the experiment, however, this relationship was reversed. That is, the rats were allowed continuous access to water 24 hours a day, but were prevented from access to the activity wheel except for 1 hour a day. In this unusual situation, it was found that if the opportunity to run in the wheel was made contingent upon licking water from a tube, the rats spent between three and five times as long drinking during that hour than they did when this contingency was not in effect. That is, operant conditioning occurred with the response of drinking water being reinforced with access to the activity wheel. Such experiments establish that it is not a 'law of nature' that wheel turning by rats can be reinforced with water; instead, this result depends on the usual practice of depriving rats of water, but not activity, prior to the experiment. If the conditions are reversed, then running in the wheel can be shown to reinforce drinking. In an earlier study by Premack, the same strategy was adopted with children and the two activities of eating candy or playing a pinball machine. When the children were hungry they would operate the pinball machine (an operant response) in order to obtain candy (a reinforcer), but when they were not hungry they would eat candy (an operant response) in order to obtain access to the pinball machine (now a reinforcer)!

The concept of 'a reinforcer' is evidently a relative one; a fact that we should especially bear in mind before uncritically calling any particular stimulus in the everyday world a reinforcer. Following the line of analysis started by Premack, other researchers (see Leslie, 1996, Chapter 4 for a review) have demonstrated that the amount of operant response required and the amount of access to the reinforcer that follows must also be taken into account to specify the reinforcement relationship. Most generally, it appears that reinforcement involves a set of relationships between environmental events in which the individual is 'deprived' of the currently preferred rate of access to the reinforcer unless the operant response increases above its currently preferred rate. This is called the *response-deprivation principle* (Allison and Timberlake, 1974; see also Leslie, 1996, Chapter 4, for a brief formal statement of the principle).

As we have now defined reinforcement with reference to the current behavioural repertoire, we should take care – in the laboratory or in real-world applications – not to presume that a stimulus will necessarily continue to be a reinforcer if the conditions are radically changed. It also follows that reinforcement cannot essentially be linked to biological needs or corresponding drives in the way that Hull (1943) suggested. However, it remains true that it is often possible to use the reduction of a basic need, such as the presentation of water for a thirsty animal or food for a hungry one, as a reinforcing operation, and that for practical purposes reinforcers are often 'trans-situational', or effective in many situations. This is particularly true with human behaviour, which is strongly affected by conditioned reinforcement as will be described in the next chapter.

## 3.9 STIMULUS CONTROL

In order to complete our account of the basic elements of operant conditioning, we need to consider an issue that is also relevant to classical conditioning. Ever since Pavlov (1927) extended the concept of the reflex to the study of conditioned reflexes in classical conditioning, behavioural scientists have sought to analyse the control exerted by stimuli over behaviour. Many stimulus classes – that is, sets of similar or related stimuli – exert control over behaviour in the sense that certain responses become much more probable (or much less probable) when a member of the stimulus class is present. As with the other phenomena that we have introduced, such *stimulus control* is a characteristic not only of human behaviour but also that of many other animal species. Consequently, we will be able to draw on the results of experimental work with various species in order to illustrate its features. However, we will begin by identifying some defining characteristics of stimuli and stimulus classes.

The environment around us has measurable physical dimensions. Thus, we talk about atmospheric pressure, ambient temperature, light energy with a given wavelength, sounds of certain frequencies and so on. We can describe the stimuli present in the environment, or those explicitly presented during experiments, in terms of those physical dimensions. However, from our point of view, this multidimensional physical environment has some especially important aspects. The effective stimulus class, the range of events that influences the behaviour of an individual in their natural environment or in an experiment, is more restricted than the whole range of events that make up the physically defined environment for two reasons.

1. The effective stimulus class has only those properties than can be perceived by the individual organism. It makes perfectly good sense to speak of a projector displaying a field of ultraviolet radiation on a screen, but as we will be unable to see it (although a honey bee could) it is not a stimulus for us because it could not enter into a relationship with our behaviour. More subtly, if your arm is jabbed by the points of two needles, you will only feel one prick if the needles are close enough together. In this case, the distance between the two is below the threshold for its detection.
2. At any given time, behaviour may be influenced by some, but not all, of the stimulus properties potentially perceivable by the individual organism.

We can summarize these two restrictions on the effective stimulus class as what the organism *can* learn about the stimulus, and what the organism *does* learn about the stimulus. In terms of the classical divisions of psychology, these topics fall into the areas of 'perception' and 'learning' respectively. In this chapter, as elsewhere, we are primarily concerned with learned behaviour (our general task being to account for how the behaviour of the individual changes as a consequence of its history since birth of interaction with its environment), but we will start by considering some aspects of stimulus perception.

## 3.10 PERCEPTUAL STIMULUS CLASSES

The prevailing environment of an organism (its 'psychological' environment) may be considered to be the pattern or configuration of all energies, present at any given time, that are capable of having a systematic effect on behaviour. These energies are only a small subset of the energies studied by physicists. They are restricted to those that can be detected by the specialized anatomical structures, or *receptors*, that organisms have for receiving certain energies and for transforming them into electrical nerve impulses. The eye is specialized for the reception of a limited range of electromagnetic radiation, the ear for a limited range of air-pressure vibrations, the tongue and nose for certain chemical energies. Receptors in the skin detect mechanical pressure and thermal changes. There are receptors within the muscles and joints of the body that detect the movement of the muscles and joints in which they are embedded. A complete specification of the patterns of electromagnetic, mechanical, chemical and thermal energies, impinging on an organism's receptors at any time, can rarely be undertaken. Fortunately, it is not usually necessary, as behaviour can come under the selective control of only limited parts or features of the energy configurations that make up what we call the physical environment.

For purposes of simple illustration, we will only use examples in the rest of this section that relate to visual perceptual stimulus classes. A stimulus is a part of the environment and can be described in terms of its physical dimensions. In manipulating the visual environment, we frequently confine our experimental changes to one of the fundamental dimensions by which physicists describe light. For our purposes, light may be considered to be a limited range of electromagnetic disturbance, radiated at $3 \times 10^{10}$ centimetres/second in wave form. Wavelength is one important dimension of electromagnetic radiation, and part of that dimension is a stimulus dimension to which the different verbal responses we call colours have been attached. The wavelengths that we call light comprise the very small portion from about 380 to 760 nanometres (1 nanometre = $10^{-9}$ metres) of the entire electromagnetic spectrum.

Nearly all animals respond to differences in amplitude or intensity of light waves (we call the corresponding response dimension 'brightness'), but only a limited number of species have receptors specialized for detecting changes in wavelength in the range 380 to 760 nanometres, and are thus said to have colour vision; pigeons, humans, snakes and monkeys are examples of animals that do. Others, such as rats and dogs, are said to be colour-blind because differences in wavelength alone cannot be learned about and thus come to control differential responding.

The wavelengths that occur in the rainbow, and that are perceived by us as colours (red, orange, yellow, green, blue, indigo, violet), are called 'pure spectral lights' because they contain only one wavelength. Most lights, including reflected light that reaches the eye from surfaces such as tables, chairs, blackboards and lawns, are far from pure in this sense. Generally, even the light from a homogeneously coloured surface or a lamp is made up of a large mixture of different wavelengths. Those wavelengths that are predominant usually determine the colour-naming response we make. Some mixtures of light, however, are not named by their predominating wavelengths. For example, the word 'purple' is never used to name a pure spectral light of one wavelength; 'purple' is the colour name for a mixture of red and blue. The lights we call white and the surfaces we call grey radiate heterogeneous mixtures of nearly all visible wavelengths, and no single wavelength predominates in such lights.

Visual stimulus dimensions are not confined to different wavelength distributions and intensities of isolated patches of light. Relevant dimensions that can control behaviour may be defined to include spatial combinations of the fundamental dimensions of wavelength and intensity. For instance, the relative intensities of two adjacent light regions can be a powerful controlling stimulus dimension, determining the brightness response that an observer will make to a portion of the pattern. That is, a grey patch may be seen as bright if surrounded by a less intense surround, and as dull if surrounded by an area of higher intensity. An example of this effect is shown in Figure 3.9.

Note that in this discussion we use one set of terms to describe stimulus dimensions and another set to describe corresponding behavioural responses. Although there are lawful correlations between these stimulus and response dimensions, labels for stimuli and responses should not be confused. Frequency and intensity of light energy are stimulus dimensions; colour and brightness are response dimensions. Frequency and intensity of sound energy are stimulus dimensions; pitch and loudness (or volume) are response dimensions. Smell, taste, temperature and weight are response terms associated with the stimulus dimensions of chemical structure, thermal energy,

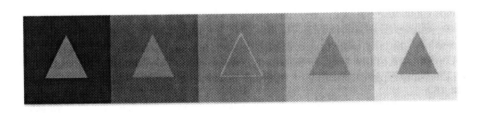

**Figure 3.9** The relative stimulus intensity effect: the grey triangle looks dull in the right panel and bright in the left panel because of the change in brightness of the surround

quantitative force and so on. Recognition of the difference between the terms appropriate for describing stimuli and those for describing responses will prevent a great deal of confusion.

A perceptual stimulus class consists of stimuli that lie along a physical dimension, such as those of frequency or intensity of light or sound. Instances of a class may vary somewhat along that dimension, but still produce the same response. For example, light stimuli in the range 680 to 720 nanometres will be labelled as red, and thus fall into the same perceptual class. While perceptual stimulus classes seem to be determined in part by the evolutionary history of the species – as we have noted not all animal species have colour vision, for example – we will see in the next chapter that animal and human behaviour also comes under the control of stimulus classes that are established through the learning history of the individual.

## 3.11 STIMULUS CONTROL IN CLASSICAL CONDITIONING

The first major experimental work on stimulus control was Pavlov's study of differentiation. In a straightforward elaboration of the basic experiment, one stimulus (termed the CS+) was paired with food (the US) and, once the CS+ had begun to reliably elicit a conditioned response, another stimulus (CS–) was introduced which was not followed by food. The CS+ (always paired with food) and the CS– (never paired with food) were then presented alternately, in a random sequence. The results of two of Pavlov's experiments are as follows. In the first, CS+ was a rotating disk and CS– was the same object, rotating in the other direction. In the second, the two stimuli were a tone and its semitone. In both experiments, before the differentiation phase began CS+ had been established as an eliciting stimulus for a conditioned response. When CS– was introduced, the response to it was, at first, slight. With continued presentations of both CS+, followed by food, and of CS–, not followed by food, the response to CS– increased until it approached that to CS+. Following this rise, there was a decline in the response to CS– until it reached zero. The ability of CS+ to elicit a conditioned response continued undiminished, and a *discrimination* was established between the two stimuli. The results of these two experiments are illustrated graphically in Figure 3.10. It appears that the similarity of CS+ and CS– initially induces a response to CS–, but subsequently the fact that the US does not follow the CS– results in reduction of responding to that stimulus. (The similar phenomenon of operant discrimination is described in Section 4.15.)

Simple experiments using more than one conditioned stimulus reveal other interesting features of classical conditioning. For example, many classical conditioning experiments show that the strength of the conditioned response increases rapidly over early trials, but with additional trials these increases

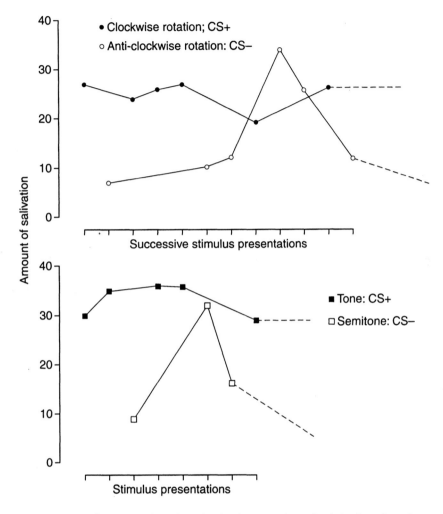

**Figure 3.10** Data from Pavlov (1927) on the development of two discriminations; in each case, a number of earlier CS+ food trials had occurred before the ones shown here, but the first few CS– trials are shown; dotted lines indicate Pavlov's verbal report of the effects of subsequent training – CS+ responding was maintained while CS– responding decreased to zero

become smaller and finally stop (we say that the strength of the conditioned response has reached an asymptote). However, Kamin (1968) was the first to demonstrate that not every CS paired with a US will result in a conditioned response that increases in this fashion. He showed that one can obtain a *blocking effect* in the following manner. If CS1 (for example, a light) is paired with a US over number of trials, there will be an increase in the conditioned response strength to a high asymptotic value, but if CS2 (for example, a tone) is then introduced and presented for a number of trials at the same time as CS1, and paired with the same US, not much conditioning to CS2 will occur. That is, in subsequent trials, presentation of CS1 alone will elicit a substantial conditioned response, but presentation of CS2 alone will not.

One further stimulus-control phenomenon in classical conditioning is related to the biological significance of conditioning. Pavlov discovered that if CS1 is a stimulus of high intensity and CS2 is a weaker stimulus, and the two are presented together and followed by a US, then only CS1 will come to elicit a strong conditioned response. We say that conditioning to CS2 has been overshadowed by conditioning to CS1, and this phenomenon is called *overshadowing*. An interesting type of overshadowing can occur if CS1 and CS2 are from different sensory modalities (e.g., vision and taste). Then the overshadowing that occurs depends on the nature of the US. For example, Garcia and Koelling (1966) found that in an experiment with rats, if CS1 was lights and noise, and CS2 was the taste of a liquid, then conditioning would occur to CS1 (but not CS2) if the US was a painful electric shock, and conditioning would occur to CS2 (but not CS1) if the US was a treatment that caused a stomach upset. There are clearly 'rules' – further aspects of what Seligman (1970) called preparedness – determining which potential CS comes to elicit a conditioned response

The phenomena of discrimination, blocking and overshadowing indicate that classical conditioning provides a sophisticated set of processes whereby relevant classes of stimuli gain control over behaviour, while irrelevant stimuli do not. This is very much what Pavlov (1927) believed when he presented his original findings and contradicts the contemporary popular notion that 'Pavlovian reactions' are somehow not part of intelligent behaviour (see also Rescorla, 1988).

At this point, we can provide a more formal definition of the conditions under which classical conditioning will occur. Pavlov asserted that the essential element of the classical conditioning procedure was the pairing of CS and US. Simple though the pairing operation seems, it actually confounds two distinct features: temporal contiguity and contingency. The CS is contiguous with the US if the US occurs immediately after the CS ('temporal contiguity' means 'touching in time'), and the US is contingent upon the CS if the occurrence of the CS predicts (and thus is correlated with) the occurrence of the US. This distinction is illustrated in Figure 3.11. Panel (a) shows the conventional pairing procedure involving both contiguity and contingency; panel (b) shows a procedure that gives contiguity while minimizing contingency; panel (c) gives contingency with minimal contiguity; and panel (d) shows a procedure in which US never follows CS, thus giving no contiguity and a negative contingency. It is a negative contingency because the CS now predicts when the US will not occur.

We can make predictions about the outcomes of the various procedures in Figure 3.11. If contiguity is all-important, then (a) and (b) should produce

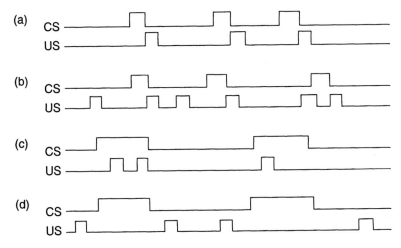

**Figure 3.11** Timelines showing varying contiguity and contingency of CS and US (see text for details)

conditioning, the effect of (c) will be weak and (d) will have no effect. If contingency is the crucial factor, then (a) and (c) will produce conditioning, while (b) is ineffective and (d) might produce an inhibitory CS. The data show that contingency is more important: procedure (c) is effective, while (b) often is not. For example, Rescorla (1968) manipulated the probability of a US occurring in each 2 minutes, both within the CS and in the inter-trial interval, the interval between CS's. He found that conditioning only occurred when the probability of the US occurring was greater during the CS than in its absence. Also, the greater the difference in probability, the greater the conditioned response.

Rescorla's results show that contingency between CS and US is important in classical conditioning, just as is the contingency between response and reinforcer in operant conditioning. However, Pavlov's idea of contiguity cannot be ignored totally because the overall temporal parameters are important: conditioning will not occur if either the CS or the inter-trial interval is too long. All the findings reviewed showed that it is 'relevance' in various senses that determines whether a CS–US relationship results in classical conditioning.

## 3.12 THE THREE-TERM RELATIONSHIP OF OPERANT CONDITIONING

Having defined stimulus classes and stimulus control, we can complete our definition of the key elements of operant conditioning. In describing operant conditioning, we have so far used only two terms: the operant response and the reinforcing stimulus. However, this relationship is established, either implicitly or explicitly, under certain stimulus conditions: there is a particular context, a set of stimuli that specify the occasions on which the response can be reinforced. In an experiment, these may be simply the stimuli arising from being in the apparatus and having the opportunity to make the response. Our general account of operant conditioning should thus include this feature. We will complete our basic account of operant conditioning as a *three-term relationship* by including the *discriminative stimulus*.

Consider the example of the lever–pressing response of a hungry rat in a Skinner box being reinforced with food. The complex of stimuli arising from 'being in the Skinner box' stand in an obvious relationship to reinforced lever pressing; after all, this is the only location where the rat has the opportunity to lever press. The experimenter may also arrange that a discriminative stimulus ($S^D$) is provided that explicitly signals when lever pressing may be reinforced. This may simply be the house-light in the ceiling of the Skinner box, or it may be an additional auditory or visual signal. In either case, the situation is one in which *the $S^D$ sets the occasion for reinforcement*. The $S^D$ is thus a stimulus that does not elicit responding, but in its presence responses are emitted and reinforced. When the $S^D$ is effective, and response rates are higher in its presence than in its absence, we say that it exerts *stimulus control*.

The three-term relationship between the discriminative stimulus, operant response, and reinforcing stimulus, can be written thus:

$$S^D: R \rightarrow S+$$

This means: 'In the presence of the discriminative stimulus, $S^D$, if an instance of the operant response, R, occurs, it is followed by presentation of the reinforcing stimulus, S+.' Remember that operant conditioning is said to occur only if this contingency results in an increase in the frequency of the operant response in the presence of the discriminative stimulus.

For our present example:

$S^D$ is the discriminative stimulus, the house-light
R is the operant response, the lever press
S+ is the reinforcing stimulus, the delivery of a food pellet.

The use of an $S^D$ implies that at times during the experiment this stimulus is not present. It may simply be absent (for example, house-light switched off), or may be replaced with a different one (for example, a steadily illuminated house-light might be replaced with a flashing one). In either case, we refer to the alternate stimulus situation, which generally signals the absence of the reinforcement contingency, as S$^\Delta$ ('S-delta'). S$^D$ and S$^\Delta$ are often referred to as positive and negative discriminative stimuli. If a higher rate of responding occurs during S$^D$ than during S$^\Delta$, then this is a simple example of discrimination learning (this is discussed in the next chapter).

Both an S$^D$ in operant conditioning procedures and a CS in classical conditioning exert stimulus control. The differences between the two lie in the nature of the behavioural control – an S$^D$ sets the occasion for a higher frequency of a reinforced response, while a CS elicits a response – and the type of conditioning history – operant or classical – that led to that stimulus gaining control over the behaviour.

## 3.13 THE ABC OF BEHAVIOUR ANALYSIS

In the previous sections, we followed the usual conventions of describing relevant aspects of the environment as 'stimuli' and categories of behaviour as 'responses'. The three-term relationship of operant conditioning thus consists of two stimuli (S$^D$ and S+) and a response class (R), while only two stimuli (CS and US) are used to specify the procedure of classical conditioning. There is, however, an alternative labelling system available for operant conditioning, which is easier to remember.

As we have already seen, a response class is an aspect of *Behaviour*, and reinforcing stimuli are *Consequences* of behaviour. If we adopt the term *Antecedent* (or antecedent stimulus) instead of discriminative stimulus or context, we can rewrite the three-term relationship of operant conditioning as:

A: B → C

Which means: 'In the presence of the *Antecedent* stimulus, if an instance of the *Behaviour* occurs, it is followed by presentation of the *Consequence*.' As previously stated, this is only an instance of operant conditioning if this reinforcement contingency results in an increase in the frequency of the operant behaviour in the presence of the antecedent stimulus.

The acronym 'ABC' for this is memorable, and points up important issues. In the first place, A, B and C generally go together. That is, all three must be identified to specify an operant conditioning process, and each term is defined with respect to the others. Second, when we come to discuss ways of changing human behaviour, B, we find that we can adopt two strategies: we can change the antecedents of the behaviour, A, or we can change the consequences, C. Thus the acronym ABC summarizes our possible intervention strategies as well as reminding us of the key concepts and their interrelatedness (see Chapter 6).

## 3.14 SUMMARY

The purpose of this chapter has been to explain the key features of two fundamental behavioural processes: classical conditioning and operant conditioning. These are general behavioural processes, in that they occur with many types of stimuli and responses, and with individuals from many species. Both classical conditioning and operant conditioning are explained in part by carefully presenting simple experimental procedures and their behavioural outcomes. Classical conditioning occurs when a CS and US are presented in a sequence where CS presentation is correlated with subsequent US presentation, provided this is not blocked or overshadowed by other CS–US relationships.

Operant conditioning is defined within the three-term relationship of discriminative stimulus ($S^D$), operant response (R) and reinforcing stimulus (S+). Operant conditioning occurs when the frequency of R increases in the presence of $S^D$ because of the contingent presentation of S+. Operant response classes are usually functionally defined – that is, in terms of the effect that instances of the response class have on the environment. The responses studied in experiments (such as those using Skinner boxes) are often arbitrarily selected but the results obtained generalize to many other response classes.

Reinforcing stimuli are often related to the biological needs of the individual organism (for example, food may be used as a reinforcer for an operant response in a hungry animal), but any stimulus of which the organism is currently deprived may in principle be used as a reinforcer. A reinforcing stimulus functions in a specified context if, and only if, contingent presentation of the reinforcing stimulus leads to an increase in frequency of the operant response.

A stimulus, or stimulus class, consists of some of those aspects of the environment that can be detected by the perceptual systems of the organism. Stimulus control exists when presentation of a stimulus – a CS in a classical conditioning procedure or an $S^D$ in an operant conditioning procedure – results in a response being elicited in the first case or in an increase in the frequency of the operant response in the second case.

The use of the alternative terms – antecedent, behaviour and consequence (A, B and C, corresponding to the discriminative stimulus, operant response and reinforcing stimulus respectively) – for the three-term relationship of operant conditioning, makes them easy to remember.

## Study question for Chapter 3

When students carry out simple experiments, such as the one described in Section 3.4, they sometimes infer mental processes in the rat that takes part in the experiment. They may state, for example, that 'The rat began to press the lever frequently once he knew that it produced food.' Behaviour analysts regard this sort of inference as unscientific, unhelpful and almost certainly untrue. How many reasons can you find that might support the behaviour analysts' criticisms?

Now check your answer with my suggestion in the 'Possible answers to study questions' section, see page 220.

# Further Principles of Behaviour Analysis

4

The purpose of this chapter is to provide enough further information about behavioural processes investigated in the laboratory to be able to make sense of the material in the remaining chapters. Those chapters will apply the principles of behaviour analysis in various ways to understanding the phenomena of behavioural neuroscience and language and cognition, and to resolving human behavioural problems. While the contents of Chapter 3 were essential and basic, the contents of this chapter comprise a selection of the many ways in which the science of behaviour analysis has developed from the basic findings reported in Chapter 3. A feature of this chapter is that it starts with a number of topics that have been investigated in experiments using non-human animals, and moves on to topics that are most often studied in human learning. This reflects the *parsimonious* and *comparative* approach of behaviour analysis. In this context, the use of parsimonious explanation means that we attempt to use the minimum number of explanatory principles we can. Thus where a principle that explains behaviour in non-human animal behaviour may also apply to human behaviour, that possibility is investigated. The comparative approach, which originated with Charles Darwin, indicates that we should expect to find – through comparisons between species – that behavioural processes are common to many related species, but that more complex processes may be seen in humans than in other species. The later sections of this chapter discuss two processes with great influence on human behaviour. These are stimulus equivalence, which may turn out to be a behavioural process that can be seen in complete form only in human behaviour, and modelling, which does occur in some other species but is predominantly an influence on human behaviour.

# 4.1 ALTERNATIVE TYPES OF REINFORCEMENT IN OPERANT CONDITIONING

As defined in Chapter 3, operant conditioning involves a three-term relationship, and the contingent presentation of a reinforcing stimulus (S+) results in an increase in the frequency of the operant response. This version of operant conditioning is, however, only one of several types of reinforcement contingency. If we consider the possible role of operant conditioning from an evolutionary perspective, operant conditioning of this type is clearly biologically useful. That is, it provides a mechanism by which the behaviour of individual organisms can adapt to the circumstances encountered, thus enhancing the survival of those organisms. However, this particular behavioural process, whereby a response class increases because it results in certain consequences, is only one of a number of relationships that may benefit the organism. In general, reinforcement contingencies can modify the frequency of an operant response through either the *presentation* or the *removal* of stimuli, and they can result in either the *increase* or the *decrease* of the operant response.

The four variations are presented in Table 4.1, which gives the name *positive reinforcement* to the type of operant conditioning already discussed in which contingent presentation of a reinforcing stimulus results in an increase in the frequency of the operant response. The other three types of reinforcement contingency – *negative reinforcement, punishment* and *time out* – will be described in the first part of this chapter.

**Table 4.1** Four possible types of reinforcement contingency

|  | Contingent stimulus is presented | Contingent stimulus is removed |
| --- | --- | --- |
| Operant response is increased | Positive reinforcement | Negative reinforcement |
| Operant response is decreased | Punishment | Time out |

## 4.2 AVERSIVE CONTINGENCIES

Negative reinforcement can occur through the response-contingent removal or postponement of aversive events. These, in turn, can be defined as those events (for example, those that cause pain) that the organism is motivated to remove. Contingencies involving relationships between these types of event and behaviour are called *aversive contingencies*.

## Escape

Operant conditioning can occur through the response-contingent removal of certain environmental events. We see that birds find shelter during rainstorms, dogs move to shady spots when the summer sun beats down upon them and people close windows when the roar of traffic is loud. In these instances, behaviour is emitted that removes or terminates some environmental event: rain, heat or light, and noise, in the examples given. These observations suggest the existence of a distinctive class of reinforcing events. Because the operation that defines these events as reinforcing is their removal, and is opposite in character to that of positive reinforcers, they are known as *negative reinforcers*, and we use the symbol 'S–' for a stimulus of this type. In general, negative reinforcers constitute those events whose *removal, termination, or reduction in intensity* will increase or maintain the frequency of operant behaviour. This process is called *negative reinforcement*. Because the events that will function in this way are often those regarded as unpleasant or even painful, we will call them aversive events, and the negative reinforcement procedure is one way of defining *aversive events*, or aversive stimuli.

There are two important behavioural processes involving negative reinforcement: *escape* and *avoidance*. In the *escape procedure*, an aversive stimulus is presented and termination of that stimulus is contingent upon the occurrence of a specified operant response. If this contingency results in an increase in frequency of the response, and in the other associated behavioural changes described for positive reinforcement in Chapter 3, then *escape learning* has occurred.

We can represent the escape procedure symbolically by the following three-term relationship:

$$S-: R \rightarrow S^0$$

where

S– is the aversive stimulus, which is the discriminative stimulus or antecedent (A)
R is the specified operant response or behaviour (B)
$S^0$ is the absence of aversive stimulus, which is the reinforcing event or consequence (C).

Note the following important points.

1. Escape learning, as defined here, is a form of operant conditioning, and there is a three-term relationship between antecedent S–, behaviour R and consequence $S^0$.
2. The stimulus, S–, is designated as aversive, and its termination as negatively reinforcing, on the basis of the results of the experiment. The experiment, therefore, can be seen as a test of the aversiveness of the stimulus.
3. Unlike the other reinforcement contingencies in Table 4.1, there is a connection between the discriminative stimulus or antecedent, which is the presentation of S–, and the reinforcing stimulus or consequence, which is the removal of S–.

Typically, an experiment involves a number of trials, each terminating after a correct response or a fixed period of exposure to the aversive stimulus, separated by inter-trial intervals in which no stimuli are presented. Experimental studies of escape have generally used apparatus in which a long series of trials (S– presentations) can be presented at appropriate intervals without the participant having to be removed. In the Skinner box, for example, lever presses can be arranged to terminate electric shocks coming from the grid floor. Studies in which the strength of the aversive stimulus has been varied have found that escape behaviour increases in frequency as the intensity of the aversive stimulus increases, but escape behaviour may reach a maximum rate and then decline if the aversive-stimulus intensity is made very great. The decline in responding associated with very intense aversive events is mainly due to a general suppressive (emotional) effect of strong aversive stimuli.

Ethical concerns have limited the number of experiments on escape behaviour with human participants. That is, we are reluctant to carry out, or sanction others carrying out, experiments that necessarily involve people being presented with aversive events. Our concern is perfectly reasonable – as is concern with the ethics of carrying out experiments with non-human animals that involve aversive stimuli – but it can be argued that it is misplaced because escape behaviour is very important in humans as in other species. Imagine the danger a young child would be in if she was incapable of escape learning when, for example, she put her hand too near a flame. Consequently, our scientific curiosity should be aroused and, more importantly, a better knowledge of how it occurs in humans would enable us to devise *intervention strategies* for significant human problems. Consider the example of self-injurious behaviour, a very distressing problem that greatly reduces the quality of life of a large number of people with moderate or severe learning disabilities (approaches to this problem are discussed in Chapter 6). One way of conceptualizing this phenomenon would be as a failure of escape learning that normally occurs. For most of us, the pain of striking our head on a wall, for example, rapidly leads to a change in behaviour and this is a form of escape learning. It may be that some people lack the capacity to readily learn in this way or, more likely, that other escape contingencies (perhaps escape from social pressures) have a greater influence on their behaviour. As with all forms of conditioning, we need basic research on escape procedures with human behaviour, and comparative studies with other species, in order to understand the behavioural processes and to design effective interventions for serious behavioural problems.

## Avoidance

Consider the escape paradigm applied to the example of someone walking in the rain:

| S−: | R → | S⁰ |
|---|---|---|
| rain falling | put up umbrella | rain escaped |

This seems to be a clear case of escape behaviour; in the presence of the rain (A), putting up the umbrella (B) is reinforced by escape from the rain (C). Consider, however, another element of this incident: the person was carrying an umbrella. Can we explain the 'umbrella-carrying response' in terms of an operant reinforcement contingency? It seems likely that umbrella-carrying on a showery day is reinforced by the avoidance of getting wet that would otherwise occur. We can thus state:

| $S^D$: | R → | $S^0$ |
|---|---|---|
| showery day | carry an umbrella | rain avoided |

Note the differences between this three-term relationship and the one for escape. The discriminative stimulus ($S^D$) or antecedent (A) for making the umbrella-carrying response (B) is not now an aversive stimulus as well: it need not actually be raining when we leave the house for us to take an umbrella. Furthermore, the consequence of making the response is rather different. In the escape paradigm, S– offset occurs as soon as the response is made. *In the avoidance paradigm, S⁻ is prevented from occurring*, and thus avoided, by the response.

In an experimental avoidance procedure, a stimulus is programmed to occur unless a specified operant response occurs. Occurrence of that response cancels or postpones these stimulus presentations. If this contingency results in an increase in frequency of that response, then *avoidance learning* has occurred, and the stimulus has negative reinforcement properties for that response. Notice that the avoidance procedure supplements the escape paradigm in giving us a second, independent, way of discovering negative reinforcers, and thus defining aversive stimuli.

Representing avoidance diagrammatically is awkward, because the crucial element is the postponement or cancellation of an event that has not yet occurred. Figure 4.1 illustrates 'timelines' for two types of *avoidance schedule*, which have often been used in experimental studies. In free operant avoidance (Figure 4.1a), aversive stimuli occur at regular intervals unless an operant response occurs. If it does, the next aversive stimulus is postponed for a period of time. On this schedule, no aversive stimuli will ever be delivered if each response follows the preceding one within the specified interval. In discriminated avoidance (Figure 4.1b), a discriminative stimulus (S^D) precedes each aversive stimulus delivery. A response during the 'warning signal' S^D cancels the forthcoming aversive stimulus and terminates the S^D. Responses

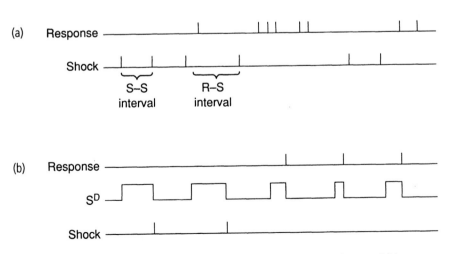

**Figure 4.1** Timelines illustrating the procedures of (a) free operant avoidance and (b) discriminated avoidance

during the inter-trial interval have no effect. Every aversive stimulus will be avoided if one response occurs during each $S^D$.

Many experimental studies with non-human animals have shown that animals will learn to respond effectively and thus, after a certain amount of training, avoid virtually all the aversive stimuli that might occur. This is a surprising finding: it seems highly intelligent to be able to respond in a way that improves the future conditions. Consequently, the ability of animals to solve problems of this type, in Thorndike's terminology, attracted a lot of interest from experimenters and theoreticians, and we will briefly review some of the issues.

Everyday descriptions of avoidance behaviour are couched in purposive terms. In the case of avoidance, we say that we turn the wheel of a skidding car away from the direction of the skid to avoid a crash, that one builds a bridge in a certain way to avoid its collapsing, that a deer flees in order to avoid a pursuing wolf. As discussed earlier, the term 'to', or 'in order to', imputes a purposive quality to the behaviour, and such explanations are generally rejected by scientists on the grounds that they purport to let a future (and therefore non-existent) event be the cause of a present (existing) event. For this reason, and to provide a parsimonious explanation of how non-human animals could solve the apparently complex problem of avoidance learning, behaviour theorists sought to explain the facts of avoidance by a mechanism that was analogous to positive reinforcement or escape behaviour. However, this is difficult to do because, in both positive reinforcement and escape learning, behaviour is reinforced by making a stimulus change consequent upon that behaviour. In avoidance learning, however, the aversive stimulus is present neither after the response nor before it. Rather, it occurs intermittently in the absence of responding.

There are at least two routes to a solution of this problem.

1. Perhaps there is a stimulus, or stimulus change, which is a consequence of responding and acquires the power to reinforce avoidance responses. If this is the case, then avoidance learning may be described in similar terms to positive reinforcement or escape learning. For example, in the procedure of Figure 4.1b, the offset of the $S^D$ (but not the onset) may act as a reinforcing stimulus because it signals a 'safe' period when no aversive stimuli will be presented.

2. Perhaps the occurrence of a reduced frequency of aversive events over a period of time following the operant response is sufficient to act as a reinforcing stimulus. After all, if a number of operant responses occur there will be a low or zero rate of aversive events, but if no operant responses occur there will be a high rate of aversive events.

A review of the extensive experimental research literature shows that, in various non-human species, avoidance behaviour can be maintained by both types of effect (see Leslie, 1996, Chapter 8, for a review). This suggests that while short-term consequences may have big effects on operant behaviour (as we have seen with positive reinforcement and escape learning procedures), consequences over a longer period may also be effective (for example, the occurrence of a period of time with a lower frequency of aversive events in an avoidance learning procedure). Learning in laboratory animals (pigeons and rats, for example) clearly includes an ability to learn from relationships between behaviour and long-delayed consequences, as well as the immediate consequences that are more often studied in experiments.

# Punishment

We define punishment, similarly to other behavioural processes, as a procedure with a characteristic outcome. In the punishment procedure, a stimulus is made contingent upon a specified response. If a variety of characteristic effects occur, particularly a reduction in frequency or suppression of that response, then we say that punishment has occurred, and that the contingent stimulus is a punisher, a punishing stimulus or an aversive stimulus. We can represent the procedure as:

$$R \rightarrow S-$$

where

R is the specified response or behaviour (B), and
S− is an aversive stimulus, or punishing consequence (C).

As with escape and avoidance procedures, the punishment paradigm provides a way of assessing the aversiveness of contingent stimuli. However, note that in parallel with all other operant procedures, the effect of the contingent stimulus depends on the particular situation or antecedent (A), the particular response selected for study, and other contextual variables. We cannot assume, for example, that the verbal command, 'Sssh!', which effectively silences a child talking in church, will also have this effect in a schoolroom. Neither can we assume that a stimulus identified as an effective punishing consequence, or punisher, for one operant will necessarily effectively punish another operant behaviour, or that a stimulus found aversive from escape or avoidance procedures will necessarily act as a punisher.

In ordinary language, the word 'punishment' is used ambiguously. It can either mean the delivery of an aversive stimulus contingent upon a response, as here, or simply the delivery of an aversive stimulus in no particular relation to behaviour. We have removed this ambiguity, and there are important behavioural differences between the two procedures. Simple delivery of an aversive stimulus tends to disrupt behaviour generally, but not selectively reduce any particular category of behaviour. We also depart from ordinary language in specifying that punishment has only occurred when a particular behavioural *effect* is seen.

Early laboratory work with non-human animals on punishment (including some findings of Skinner, 1938) appeared to support the conclusion that punishment yields only a transient effect on operant behaviour, and this conclusion is still occasionally quoted. However, as long ago as 1966, an authoritative review was produced by Azrin and Holz of later findings where reliable punishment effects were obtained. They pointed out that a number of methodological requirements must be met to enable punishment phenomena to be investigated successfully, and these were not always achieved in the early studies. There must be a reliable methodology for maintaining operant behaviour in the absence of punishment, which is supplied by the use of schedules of intermittent positive reinforcement (these are discussed in Chapter 5), and there must be a punishing stimulus that can be defined in terms of physical measurements (so that it can reliably be reproduced), delivered in a consistent manner to the experimental participant, and that cannot be escaped from (for example, by leaving the experimental situation). The punishing

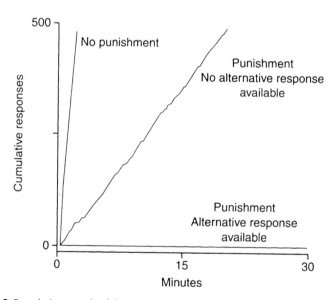

**Figure 4.2** Cumulative records of the punished responding of human participants on a variable-interval schedule of reinforcement under three conditions; when an alternative response was available, punishment totally suppressed responding (Azrin and Holz, 1966, based on data from Herman and Azrin, 1964)

stimulus should also be one that does not elicit strong behavioural responses itself, and that can be varied in intensity over a large range. From the 1960s, use of intermittently reinforced operant behaviour in Skinner boxes, with electric shock delivered as the punishing stimulus, met all these requirements. The main conclusions of Azrin and Holz's (1966) review were consistent with the hypothesis that punishment can have effects that are broadly opposite to those of positive reinforcement: within limits, more intense and more frequent punishment produces greater response suppression, provided that the punishing stimulus is reliable and immediately follows the response. Other factors they identified as contributing to punishment effectiveness were that long periods of punishment should be avoided, and that punishment effectiveness increases when an alternative (reinforced) response is available. Not all the data they reviewed was from non-human studies, and Figure 4.2 shows a clear effect of punishment (by 'an annoying buzzer sound') on human operant behaviour, which was greatly enhanced when an alternative reinforced response was also available.

## 4.3 AVERSIVE CLASSICAL CONDITIONING

Escape, avoidance and punishment procedures all involve programmed relationships between responses and aversive stimuli. The other general class of aversive contingencies involves relationships between neutral (conditioned) stimuli and aversive stimuli, and is a variety of classical conditioning. Classical conditioning can occur in procedures that were designed to demonstrate the operant conditioning phenomena of escape, avoidance or punishment. This can happen because the most important relation may turn out to be that between the context and the aversive event, without regard to the contingency involving an operant response. In fact, it was this type of effect that was probably responsible for some of the early experiments from which it was concluded that 'punishment doesn't work', such as those by Skinner (1938) referred to in the previous paragraph. The problem can be illustrated as follows. There is an experimental participant (e.g., a laboratory rat) in a stimulus context (e.g., a Skinner box), and a contingency has been arranged between a particular response (e.g., a lever press) and an aversive consequence (e.g., a shock delivered through the floor). This is planned as an operant punishment procedure, but it also contains this relationship:

CS          –          US
Skinner box            Shock

There will be repeated pairings between the Skinner box and an aversive event, which can result in classically conditioned responses (typically, of fear and immobility) in the apparatus. That is, it may be that the effective relation is between the context and the shock, without regard to the behaviour of pressing the lever. In order not to get this result, the procedures described in the previous paragraph for the effective use of punishment should be followed. In particular, the aversive stimulus used should not be too intense and should not elicit a strong behavioural response itself. These findings can be seen as a 'nuisance' (given that the classical conditioning was not the main focus of study), but are better taken as illustrations of how operant and classical conditioning interact in laboratory settings as well as in natural settings.

Aversive classical conditioning is studied directly when contingencies are arranged between CSs and aversive USs. Many aspects of the resultant process parallel appetitive classical conditioning. Indeed, many Pavlovian phenomena were originally demonstrated with aversive conditioning. However, all these studies involve restrained organisms. That is, in order to measure the unconditioned and conditioned responses, an apparatus was used that kept the animal in one place. If freely moving participants are used, some effects are seen in aversive classical conditioning that distinguish it from appetitive classical conditioning.

Some of these are so-called species-typical aversive behaviours. That is, they are the actions that members of that species usually engage in when in a dangerous situation. One simple effect of this type is that if an unrestrained animal is presented with a CS, which has on several previous occasions been followed by an aversive event, it may simply run away from the location of the CS. As with many of the effects seen in classical conditioning, this makes good biological sense because it removes the animal from apparent danger. A related effect of aversive classical conditioning is that suppression or disruption of ongoing operant behaviour can be elicited by an aversive CS. This is called conditioned suppression and is discussed in Chapter 5, because it is a widely used technique in behavioural neuroscience.

## 4.4 TIME OUT: THE CONTINGENT REMOVAL OF POSITIVE EVENTS

The types of reinforcement contingency listed in Table 4.1 include: positive reinforcement, where operant behaviour is increased by contingent presentations of stimuli; along with negative reinforcement, where operant behaviour is increased by contingent removal of stimuli; and punishment, where operant behaviour is increased by contingent presentations of stimuli. The fourth variation, the removal of positive events contingent on responding can also be used to decrease behaviour. Because this contingency has been used more widely in application to human problem behaviours than in animal laboratory studies, we will discuss applied human studies here. In time out from positive reinforcement, the person is removed from all positively reinforcing events for a brief period of time. Time out can be either exclusionary or non-exclusionary. With *exclusionary time out*, the person is removed from the current environment where the unwanted behaviour is occurring, and placed in a barren room (usually termed a 'time-out room') where no reinforcing items are available for a brief time period. Exclusionary time out is a useful method for dealing with tantrums and aggression, as such behaviours can be disruptive to others in the setting (for example, other students in a classroom). Once the brief time period has elapsed and the individual is observed not to be engaging in the aberrant behaviour then they are allowed to return to the original activities. Brief periods in time out seem to be as effective as extended time-out periods in reducing maladaptive or disruptive behaviour, and extended time-out periods might well interfere with ongoing educational activity for the person concerned.

An alternative to exclusionary time out is *non-exclusionary time out*, where the individual remains in the setting where the unwanted behaviour occurs. However, the person does not have access to reinforcers in this setting for a brief period of time. This is generally a more acceptable procedure to professionals and parents because the person is not placed in isolation. Additionally, the person has the opportunity to continue to engage in educational activities while they are in the time-out condition. In a typical study of this technique, staff removed a child away from toys and other children to a corner of the classroom whenever the designated disruptive behaviour occurred. The child was told to remain in the corner and observe the other children playing. Staff then returned to the child after 1 minute and asked the child if he was ready to return to the group. If the child was not engaged in the unwanted behaviour (e.g., tantrums) and indicated that he wanted to return to the group then he was allowed to play again. This technique is effective in reducing overall levels of disruption and aggression in a class of pre-school children. In Chapter 6 we will compare the utility of this technique with others designed to change behaviour in this type of context. We will also discuss in Chapter 6 the ethics of introducing any type of operant contingency designed to reduce the frequency of human operant behaviour.

## 4.5 CONDITIONED REINFORCEMENT

It is apparent that some of the special consequences that we have been calling reinforcers, and that have been used in positive reinforcement procedures, have a more natural or biological primacy than others: we have already noted (Section 3.8) that this led to Hull's (1943) theory that biological need or drive reduction was crucial to reinforcement. Food, water and sex seem to fall into a different, more 'basic', category than books, money and cars; yet people, at one time or another, work for all of the things in the latter category, and these thus meet our definition of a reinforcing stimulus. We can distinguish between these two categories by the manner in which a stimulus comes to be effective as a reinforcer. For each individual, there exists a class of reinforcers whose powers are a biological consequence of the individual's membership of a certain species. Possibilities of reinforcement that come built into the organism in this way define the *primary or unconditioned reinforcers*, but there is also a second group of *conditioned reinforcers*, which appear more variable and less predictable from individual to individual than the primary ones.

Money, cars, holidays, prestige, honour and the countless other arbitrary things that human beings work for, constitute a vast range of reinforcers. But many of these objects and events have no value for us at birth. Clearly, they must have *acquired* their capacity to reinforce behaviour at some time during each individual's past history. A particular past history is necessary; people of different generations, for example, do not have the same taste in popular music, and even people of the same age do not all like the same pieces of music or the same novels. The context or discriminative stimulus is also important: the business executive may enjoy a telephone call from a friend when work is slack, but be irritated by it occurring during an important meeting.

While the importance of conditioned reinforcers is much more evident in human behaviour than in the behaviour of other species, the ways in which previously unimportant stimuli (lights, noises etc.) come to have conditioned reinforcing value have been investigated extensively in laboratory experiments with other animal species. It turns out that a relatively simple rule determines when a stimulus acquires conditioned reinforcing value: a stimulus acquires conditioned reinforcing value if it signals a reduction in the delay of (unconditioned) reinforcement (Fantino, 1977). Extrapolating this principle to human development, we would expect children to be reinforced by access to stimuli that signal forthcoming mealtimes, other treats, or a period of parental affection. Because the stimuli that have these functions vary from one child's experience to another's, we would anticipate that conditioned reinforcers vary in value from individual to individual. As children grow up and their social lives become more complex, those conditioned reinforcers established earlier in life form the basis for establishing the reinforcing value of further events. By this means, some of the events that are important (and have the function of conditioned reinforcement for classes of operant behaviour) for an individual may become quite subtle and personal.

The stimulus that seems to have most general properties as a conditioned reinforcer is, of course, money. Money has the culturally defined property of being exchangeable for just about any other item: it therefore has the capacity to reduce the delay of many types of reinforcement. We can define a *generalized conditioned reinforcer* as one that has acquired reinforcing value through signalling a reduction in delay (or presentation) of many different primary reinforcers and previously established conditioned reinforcers. Money fits this definition, but it is still not a perfectly generalized conditioned reinforcer, because we still tend to prefer some forms of money to others. Thus, we might prefer gold coins to notes, or refuse to put our money in the bank and keep the cash at home instead. These 'irrational' habits presumably reflect the fact the reinforcing value of money is acquired and affected by details of the past histories of individuals. Generalized conditioned reinforcers are often used to increase adaptive behaviour in applied or clinical settings, and we will discuss examples of this in Chapter 6.

This discussion has been about conditioned positive reinforcers – that is, events that have a reinforcing value because they have signalled forthcoming positive reinforcers. There is also a class of conditioned negative reinforcers. These events, which are also called conditioned aversive stimuli, are established through a history of signalling forthcoming aversive events. Of course, this may occur with a CS that precedes an aversive US, as described in Section 4.3, and those CS's are indeed also conditioned negative reinforcers. This fits in with our everyday experience: we wish to escape from or avoid stimuli that have been presented with, or have preceded, aversive events. We may not wish, for example, to re-visit a building where we had a job interview resulting in failure, and we may not wish to be with someone who has previously told us bad news.

## 4.6 EXTINCTION OF OPERANT BEHAVIOUR

Operant conditioning results in changes in the behavioural repertoire. It provides a method by which the organism adapts to its own circumstances by selectively increasing the frequency of responses that are followed by reinforcing stimuli. It is not surprising to find that if a previously reinforced operant response is no longer followed by its usual reinforcing consequence, the frequency of the operant declines. This behavioural process is called *extinction*. We shall see in a later section of this chapter that operant extinction has the same overall effect as the related process of extinction following classical conditioning, first studied by I.P. Pavlov (Pavlov, 1927). This overall effect, common to the two conditioning processes, is the reduction in frequency of a specific response. In both cases, the process broadly reverses the effects of conditioning once the circumstances, or contingencies, that resulted in conditioning have been removed or substantially changed. However, there are also a number of associated phenomena specific to operant extinction. Not surprisingly, both operant extinction and classical extinction exert important influences on human behaviour.

Operant extinction occurs when the reinforcement contingency that produced operant conditioning is removed, but this can be done in at least two ways. Following operant conditioning, the normal operation is to cease presenting the reinforcing stimulus at all – and most of the findings reported here are based on this procedure – but there is an alternative. As it is the particular relationship, or contingency, between operant response and reinforcer that defines operant conditioning and brings about changes in behaviour, then any operation that removes the contingency constitutes extinction. Thus, a procedure in which the reinforcing stimulus continues to occur, but is no longer dependent on occurrences of the operant response, can result in extinction.

Note that the word 'extinction' is used in two different ways (and a similar distinction was made earlier in discussing the term 'punishment'). Extinction refers to the experimental procedure, or operation, of breaking the contingency between response and reinforcer. However, it is also a name for the observed resulting decline in the frequency of the response when that operation is carried out. We call this change in behaviour the extinction process. A response is said to have been extinguished if the frequency has fallen close to its operant level as a result of there no longer being a contingency between that behaviour and the reinforcer. There are, of course, other methods of reducing the frequency of a response (such as punishment – see Section 4.2), but these are not called extinction.

The decline in the rate of the once-reinforced response is the best-documented effect of extinction. The response rate is highest at the start of extinction, just after reinforcement is withdrawn, and gradually diminishes over a period of time. There can be said to be an 'extinction curve' (the converse of a 'learning curve'), because a graph of response rate over time would usually show a steady decline in response rate. Some researchers have found that the extinction process is due principally to a gradual increase in the number of inactive periods over time, and that when the organism responds it does so at the high rate that was previously shown during reinforcement. Accompanying the overall decline in response rate in extinction, there is often seen a transitory increase in rate, or *extinction burst*, at the very beginning of extinction. A possible reason for this transient effect is discussed in the next section.

The effects of extinction are by no means confined to frequency changes in the selected response. Changes occur in the form of the behaviour and its organization during extinction. In a classic study by Antonitis (1951), in which the operant under study involved a rat poking its nose through a slot in the wall (see Figure 4.3), the effects of several sessions of extinction interspersed with reinforcement were measured. One wall of the chamber used by Antonitis contained a horizontal slot, 50 centimetres long. Whenever the rat poked its nose into the slot, a light beam was broken, causing a photograph of the rat to be made at the exact instant of the response. By reinforcing nose poking with food, the frequency of this behaviour was first increased above operant level. Subsequently, nose poking was extinguished, reconditioned, re-extinguished, and reconditioned again. Antonitis found that response position and angle

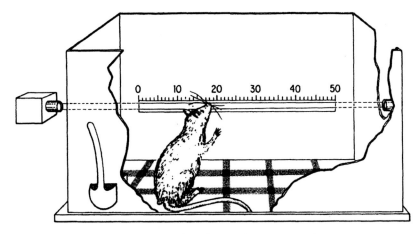

**Figure 4.3** Apparatus used by Antonitis (1951) to reinforce a nose-poking response

tended to become stereotyped during reinforcement: the animal confined its responses to a rather restricted region of the slot. Extinction, however, produced *variability* in nose poking at least as great as that observed during operant level; the animal varied its responses over the entire length of the slot. Finally, reconditioning resulted in even more stereotyped behaviour (more restricted responses) than the original conditioning had produced. It is also found that while a sequence of behaviour (e.g., the occurrence of the operant response followed by the response required to retrieve the food pellet or other reinforcer) becomes stereotyped during operant conditioning, this sequence breaks down during extinction.

The occurrence of increased variability in behaviour is a general effect of extinction. This makes the behavioural repertoire more like the behaviour seen prior to conditioning, and it is also adaptive in a biological sense. That is, if the behaviour that was previously effective (e.g., in obtaining food) is no longer effective, it is likely that other variants in behaviour will be more useful. We often experience this sort of change in our own behaviour. If you are writing with a pen and the ink ceases to flow, you automatically begin to press harder, shake the pen, or scribble on spare paper with it; if your usual hand movement fails to open the door you immediately try more vigorous actions, and so on.

## 4.7 EXTINCTION-INDUCED AGGRESSION

Some responses that are reduced in frequency when an operant is reinforced (in the case of a rat reinforced with food these may include grooming and investigatory behaviour) increase again during extinction. More surprisingly, some 'new' behaviour may be seen. That is, responses occur that were not seen during reinforcement and had effectively zero operant level prior to reinforcement. The most remarkable of these is aggression. Azrin, Hutchinson and Hake (1966) trained a hungry pigeon to peck a disk for food. When the pigeon in the experiment had acquired key pecking behaviour, a second 'target' pigeon, immobilized in a specially designed box, was introduced into the experimental compartment (see Figure 4.4). The box holding the target pigeon was mounted on an assembly that caused a switch underneath to close whenever the box was jiggled vigorously. The assembly was carefully balanced so that the normal spontaneous movements of the target pigeon were insufficient to close the switch, whereas any forceful attacks that the experimental pigeon might direct against the body of the target pigeon would be recorded. Attacks occurred predictably: whenever its reinforcement contingencies were abruptly changed from reinforcement of pecking to extinction, the experimental pigeon invariably attacked the target pigeon. The attacks were vicious and aggressive, lasting up to 10 minutes.

Other experiments have established a considerable degree of generality for this result by demonstrating that extinction-induced aggression can be obtained with various species and reinforcers. The important point to remember is that these attacks do not occur simply because no reinforcement

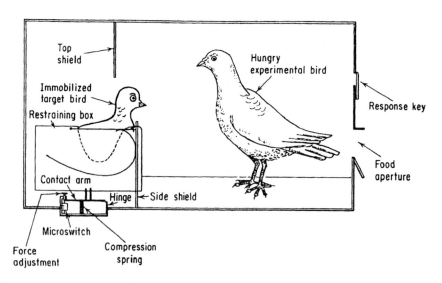

**Figure 4.4** Apparatus used for measuring extinction-induced aggression in a pigeon in a Skinner box (Azrin *et al.*, 1966)

is available, but because reinforcement was previously available and has now been discontinued. The behaviour seen can be classed as 'emotional', as certain transitions to conditions where reinforcement is no longer available tend to make all of us emotional in some sense. Children cry when they lose their toys, and even adults sometimes assault vending machines that take their money without giving anything out. As noted in the previous section, this type of variation in behaviour is sometimes adaptive (the crying child may be comforted, and the assaulted vending machine sometimes pays out). The transient increase in operant behaviour, or extinction burst, often seen at this stage is also emotional and is potentially adaptive behaviour.

## 4.8 RESISTANCE TO EXTINCTION

Were the extinction process allowed to go to completion, the operant-level state might eventually be reached; that is, the frequency of the operant response might return to the before-conditioning level. The time taken for this to occur could then be used as an index of the individual's persistence in the face of extinction, and thus of the strength of responding before extinction was begun. In actual experiments, however, a return to operant level is rarely reached, and more practical measures of persistence are based on how fast the response rate declines during extinction. For instance, the number of responses emitted, or the amount of time, up until the point at which some low-rate criterion (such as a period of 5 minutes with no responses) is met, are called resistance-to-extinction measures.

Resistance to extinction provides a quantitative behavioural index that is related in an interesting way to a number of experimental operations. In everyday life, we are often interested in how persistent a person will be in the face of no reward. A person whose resistance to extinction is low is said to 'give up too easily' or to lack 'perseverance' at a difficult task. On the other hand, too much resistance to extinction is sometimes counter-productive. The man or woman who spends too much time fruitlessly trying to patch up a broken love affair may miss a good chance for a new and better relationship.

One of the variables that has been shown to affect resistance to extinction is the number of previous reinforcements. If a large number of responses have been reinforced, resistance to extinction is greater than if only a few have been. Another variable that affects the persistence of a response in extinction is the effortfulness of the response: the greater the effort needed to complete the operant response, the more persistent the response is during extinction. Even bigger effects on resistance to extinction result from exposure to *intermittent reinforcement*, which is discussed later in this chapter (and also in Chapter 5).

## 4.9 EXTINCTION OF CLASSICALLY CONDITIONED RESPONSES

As noted in earlier chapters, not only did Pavlov (1927) carry out the initial studies of classical conditioning, he sustained a systematic research programme over many years. The investigation of extinction following conditioning was a major part of this. In parallel with operant conditioning, classical extinction occurs if the CS–US pairing is broken. This is usually achieved by repeatedly presenting the CS without the US. The result is a fairly steady diminution of the response to the CS. An example for the rabbit's nictitating membrane (blinking) response is shown in Figure 4.5. Although the data in this figure are the average performances of groups of rabbits, very similar results would be obtained from individual rabbits. In the control group, the CS and US were

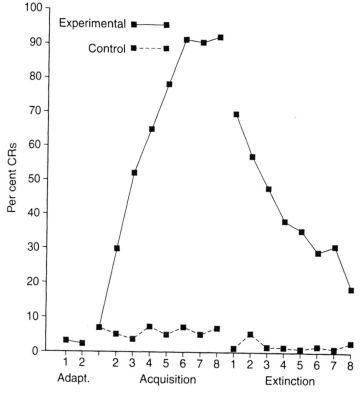

**Figure 4.5** Average percentage of CS presentations on which a classically conditioned response occurred (per cent CRs) in two groups of rabbits in acquisition and extinction (see text for details; Gormezano *et al.*, 1962)

presented but not paired together in the 'acquisition phase', and thus conditioning did not occur in that group. The experimental group showed conditioning occurring rapidly over 5 days, then reaching a steady asymptotic level. In extinction, the number of conditioned responses fell fairly steadily from day to day.

If a period of time elapses after the extinction of a classically conditioned response and then the experimental participant is returned to the experimental situation and the CS is again presented, a certain amount of *spontaneous recovery* occurs. This means that a higher level of responding is observed than at the end of the previous session. Pavlov argued that this demonstrates that *inhibition* had developed during the first extinction session and had dissipated, to some extent, before the next test, thus allowing the response to recover. This a one of a number of inhibitory phenomena discovered in the experiments of Pavlov and his associates. Pavlov, who was trained as a physiologist, presumed that inhibitory (response-suppressing) processes as well as excitatory (response-eliciting) processes will occur in conditioning. Behavioural psychologists were at first sceptical. That is, they were not sure that inhibitory concepts were needed to explain behavioural processes. After all, a response either occurs or fails to occur; we need not necessarily infer from its absence that it is inhibited, it might simply be that the stimulus no longer elicits a response. However, spontaneous recovery does suggest that some process occurs on the extinction trials that dissipates over a longer period, leading to later recovery of responding. The same effect is seen following operant extinction. That is, if the experimental participant is returned to the experimental situation some time later, renewed operant responding occurs for a while. Note that the term 'spontaneous recovery' only refers to the recovery of responding while extinction is still in effect, in either classical conditioning or operant conditioning.

## 4.10 INTERMITTENT REINFORCEMENT

So far, we have restricted our discussions of operant behaviour to examples where every occurrence of the operant response is followed by delivery of the reinforcing stimulus, and examples of extinction, where that contingency is removed. If we change the conditions so that the reinforcing stimulus occurs only after some of the designated responses, we have defined the general procedure of *intermittent reinforcement*. Intermittent reinforcement procedures can be arranged in a number of ways, with varying rules, or schedules, determining which individual responses are followed by the reinforcing stimulus.

It has been found that intermittent reinforcement procedures have great utility for generating stable, long-term baselines of learned behaviour, against which effects of drugs, physiological manipulations, classical conditioning, and motivational factors can be studied. These applications of the principles of behavioural analysis have been very important for the development of behavioural neuroscience. Consequently, the ways in which reinforcement can be arranged to produce *schedules of intermittent reinforcement*, the behaviour that ensues, and the effects of neurological interventions, will be explained in

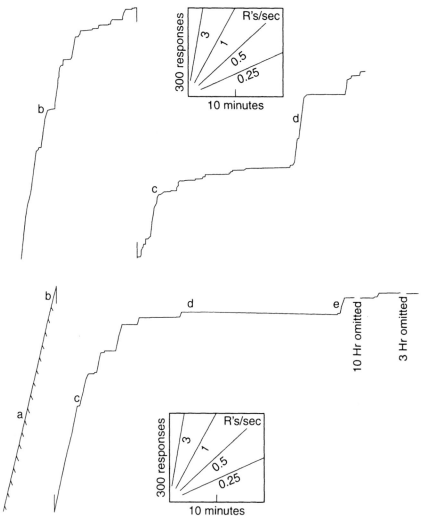

**Figure 4.6** Cumulative records of two pigeons during extinction after a short period of time on a fixed-ratio 60 schedule of reinforcement. The lower record includes (at left side), the record of prior reinforced responding; reinforcements are indicated by vertical marks. (Ferster and Skinner, 1957)

Chapter 5. The general significance of reinforcement schedules will be explained briefly here.

Any schedule of reinforcement arranges that some instances of the operant response result in delivery of the reinforcing stimulus, while other instances of the same response are ineffective. Such a schedule is usually introduced following a training period where every instance of the operant response is reinforced. The main effects on behaviour are surprising: more operant responding occurs than in the continuous reinforcement situation where every response is reinforced, and responding is now more resistant to extinction. The classic report of studies of schedules of reinforcement is that of Ferster and Skinner (1957). Among many other studies, they report the effects of extinction on operant key pecking by pigeons that had been trained for a short time on a fixed-ratio 60 schedule of intermittent reinforcement. This schedule, which will be described in detail in Chapter 6, requires 60 responses to be made before a reinforcer is delivered. Figure 4.6 shows cumulative records from two pigeons. In one case, the record from the fixed-ratio schedule is included and indicates the high rate of responding that occurs with this high response requirement for reinforcement. In both cases, the record for extinction shows that many hundreds of responses are made, mostly at a fast rate, before extinction of responding occurs.

These types of finding in the laboratory with non-human animals suggest that we should also find that intermittent reinforcement has powerful effects on human behaviour. We will see in Chapter 6 that this is the case, and intermittent reinforcement produces greater resistance to extinction in procedures that are designed to change human behaviour. However, schedules of intermittent reinforcement, such as the one illustrated in Figure 4.6, do not generally produce the same consistent patterns of behaviour with human participants. Instead, humans in such artificial situations (e.g., being asked to press a button repeatedly without being told what the likely 'reward' is) tend to generate verbal rules to guide their performance. This issue will be discussed in Chapter 7, because it concerns language and cognition.

## 4.11 DIFFERENTIAL REINFORCEMENT SCHEDULES

Positive reinforcement increases the frequency of operant behaviour and schedules of intermittent reinforcement tend to increase further the frequency and persistence of behaviour. However, psychologists working with human behavioural problems are often seeking ways to reduce behaviour that is disruptive or counter-productive, and a variety of procedures have been devised that indirectly reinforce reductions in a target behaviour. These include *differential reinforcement of other behaviour* (DRO), *differential reinforcement of incompatible behaviour* (DRI), and *differential reinforcement of alternative behaviour* (DRA). As implied by their titles, these procedures or schedules reinforce various categories of behaviour other than the target behaviour, but their effectiveness is measured primarily by the reduction in the target behaviour that occurs. The 'schedule of choice' will depend on details of the situation, but many effective interventions using these schedules have been reported. Some of these are described in Chapter 6.

## 4.12  INTERIM SUMMARY

Whereas Chapter 3 dealt with only the basic constituents of operant conditioning and classical conditioning, the first half of this chapter has been concerned with alternative types of operant conditioning, and the effects of extinction and intermittent reinforcement. The discussion has thus been mainly about the relationships between operant behaviour (B) and its consequences (C). In the next part of the chapter, we will concentrate on the role of the antecedent stimulus (A) in changing operant behaviour. As will be seen, a number of the effects in operant conditioning occur in a similar fashion in classical conditioning. In the terminology of behaviour analysis, we will be identifying further aspects of *stimulus control*, which are additional to the basic ideas presented in Chapter 3.

## 4.13  STIMULUS GENERALIZATION

Stimulus generalization is seen in crude form when a child learning to speak refers to all furry objects as 'cats', and calls all male adults 'Daddy'. It is exemplified in our own behaviour when we hail a stranger mistakenly because he appears to resemble a friend. The phenomenon of generalization is obviously very important, and the conditioning processes provide a useful way of studying it. It would be highly maladaptive if operant or classical conditioning produced responses that were so specifically linked to the training antecedent stimulus ($S^D$ or CS) that the response disappeared if some small 'irrelevant' feature of the stimulus changed. Conversely, it would be equally inappropriate if huge changes in the antecedent stimulus produced no change in the response.

The method of studying stimulus generalization is simple in principle. In the case of operant conditioning, once a response has been conditioned, variations are made in some well-controlled aspect of the environment and the rate or amount of responding at various stimulus values is measured. This is called *generalization testing* along a particular dimension of the antecedent stimulus. Let us consider a specific example. The apparatus shown in Figure 4.7 is a

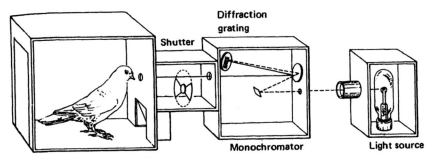

**Figure 4.7** A pigeon Skinner box fitted with an optical system to project pure light on to the pecking key

modified pigeon Skinner box in which pure light (with a single wavelength) illuminates the pecking key. The equipment permits the precise selection and presentation of any one of a large number of visible wavelengths. In an experiment performed by Guttman and Kalish (1956), birds were shaped to peck the disk, which was lit by a yellow-green light of wavelength 550 nm. Following some training, tests were made to determine to what extent the 550 nm light on the disk was specifically controlling behaviour. This test consisted of an extinction procedure in which the birds were exposed to a randomized series of successive 30-second presentations of different wavelengths, only one

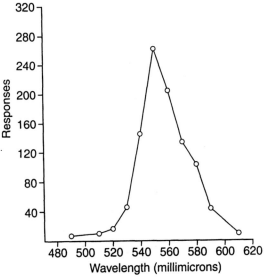

**Figure 4.8** Responses emitted in the presence of 11 different wavelengths, projected one at a time on the pecking key

of which was the 550 nm actually used in training. No other changes were made in the bird's environment.

When the numbers of extinction responses emitted in the presence of each of the different stimuli were calculated, they formed the curve shown in Figure 4.8. This indicates that the pigeons gave the maximum number of extinction responses only at their training stimulus, and gave progressively fewer responses at the test stimuli located progressively farther away from the training stimulus along the wavelength dimension. This curve, showing a reduction in responding as the environment changes, is known as the *generalization gradient*.

Generalization is a pervasive and often useful property of behaviour. For instance, skills learned in one environmental situation can be used in new situations. Having learned to catch a ball thrown from a distance of 5 feet, we will catch it pretty well at 10, 20 and maybe even 40 feet. Parents who teach their children to say 'thank you' at home are implicitly relying on generalization to see to it that 'thank you' will be emitted in similar circumstances outside the home. The educational system is designed on the assumption that the skills acquired in school will spread to environments outside the school. None the less, the generalization gradient is there to remind us that the more closely a training situation resembles the situation in which the behaviour will later be needed, the more effective will be the training. Schools and other agencies use this principle when they make the teaching situation as near to 'real life' as possible.

## 4.14 STIMULUS SALIENCE

As discussed in Sections 3.9 to 3.11, various factors determine whether a particular stimulus dimension will acquire control over behaviour. Among these are *discrimination training*, which is discussed in the next section of this chapter, and the salience of that stimulus dimension. By salience, we mean roughly, 'likelihood of being noticed and responded to'. Even within one stimulus dimension, certain stimulus values may be more likely to be responded to. For example, pecking is elicited in a newly hatched gull shown various monochromatic stimuli (that is, different colours), without any special training or experience. This unconditioned behaviour (we call behaviour 'unconditioned' if it occurs without or before conditioning) is most frequent at certain wavelengths and declines as the wavelength is raised or lowered, giving a graph or function that resembles a generalization gradient. There is clearly a stimulus class of a fairly narrow range of wavelengths of light that is effective in producing pecking, and this range of wavelengths corresponds to the colour of the adult gull's beak. The newly hatched chicks thus have a tendency to peck at their parents' beaks, rather than anything else, in the first few crucial hours of life and thus enhance their chance of being fed. (An adult gull will regurgitate food when a chick pecks at its bill.)

The phenomenon of overshadowing, discussed in Section 3.11, suggests that if a stimulus dimension is not the most salient of those present, it will not acquire control over responding. Pavlov (1927) demonstrated that if a compound CS, consisting of one intense and one weak component, was used in classical conditioning with dogs, very often no conditioned response was seen to the weaker component of the CS when it was presented by itself. He thus described the weaker CS as being overshadowed by the more intense CS. A similar effect can be demonstrated in operant conditioning. For example, if one group of pigeons is reinforced for pecking a key illuminated with white light and in the presence of a 30-mph flow of air, while another group has the same conditions, except that the key is unilluminated and the box is dark, subsequent tests will show that air-flow speed controls responding in the second group (that is, variation in the air-flow speed will produce a generalization gradient with the highest rate of responding at 30 mph, the training stimulus value), but not in the first group. For pigeons, the presence of a visual cue tends to overshadow other stimulus dimensions that might otherwise be effective. In this pigeons resemble people: we also attend selectively to visual information. More, formally, visual stimuli tend to overshadow other features of the environment.

Very often, human behaviour does come under the control of several features (or dimensions) of a complex stimulus. A child may learn that buses in his or her hometown are red, have six wheels, two decks and a rear door, that they are very noisy and smell of diesel oil. Visiting another town and seeing rather different vehicles, the child may still correctly identify them as buses. His or her response 'bus' is not attached to only one (or very few) of the stimulus features. With children that show autistic behaviour, on the other hand, a phenomenon has been demonstrated that resembles overshadowing. After training to make a simple manual response to obtain sweets with a compound auditory and visual discriminative stimulus, autistic and other children were tested with the auditory and visual components of the $S^D$ separately. Most of the other children responded on 100% of trials of both types, while the autistic children tended to respond differentially, some responding on 100% of one type of trial and none of the other (autistic children tend to respond to visual stimuli and not auditory ones). This abnormal stimulus control may underlie various aspects of autistic behaviour, which has often been described in terms of over-selectivity.

## 4.15 DISCRIMINATION TRAINING

We noted in Section 3.12 that the discriminative stimulus ($S^D$) sets the occasion for reinforcement, and when the $S^D$ is effective the response rate is higher in its presence than in its absence. The alternate stimulus situation, which generally signals the absence of the reinforcement contingency, is called 'S$^\Delta$' ('S-delta'), and S$^D$ and S$^\Delta$ are often referred to as positive and negative discriminative stimuli.

A number of procedures can be used for *discrimination training*, in which the following contingencies are presented:

S$^D$: R → S+ and
S$^\Delta$: R → no effect

This means that in the presence of the positive discriminative stimulus, S$^D$, if an instance of the operant response, R, occurs, it is followed by presentation of the reinforcing stimulus, S+, and in the presence of the negative discriminative stimulus, S$^\Delta$, if an instance of the operant response, R, occurs, it is *not* followed by presentation of the reinforcing stimulus.

If a procedure of this type is implemented, and the response rate is high in the presence of S$^D$, and low or zero in the presence of S$^\Delta$, then discrimination learning has occurred. In a simple Skinner box experiment, two lights of different wavelengths might be used as S$^D$ and S$^\Delta$, and presented alternately for 5-minute periods. What will be seen is that, initially, there will be generalization of responding in the presence of S$^D$, the reinforcement condition, to the extinction condition, in the presence of S$^\Delta$. Gradually,

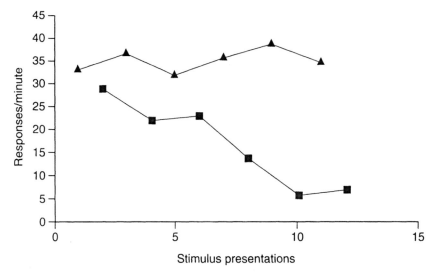

**Figure 4.9** Hypothetical data from an experiment where two discriminative stimuli are presented alternately: during S$^D$, responding is reinforced and during S$^\Delta$ responding is not reinforced; the data shown follow a period of training when only S$^D$ was presented

discrimination learning will occur and the rate of responding in the presence of $S^\Delta$ will decline towards zero. Hypothetical, but typical, data are shown in Figure 4.9.

Note that although we here define discrimination as an operant paradigm, there is a closely related classical conditioning paradigm. Earlier, in Section 3.11, we described the discrimination in classical conditioning, in which one CS (CS+) is followed by food (or another US) while another is also presented but never followed by the US. With this procedure, after a number of CS+ and CS– presentations, a greater response is elicited by CS+ than CS–. In parallel with the operant procedure, the response to CS– often tends towards zero with extended training. These related operant and classical procedures turn out to have very similar behavioural consequences.

Like reinforcement and extinction, discrimination is both a procedure and a behavioural process with a specified outcome. This interdependence between procedures and outcomes reflects the fact that behavioural phenomena are neither pieces of behaviour nor sets of environmental conditions, but interactions between the two.

Our formal definition of discrimination corresponds quite closely to our everyday use of the term. Discriminations are demonstrated at the human level by the ability to 'tell two or more things apart'. Some of us, for instance, discriminate the paintings of Monet from those of Manet, butter from margarine, or two sets of similar fingerprints. In 'telling these things apart', we are showing differential responses to them. Human discriminations vary considerably in the number of stimulus situations and response alternatives involved, as the following examples show. In every case, the necessary condition of differential reinforcement (and behaviour) associated with different environments is met.

- The discriminating movie-goer does not go to every film that arrives at his or her neighbourhood cinema. He or she goes to some, and does not go to others.
- We say that some groups of people are discriminated against when they are treated differently from the way in which other people are treated. That is, the discriminated group is treated one way and other people are treated another way.
- The professional wine-taster can discriminate a variety of wines that all taste the same to the novice. The professional's discrimination is evidenced by his or her ability to give a unique name to each one of a hundred different wines. Thus he or she makes a hundred different responses to a hundred different stimuli. Note that this is an example of how functional stimulus classes change. For the novice, there are very few stimulus classes and many wines 'taste the same' as one another; for the professional these wines are different stimuli, each controlling a range of responses, relating to the name, flavour, quality and so on.

## 4.16 STIMULUS EQUIVALENCE

Thus far we have discussed stimulus control in terms of the physical properties of stimulus classes. We have seen that, in generalization tests, human and non-human experimental participants can emit a response in the presence of a stimulus they have never encountered, as long as it is physically similar to an $S^D$ used during training. Furthermore, the more dissimilar a test stimulus is from the $S^D$ the weaker, or less frequent, is the emitted response. We have suggested that generalization and discrimination could account for aspects of complex human behaviour. However, if we examine more closely the stimulus classes that control complex aspects of our behaviour, such as social interaction, we quickly come to realize that the types of stimulus control discussed thus far are only part of the story.

Consider the following example. You are driving a car and you encounter a red traffic light: the red light acts as an $S^D$ for an avoidance response: applying the brakes of the car and stopping. However, many other stimuli could serve the same function. Here are some examples:

- a policeman stepping on to the road with a raised hand
- a passenger shouting 'Stop the car!'
- an elderly person trying to cross the road.

In this context, all four stimuli are *functionally equivalent* – that is, they control the same behaviour and thus have the same function for you. Even in the case of this very simple example it is apparent that the basis of this functional equivalence is not physical similarity: the four stimuli that are followed by the same response do not look at all similar to each other, so the behaviour could not have been learnt in the presence of one of them and then generalized to the others, in the fashion described in Section 4.13. It is thus necessary to consider alternative explanations. We might argue that each stimulus acquired control through direct training, and stopping the car has been reinforced in the presence of each of these antecedent stimuli. However, this seems a laborious method and, in the case considered here, a dangerous one, for stimuli to acquire control over behaviour. It is more likely that all four physically different stimuli are members of the same stimulus class. There have been some recent developments in behaviour analysis that provide an account of how *functional stimulus classes* that contain members with no physical similarities to each other may be formed efficiently. These developments have arisen from research on *stimulus equivalence*, or *equivalence classes*.

Before describing equivalence classes, we must describe the more complex discrimination training procedure most commonly employed to study them, which is *matching-to-sample training*. The experiments have usually been carried out on human experimental participants and, for convenience, computer-generated images are often used as stimuli. Stimuli are usually nonsense syllables or random shapes, and thus have no meaning for the experimental participants prior to the experiment. The procedure involves presenting a stimulus, referred to as the *sample*, centrally near the top of a computer display screen (see Figure 4.10). Several (usually three) *comparison* stimuli are presented simultaneously at the bottom of the screen. The experimental participant's task is to learn through trial and error which comparison goes with the sample. Choices are made by striking an appropriate key, and feedback on correct choices is given automatically by the computer. It is important to note that the 'correct' response is defined by the experimenter and that there is no logical connection or physical similarity between the sample stimulus and any of the comparison stimuli.

Given sufficient training, human and non-human experimental participants can readily learn to match stimuli in this manner, and select the correct comparison to go with each sample that is being used in all, or a very large percentage of, trials. (In the example given, there will be a total of three different sample stimuli and three corresponding comparison stimuli.) However, it is when human experimental participants are trained on a number of related matching-to-sample tasks that some interesting *emergent relationships* are observed that have not been explicitly trained. These are observed in the case of *verbally competent* human experimental participants (those who are able to speak and use language) and they give rise to equivalence classes.

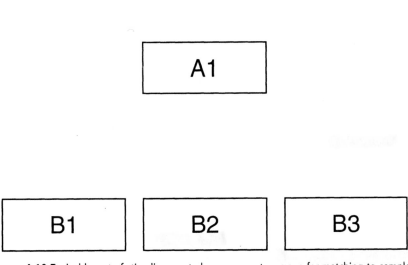

**Figure 4.10** Typical layout of stimuli presented on a computer screen for matching-to-sample training in a stimulus equivalence experiment; in this trial the sample stimulus, A1, must be matched to the correct comparison, B1, by selecting a corresponding key or touching the stimulus; the codes, A1, B1 etc. are used to identify the stimuli within the experiment and are not the stimuli seen by the experimental participant

The simplest experiment of this type involves two related matching responses. Experimental participants are initially trained to match several (typically, three) comparison stimuli (B1, B2, B3) to the same number of sample stimuli (A1, A2, A3). During a trial, either A1, A2 or A3 is presented as a sample and B1, B2 and B3 are all presented simultaneously as comparisons (as shown in Figure 4.10). Feedback is given for correct choices (which will be B1 given A1, B2 given A2 and B3 given A3) and for incorrect choices. (A difference between 'feedback' and 'reinforcement' is that we use feedback to describe a procedure in which information is provided to the participant on each occasion on which they make a response. They are told whether this is 'correct' or 'incorrect' and this feedback is usually presumed to act as reinforcement for the correct responses.) Once criterion performance is achieved on the matching-to-sample task, which typically involves making correct responses on more than 90% of a batch of trials, a second phase of training begins. In this phase either B1, B2 or B3 appears as a sample and three new comparisons – C1, C2 and C3 – appear. Correct choices will now be C1 given B1, C2 given B2 and C3 given B3. Note that the 'B stimuli' are used as samples at this stage, while they were used as comparisons in the earlier stage. Once again, there is generally no physical resemblance or logical relationship between the B sample stimuli and the C comparison stimuli that must now be selected to go with them, just as there was no such A-to-B relationship in the earlier phase. Again, training continues until a criterion level of correct responding is achieved.

If tested at this stage on certain untrained matching responses, verbally competent human experimental participants may respond correctly. For example, they will correctly match the appropriate A stimuli with the B stimuli, if the B stimuli appear as samples and the A stimuli appear as comparisons. This emergent matching response is referred to as *symmetry*, because it is the reverse of the relationship that had previously been trained. Similarly, they will correctly match the appropriate B stimuli to C stimuli, another type of symmetry response. If the A stimuli are presented as both sample and comparisons, they correctly match each A stimulus with itself. This is referred to as *reflexivity*, and will be observed in the case of B and C stimuli also. As reflexivity essentially involves successfully matching something to itself, it seems most unsurprising but, as we shall see later, it is not normally a consequence of matching-to-sample training in non-human species. If the A stimuli appear as samples and the C stimuli as comparisons, verbally competent human participants will correctly match C stimuli to the appropriate A stimuli. This is called *transitivity*. They will also show *combined symmetry and transitivity*, which is observed when the C stimuli are presented as samples and the A stimuli as comparisons. When all these matching responses are observed, a stimulus equivalence class (involving A, B and C) is said to have been formed, because each member of the class is treated equivalently (Sidman, 1971, 1990 and 1994). These stimulus relations are illustrated in Figure 4.11.

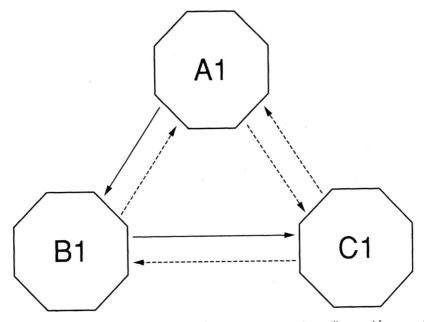

**Figure 4.11** Training and outcome of a stimulus equivalence experiment illustrated for one set of stimuli, A1, B1 and C1; as described in the text, the relations A1–B1 and B1–C1 were trained (these are indicated with solid lines) and the other four relations (dashed lines) are found to exist when tested along with the relations A1–A1, B1–B1 and C1–C1

The notion that physically unrelated stimuli are treated as equivalent when they are members of the same class is a formal statement of something that is very familiar to us. For example, the written word 'shoe', the spoken word 'shoe' and a picture of a shoe are all said to refer to the same thing, and a child could be taught to treat them as equivalent through matching-to-sample training (Sidman, 1990). However, this may be a uniquely human capacity. While A-to-B and B-to-C training is sufficient to produce equivalence classes in verbally competent humans, animals of other species (including chimpanzees, see Dugdale and Lowe, 2000) may succeed in reaching criterion performances on the matching-to-sample tasks but not show any emergent relationships. They may not, for example, even match stimuli to themselves (such as A1 to A1) without explicit training.

A striking feature of equivalence classes is that as the number of members (stimuli) increases, the number of emergent matching responses increases dramatically. For example, training two relationships (A to B and B to C) produces a three-member class with a further seven matching relationships emerging (A to A, B to B, C to C, B to A, C to B, A to C, C to A, a total of

$3^2 - 2 = 7$) but training four relationships (A to B, B to C, C to D, D to E produces a five-member class with a further 21 matching relationships emerging ($5^2 - 4 = 21$). 'Natural' stimulus equivalence classes (that is, those that enter into relationships with human behaviour in real-life settings) may have very many members with a huge number of emerging matching responses. This fact, along with the account of generalization between physically similar stimuli we gave earlier in this chapter, gives us a way of dealing with some long-standing philosophical problems. Philosophers have posed questions such as 'What is the essential feature of a chair? How do we decide what is, and what is not, an example of a chair?' We now have the elements of a general answer to this question, and many like it. A chair is a class of stimuli that are functionally equivalent in allowing us to make the response of sitting down. Some members of the class have physical similarities, but a new design of chair (which does not have those physical features) can be added to the class and subsequently be seen to be as 'chair-like' as the more conventional members of the class. It is worth noting that every individual will have their own 'class of chairs': someone who has never encountered a particular new design of chair may not identify it as a chair. This type of example suggests that some of the traditional philosophical questions may be misconceived, and that there are no absolute or essential features of 'being a chair'. We will discuss some of these ideas again in Chapter 7.

As noted above, a key feature of equivalence classes is that, under certain circumstances, behaviours controlled by one member of a class may be controlled by other members of the class without explicit training. This is called *transfer of function,* and it is this characteristic of equivalence that provides an account of how physically dissimilar stimuli may control the same behaviour without the need for explicit training, and thus be functionally equivalent. That is, a pattern of behaviour under the control of an $S^D$ may be transferred 'automatically' to other stimuli that are in an equivalence class with that stimulus. For example, if you typically talk in a certain way with same-sex friends, you may start to talk in this way to any new same-sex friend that you make, without a history of reinforcement for talking to that person in that way. Clearly, this is a powerful method of extending a person's behavioural repertoire. It may also contribute to less desirable outcomes by providing a rapid method of attaching fear and anxious behaviour to specific situations that were not previously feared.

This could happen in a number of ways. Most straightforwardly, if we suppose that a young child has a stimulus class of 'places where frightening things happen', then he or she may go to some lengths to avoid being in those places, may show extreme fear if encountering one of them by accident, and so on. Any stimulus that is added to the class will then control the whole range of fear-related behaviours, and it may be very easy to introduce a new member to the class. For example, the child may go into a strange room and be somewhat frightened by a sudden noise, and this may be sufficient for this place to become a new member of that stimulus class and thus control the whole range of fear-related responses. Alternatively, saying to the child 'You are frightened of monsters, aren't you? Well, there are monsters in the wood-shed!', may be sufficient to produce an aversion to *all* wood-sheds. Finally, a frightening experience in one particular store might produce a fear of all public places because, for that child, they are all members of the same stimulus class.

In summary, it is possible to demonstrate in experiments how stimulus classes can be established that have many physically dissimilar members, and to show transfer of function. That is, a function acquired by one member of the class is transferred to all the other members of the class. Because verbally competent humans readily show this behaviour, this suggests that stimulus equivalence may be intimately related to our ability to use language itself. This idea has led to much further research, and some of this is introduced in Chapter 7. Chapter 7 will also deal with language, or verbal behaviour, more generally.

## 4.17 OBSERVATIONAL LEARNING AND MODELLING

Behaviour analysis has been mostly concerned with the selection of behaviour by reinforcement contingencies, and less with how variation in behaviour occurs. The operants selected for experimental study have usually been simple acts that can be shaped if necessary through reinforcement of successive approximations (lever pressing, key pecking, button pressing and so on). Similarly, although it is acknowledged that classical conditioning can produce diverse effects on behaviour, investigators have normally looked in detail at a single, relatively simple, aspect of behaviour (salivation, eye-blinks, heart rate and so forth). Thus, neither operant nor classical-conditioning techniques are oriented to the analysis of the *acquisition of complex behavioural sequences*. However, it is a compelling fact that humans readily acquire such sequences, and do so very rapidly.

Many examples of acquiring 'new' and often complex behaviour seem to depend on *observation*. For example, the new factory worker may be shown how the machine works by the supervisor, and then he or she can operate it himself or herself immediately with reasonable efficiency. His or her subsequent improvement towards being a skilled operator depends on feedback (reinforcement) from the machine and from co-workers, but the initial acquisition is very rapid. We might crudely conceptualize it thus:

| $S^D$ | : | R | $\rightarrow$ | $S+$ |
|---|---|---|---|---|
| operation of machine by supervisor | | copying supervisor's behaviour | | successful operation of machine |

If an *observer* acquires a new response pattern or behaviour sequence by observation of another individual, this is an instance of *modelling*. There are two important types of modelling influence. The first is the one we have described, and is called the *response acquisition effect* of modelling. Observation of a *model* (another person) may also lead to the inhibition or facilitation of already learned behaviour. For example, observing someone else making jokes about a taboo subject and gaining approval may lead to the observer telling similar jokes. This is called the *response modulation effect*. Before attempting an analysis of modelling processes, we will describe a study that demonstrates the effectiveness of modelling, both on response acquisition and response modulation.

## 4.18 CHILDREN'S BEHAVIOUR AFTER OBSERVING AGGRESSIVE MODELS

Bandura and associates carried out a series of studies showing the powerful effects on children of short periods of observing adults or children modelling specific behaviours. In a typical study (Bandura, 1965), children (aged 42 to 71 months) watched film of an adult who produced several novel physical and verbal aggressive behaviours.

The film lasted 5 minutes and involved an adult approaching an adult-sized plastic doll and ordering it out of the way. Then the model (the adult) laid the doll on its side, sat on it, and punched it on the nose. This was followed by hitting it on the head with a mallet and then kicking it round the room. Finally, the model threw rubber balls at the doll. Each act of physical aggression was accompanied by a particular verbal aggressive response. Following this performance, the children observing the film saw one of three closing scenes: another adult appeared with candies and soft drinks, and congratulated the model, giving the model food and drink (model-rewarded group); or the second adult came in and reprimanded the model, while spanking the model with a rolled-up magazine (model-punished group); for a third group of children, the film ended before the second adult arrived (no-consequences group).

Immediately after watching the film, each child was taken to a room containing a similar large doll, a mallet, balls and a number of other toys not seen in the film. The child spent 10 minutes alone in this room, where they could be observed through a one-way mirror. The experimenter then entered, carrying soft drinks and pictures. These were offered to the child as rewards if he or she could imitate what the model had done in the film. Each modelled behaviour that the child produced was reinforced with a drink or a picture.

The results from both parts of the experiment are shown separately for boys and girls in Figure 4.12. The most notable feature of the data is the generally

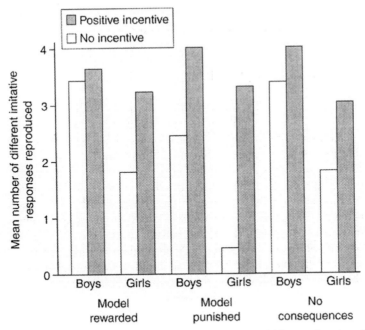

**Figure 4.12** Mean number of aggressive behaviours shown by children, as function of consequences for the model, sex of child and whether the child was reinforced ('positive incentive') or not reinforced ('no incentive') for showing imitative behaviour (Bandura, 1965)

high level of modelled behaviour. After watching a short film, a number of conditions produced mean levels of between three and four different modelled behaviours out of a possible maximum of eight (four physical acts and four verbal behaviours). Apart from this, the sex of the children, the consequences for the model and the consequences for the children all influenced behaviour. In the first observation period, when no reinforcement was provided, the boys reproduced more of the model's aggressive acts than the girls. In the second period, however, when modelling was reinforced, all groups considerably increased modelling behaviour and the differences between the sexes were largely eliminated. These two phases demonstrate: (i) that some imitation occurs without visible reinforcement for the participants (this is the response acquisition effect); (ii) some modelled responses are acquired that may not be performed unless explicitly reinforced; and (iii) the sex difference in aggressive behaviour diminishes when aggression is reinforced.

In the first observation period, the amount of imitated behaviour was also influenced by the observed consequences of the behaviour for the model. If the model had been seen to be punished for the aggressive behaviour, the children showed less aggression. The effect was particularly dramatic for the girls in the model-punished group. They imitated an average of fewer than 0.5 aggressive acts in the first period, but increased this to more than 3.0 when subsequently reinforced for aggressive acts. This exemplifies a powerful response modulation effect: performance of aggressive behaviour was jointly influenced by the observed consequences for the model and the available consequences for the participant.

In Bandura's (1965) study, observation of the adult model for a short period of time was a sufficient condition for the children to imitate some of the model's behaviour without reinforcement or explicit instructions. This is a remarkable finding and suggests that modelling may be responsible for the acquisition of many social and complex behaviours. After all, we spend a great deal of time observing the behaviour of others. However, we obviously do not acquire all the behaviour we observe. In fact, further studies have shown that observers tend to imitate behaviour shown by high-status models, behaviour of models that are supportive of them, and behaviour observed in several models. Modelling, therefore, can produce a 'group identification' effect whereby behaviour, initially shown by leaders, is rapidly transmitted to the whole group. This effect is readily observed in groups of adolescents, who seem to all wear the same clothes, have the same interests, etc.

## 4.19 WHY DOES MODELLING OCCUR?

It is possible that copying the behaviour of a model is maintained by *conditioned reinforcement*. We all have a history of being reinforced for behavioural similarity, or imitating the behaviour of a model. During language acquisition by a young child, for example, parents often spend long periods of time coaxing the child to repeat a particular word or phrase. When the child finally produces the appropriate utterance, this *behavioural similarity* is immediately reinforced. You will recall from Section 4.5 that any event that is regularly followed by primary reinforcement, such as parental affection, may become a conditioned positive reinforcer. As behavioural similarity is often paired with reinforcement in this way, it will become a conditioned reinforcer. It can then act to reinforce modelling behaviour when it occurs. The paradigm would be:

$$S^D \quad : \quad R \quad \rightarrow \quad S+$$

model's behaviour      imitate model      behavioural similarity

where the last term, S+, is a conditioned reinforcer. Behavioural similarity would only acquire and retain conditioned reinforcing properties if it was explicitly reinforced in a variety of situations. Non-reinforced imitation in the test situation can then be described as *generalized imitation*, because imitative behaviour is generalizing from reinforced to non-reinforced situations. The term 'generalized imitation' can be used to describe most instances of imitation because many of them are not followed by an explicit reinforcer.

Up until this point in this book, the events that have been identified as reinforcing stimuli have all been clearly located outside the organism. That is, if a food is delivered to a hungry pigeon following a peck, if a child is hugged following completion of homework, or if the boss says 'Well done!' when an employee carries out a task at work, the reinforcing event is in the environment outside the skin of the individual showing the behaviour. We are now proposing that in a modelling paradigm it is the similarity of the behaviour of the observer to the previously occurring behaviour of the model that has a reinforcing function. Because people can perceive their own behaviour, just as they can perceive external events it is logically possible that behavioural similarity can act as a reinforcer, and Gladstone and Cooley (1975) were able to demonstrate the reinforcing effects of behavioural similarity. Children were given the opportunity to model a behaviour sequence (that is, act as models) and then operate a bell, a horn or a clicker. If the appropriate one of these responses was made, the experimenter (acting as the observer) immediately imitated the behaviour the child had modelled. The other two responses had no consequences. If behavioural similarity has reinforcing properties, the child-model should select the response that resulted in imitation by the experimenter-observer. This did happen, and each of the four participants gradually switched to the response currently reinforced. This experimental study thus demonstrates the reinforcing effects of behavioural similarity.

As noted in Section 4.17, the sudden production of integrated behaviour sequences is one of the most striking features of response acquisition through modelling. This feature cannot be explained by operant reinforcement principles alone, which are concerned mainly with processes of *selection*, because a reinforcement contingency operates to increase or decrease the frequency of an existing category of behaviour relative to other categories of behaviour. However, as we have noted from time to time, we need also to investigate those processes of behavioural variation that provide the 'raw material' on which contingencies operate. In Chapters 3 and 4 we discussed classical conditioning, extinction and shaping, which are examples of these. Another type of behavioural variation occurs through observation of the behaviour of another individual. This process is extremely important in human behaviour and contributes to its richness and complexity, although it has sometimes been obtained in experimental studies with other species. An interesting study was carried out with rhesus monkeys (Mineka *et al.*, 1984). Young rhesus monkeys that had been reared in the laboratory, and thus could never have seen a snake, showed no fear of snakes. However, if they once saw a parent monkey (who had been raised in the wild and may have previously seen monkeys reacting fearfully) showing the typical fear response to a snake, they too showed a fear response on subsequent sight of a snake. This is good evidence for a modelling response acquisition effect in a non-human animal species.

# 4.20  REINFORCEMENT OF MODELLING

Given that operant reinforcement and modelling can both modify the behavioural repertoire, the joint operation of both should be a highly effective method of altering behaviour, and so it has proved. It is particularly suitable for conditions of *behavioural deficit*. A behavioural deficit means that an individual simply lacks a class of behaviour common in other individuals. Behavioural deficits have a large influence on the relationship between the individual's behaviour and the contingencies of reinforcement provided by the society in which he or she lives. Normally, the incidence of a class of behaviour – for example, talking – is continuously modified by the social environment. Someone who never speaks, however, fails to make contact with these contingencies. Their situation is quite different from that of a low-frequency talker, whose talking may have been suppressed by verbal punishment, or may subsequently increase as a result of reinforcement. In contrast, the non-talker will neither be reinforced nor punished because this behaviour does not occur.

Behavioural deficits, then, represent a severe type of behaviour problem. Baer *et al.* (1967) attempted to alleviate this problem in three children with learning disabilities (aged 9 to 12 years) with very large deficits that included failure to imitate any behaviour. The children were taught a series of discriminated operants of this form:

| $S^D$ | : | R | $\rightarrow$ | S+ |
|---|---|---|---|---|
| 'Do this' followed by demonstration by model | | behavioural similarity by child | | food |

As no imitative behaviour occurred initially, shaping was used. This involved assisting the participant, physically, to make the appropriate sequence of actions, and then delivering food reinforcement. Sessions were always conducted at mealtimes, to ensure that the food would function as a reinforcer, and the amount of assistance was gradually reduced. As training proceeded, the probability of showing imitation of a demonstrated response without this training increased in two of the three participants from zero early in training to around 80% once more than 100 different behaviours had been trained (for the third participant, a high level was reached after training on nine behaviours). These children also developed generalized imitation. This was shown by including a subgroup of modelled behaviours for which imitation was never reinforced, once the children had learnt to imitate successfully. These behaviours were imitated with about the same probability as the ones currently being reinforced.

## SUMMARY

Reinforcement contingencies in operant conditioning are relationships between specified classes of behaviour and environmental consequences, and have the effect of changing the frequency of those classes of behaviour. As this can come about through the contingent presentation of stimuli or their removal, and the consequence can be either the increase or decrease of the behaviour class, there are four types of contingency. In addition to positive reinforcement (discussed in Chapter 3), one of the other types is negative reinforcement (escape or avoidance) where the operant behaviour increases through the contingent removal or postponement of aversive events. Because of the use of aversive events (which can be defined through their effectiveness in negative reinforcement) these contingencies have usually been investigated in experimental studies with non-human animals. Negative reinforcement is effective in changing behaviour, which has seemed surprising in experimental studies of avoidance with non-human animals because in this procedure there is no reinforcing event that immediately follows a response. None the less, animals of many species can learn to respond effectively, and thus avoid aversive events in procedures where operant responses either reduce the number of aversive events over a period of time or are followed by stimuli that signal a low rate of aversive events.

Punishment is a further type of operant contingency where the specified class of behaviour is followed by contingent presentation of an aversive event, with the result that the operant is reduced in frequency. This procedure has also been dogged by controversy, but careful experiments have shown that it can have the planned effect of a selective reduction of the operant response class. The final type of contingency is time out, where the operant response class cancels stimuli that would otherwise occur. This procedure has the effect of reducing the frequency of the operant response class. Although less often studied, time out has been found to be effective, for example in applied studies with children showing disruptive behaviour.

Aversive classical conditioning occurs when a CS predicts the occurrence of an aversive US. This CS–US relation can occur in an unplanned way in negative reinforcement and punishment procedures. When this happens, the classically conditioned response may interfere with the operant response. This had led to confusion in the discussion of the effects of negative reinforcement and punishment. When aversive classical conditioning is studied directly, some effects are seen that do not occur with other forms of classical conditioning. In particular, species-typical aversive behaviours – including running away from the location of the CS – may be seen.

The learning history of the individual changes the reinforcing value of events. Events that predict or precede positive reinforcers can become conditioned positive reinforcers, while events that occur in the same relation to aversive stimuli can become conditioned negative reinforcers, or conditioned aversive stimuli. Conditioned reinforcement is very important in human psychology, because most of the time it is the relations between operant behaviour and conditioned reinforcers (rather than primary reinforcers such as food) that maintain and change our behaviour. The most potent generalized conditioned reinforcer is money, but there are many conditioned reinforcers that are specific to an individual.

Conditioned behaviour can undergo a process of extinction, resulting in the eventual reduction of the behaviour to a low level. This happens when the relationship between events that established the behaviour, whether through operant conditioning or classical conditioning, is removed. Features of the operant extinction process are the response burst early in extinction, an increase in variability of the form of the response, and extinction-induced aggression. A feature of extinction following classical conditioning is the spontaneous recovery that may occur over a period of time. This phenomenon suggests that inhibition may be involved in the extinction process.

Resistance to extinction, the amount of operant behaviour occurring before an extinction criterion is reached, is related to the amount of previous training and other features of the operant conditioning that precedes extinction. The biggest effects on resistance to extinction are produced by intermittent reinforcement procedures, where only some of the operant responses are followed by the reinforcer. Schedules of reinforcement, discussed in detail in Chapter 5, can result in thousands of responses occurring during the extinction process.

Stimulus generalization is the occurrence of a response to a stimulus that resembles, but is not identical with, the stimulus previously trained as an $S^D$ or CS. This is an important phenomenon because it allows conditioned response to 'spread' beyond the exact training stimulus. In a laboratory context, a generalization gradient can be obtained when a relevant aspect of the $S^D$ or CS is varied, and responding is seen to decline in frequency as the stimulus presented varies increasingly from the training stimulus.

Stimulus salience refers to the varying likelihood that different aspects of the physical environment have an effect on behaviour. In both operant and classical conditioning experiments, this phenomenon is termed overshadowing and results in some features of the environment and not others controlling a response. A feature that does not control behaviour when tested is said to have been overshadowed by other features.

In discrimination training, the stimulus conditions under which an operant response class is reinforced are explicitly contrasted with other conditions where that operant is not reinforced. These conditions are termed $S^D$ and $S^\Delta$ respectively. Whereas generalization is a 'failure' to tell two or more conditions apart, discrimination training is explicit training to discriminate between $S^D$ and $S^\Delta$. After sufficient training, there may be a high rate of responding in $S^D$, and little or no responding in. Discrimination training can result in many different functional stimulus classes emerging.

Human behaviour is affected by stimulus classes with physically dissimilar members that are determined by the individual's learning history. These stimulus equivalence classes are pervasive in everyday life (for example, the class consisting of the written word 'chair', the spoken word 'chair', a picture of a chair, etc.), and they can be investigated experimentally using matching-to-sample procedures. With verbally competent participants, a limited amount of training with these procedures (such as, given A1 pick B1, given B1 pick C1) can result in the emergence of many relationships between stimuli that have not been explicitly trained (such as, given A1, pick A1, given A1 pick C1, given B1 pick A1, given B1 pick A1, given B1 pick B1, given C1 pick A1, given C1 pick B1, given C1 pick C1). These stimuli are thus treated as equivalent, and appear to have the same functions as each other. That is, a function acquired by one member of the class transfers to all other class members. This finding has enormous potential for explaining rapid changes in human behaviour, including undesirable ones such as fear of many situations that have never been directly experienced. Stimulus equivalence is also related to human language and cognition, and this will be discussed further in Chapter 7.

Modelling is an important behavioural process. It provides a rapid mechanism for the acquisition of complex behaviour. In modelling, a particular behaviour is shown by one person, the model, and then may be copied or imitated by another person, the observer. This may occur as a response acquisition effect, where the observer is now able to show behaviour that they previously did not have in their repertoire, or as a response modulation effect where behaviour that had been previously acquired is now shown with high probability in the context where the model demonstrated the behaviour. Modelling does not involve a programmed reinforcing consequence following the behaviour. Experimental studies have shown that robust effects can be obtained on children's behaviour, particularly when aggressive behaviour is learnt by observing an adult model. It is possible that such modelled behaviour is maintained by conditioned reinforcing effects of behavioural similarity. The modelling procedure is an important source of 'new' human behaviour in social settings.

A common feature of people with developmental delay or learning disabilities is that they do not imitate behaviour readily. However, positive reinforcement of showing behavioural similarity leads to enhanced imitation in such individuals. Through this training, they may come to show the generalized imitation that is such an important feature of human learning.

## Study questions for Chapter 4

Here are some questions, based on a 'quiz' suggested by Catania (1999). You should be able to answer the first four of them, based on the material covered in the book so far. Question 5 may be more difficult. Which of these statements are true, and which are false?

1. In a Skinner box with two operant responses available (a chain and a lever), chain pulls produce food and lever pressing increases. This illustrates reinforcement.

2. The response classes produced by reinforcement are defined in terms of their forms or topographies.

3. Reinforcers work because they make the organism feel good or because the organism likes them.

4. If reinforcers have produced problem behaviour, the best solution is simply to take the reinforcers away: to reduce a child's bad behaviour, extinguish it.

5. Following a long string of errors, do not miss a chance to reinforce the next correct response.

Make sure that you have decided on your answers, and the reasons for them, before turning to my suggested responses.

Now check your answers with my suggestions in the 'Possible answers to study questions' section, see page 221.

# 5

# Behavioural Neuroscience

- What is behavioural neuroscience?
- Behaviour pharmacology
- 'Behavioural baselines': schedules of reinforcement
- Use of operant techniques in behaviour pharmacology
- Conditioned suppression
- Resistance to extinction after fixed-ratio training
- Behavioural effects of amphetamines
- Animal models of psychiatric and neurological disorders
- The new genetics and the use of 'transgenic animals' in behavioural studies
- Completing the circle: effects of environmental enrichment
- Summary

Chapters 1 and 2 set the scene: they provided an account of the main aims of behaviour analysis and placed it in a scientific and historical context. Chapter 3 gave an account of the basic principles, and Chapter 4 went somewhat further and sought to provide enough understanding of behaviour analysis to consider its applications to *behavioural neuroscience* and *applied behaviour analysis*, and its extension towards providing an account of human *language and cognition*. These are the topics of Chapters 5, 6 and 7 respectively.

## 5.1 WHAT IS BEHAVIOURAL NEUROSCIENCE?

In parallel with the development of scientific approaches to psychology, there were massive developments in our knowledge and understanding of the brain and central nervous system in the twentieth century and this progress has accelerated in recent years. Practitioners of both disciplines are aware that each discipline needs the other to provide a more complete account of human psychology and behaviour. However, there is a tendency to regard brain processes as more 'basic' in some sense, and to expect that psychological or behavioural processes will, in the end, be explained by brain processes. Whether or not one accepts this 'reductionist' philosophical position, scientific and practical considerations show that it is necessary to investigate both behavioural processes and brain processes, and the interaction between the two.

From a scientific perspective, behavioural processes are interesting in their own right, and knowledge of them and their applications can be developed without necessarily knowing about the correlated brain processes. Indeed, we will review many interesting findings based on such a purely behavioural strategy in the next two chapters. However, scientific curiosity would lead us to investigate, where possible, the brain processes that exist in parallel with behavioural or psychological phenomena. From the perspective of neuroscience the argument is even more compelling: we hardly ever investigate a process in the brain or central nervous without a parallel interest in its relationship to psychological functioning. As soon as we ask, 'How does this brain process affect behaviour?', we require an adequate account of behavioural processes to which we can relate our study of brain function.

From a practical point of view, parallel investigations of behavioural and neurological aspects are highly desirable. There is endless public debate as to whether certain psychiatric disorders – for example, schizophrenia – are 'really' genetic or environmental in origin. It should become clear in this chapter that this question is misstated, because there will always be a range of biological and a range of environmental influences on any aspect of human functioning. One investigation might show strong evidence of genetic factors in a disorder (e.g., if family members sharing a certain gene show evidence of the disorder while family members without the gene do not show it), and another might show evidence of a strong environmental influence (e.g., if those members of a community subjected to severe stress show the disorder, while those not stressed do not). The solution to the apparent problem here is that certain investigative strategies reveal the influence of biological or neurological factors, while others reveal the influence of environmental factors. Which is more 'important' depends on our current concern. If it is possible, for example, to reduce the stress individuals suffer as a route towards reducing psychiatric disorder, then we will be most interested in the findings and implications of the study showing environmental effects. If, on the other hand, new developments in gene therapy suggest that a targeted drug treatment is feasible, then data from the family genetics study will be crucial. Finding an effective strategy will always be made more likely if both behavioural and brain processes are understood.

In broad terms, behavioural neuroscience is the interdisciplinary field of study that seeks to use behavioural techniques to understand brain function, and to use techniques of neuroscience to elucidate behavioural processes. Psychology and neuroscience come together in various ways in this interdisciplinary field. We shall be concerned here with the contributions that have been made by behaviour analysis. This relatively narrow focus is relevant to this book, of course, but it is also justified by the considerable contribution that behaviour analysis has made in this area. In some of the sections in this chapter general strategies and techniques will be introduced, while other sections will give more detailed information on specific issues in behavioural neuroscience. With both these approaches, it should be possible for the reader to begin to frame an answer to the question 'What is behavioural neuroscience?' It should be realized that the examples given in this chapter are a small group from a huge number that could be included, as this field is developing very rapidly. A minimum of information will be given about basic neuroscience. More extensive introductory accounts are suggested in the 'Further reading' section at the end of the book.

## 5.2 BEHAVIOUR PHARMACOLOGY

The last 50 years have seen the development of the modern pharmaceutical industry. This industry has the capacity to synthesize new chemical compounds that may be useful in treating human diseases and ameliorating psychological distress of one kind or another. A major section of the industry is concerned with agents that may alter the functioning of the human central nervous system. In the development of a new drug that affects the human central nervous system many practical, legal and scientific issues must be addressed. As well as safety issues (the drug may be toxic to many species, or especially to humans, or it may damage certain types of tissues or impair certain physiological functions etc.), the drug must pass various positive tests as well. Even if it is chemically similar to a compound already in use for the treatment of anxiety, for example, it may not itself be effective. If it is effective, how should it be administered, and on what type of dosing regime?

Most of these questions cannot be addressed, in the first instance, by giving the new drug to human volunteers or patients suffering from the disease that the drug may ameliorate. This is ethically unacceptable, because of the risks to the people concerned, and is consequently illegal in most jurisdictions. Fortunately, techniques for investigation of behavioural processes in non-human animals developed at roughly the same time as a demand emerged for techniques to assess the nature of drug effects on central nervous system functions. Behavioural experiments with other species have turned out be an extremely useful way of characterizing the effects of a drug prior to assessing its effects with a human clinical population. This strategy has proved so reliable that drug companies routinely use some of the techniques described below. This in turn has led to a better understanding of the behavioural processes involved. Testing drugs on non-human animals also raises ethical concerns, and such studies are subject to strict regulation in the UK. Researchers in this area are required, by legislation, to minimize the numbers of animals involved and any suffering that might ensue.

## 5.3 'BEHAVIOURAL BASELINES': SCHEDULES OF REINFORCEMENT

We noted in Section 4.10, that intermittent reinforcement procedures have great utility for generating stable, long-term baselines of learned behaviour against which effects of drugs and other factors can be studied. The ways in which reinforcement can be arranged to produce long-term patterns of behaviour are called schedules of intermittent reinforcement.

Early experimental studies of learned behaviour were conducted by investigators who were mainly concerned with the acquisition of behaviour, and these investigators took little interest in intermittent reinforcement. However, once it was investigated, intermittent reinforcement was found to have powerful effects on behaviour. Although it is true that the acquisition of 'new' behaviour usually proceeds most smoothly when each and every response is reinforced (we will return to this point in Chapter 6), intermittent reinforcement procedures produce reliable and distinctive patterns of behaviour.

Schedules of reinforcement are experimental procedures that specify which instances of an operant response will be reinforced. I will refer to the positive reinforcement procedure, familiar from earlier chapters, in which every response is reinforced whenever it occurs as a *continuous reinforcement* schedule. A host of schedules have been devised and studied in which reinforcement is non-continuous, or *intermittent*. Each of these schedules specifies the particular condition or set of conditions that must be met before the next response is reinforced.

If we consider the relatively simple situation where only one response is to be examined and the stimulus conditions are constant, there are at least two things we have to specify: the number of responses that must occur, and the time that must elapse. Schedules involving a required *number* of responses are called *ratio schedules* (referring to the ratio of responses to reinforcers); schedules specifying a period of time are called *interval schedules* (referring to the imposed intervals of time between reinforcement). Schedules can also be either *fixed* (where every reinforcer is delivered after the same ratio or interval requirement has been fulfilled), or *variable* (where the ratios and intervals can vary within the schedule).

Here are verbal descriptions corresponding to an example of each of these four simple types of reinforcement schedule.

- Fixed ratio 10 (FR 10): the tenth operant response that occurs will be reinforced, then the tenth of the subsequent operant responses will be reinforced, and so on. The response requirement is fixed at 10 responses.
- Fixed interval 20 seconds (FI 20 seconds): the first operant response that occurs once 20 seconds have elapsed will be reinforced, then the first

response that occurs once a further 20 seconds have elapsed will be reinforced, and so on.

- Variable ratio 15 (VR 15): the operant response requirement varies with an average value of 15. Thus it might be that twenty-fifth response that occurs is reinforced, and then the tenth response, and then the thirtieth response, and so on. Over a long run, the average of these requirements will be 15.

- Variable interval 40 seconds (VI 40 seconds): the inter-reinforcement interval varies, with an average value of 40 seconds. It might be that the first operant response after 20 seconds is reinforced, then the first response after a subsequent interval of 55 seconds, then the first response after a subsequent interval of 35 seconds, and so on. Over a long run, the average of these times will be 40 seconds.

Although the procedures require a complicated verbal description, each of the four schedules we have defined generates a characteristic performance, or behavioural steady state. These states can be easily identified by looking at cumulative records (see Figure 5.1). You will recall from Chapter 3 that the cumulative recorder steps vertically, a small and fixed amount, each time a response occurs, while continuously moving horizontally at a fixed speed. So the slope of the record at any point reflects the rate of response; cessation of responding produces a flat record, while a very high response rate produces a steep one. Vertical marks on the record indicate the delivery of reinforcers.

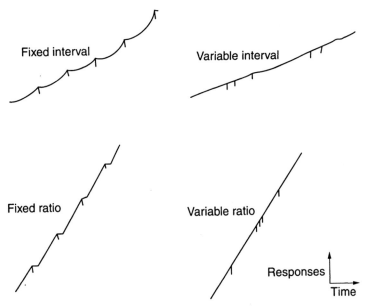

**Figure 5.1** Cumulative records of operant behaviour maintained by four types of schedule of reinforcement

Although the records in Figure 5.1 are hypothetical (rather than from actual experiments), they are in no sense idealized. Reinforcement schedules exert such powerful control over behaviour that even a previously 'untrained' rat, placed in a Skinner box by a previously untrained student or researcher, could generate one of these records after a few hours. Significantly, these performance patterns have been produced in many species, and with a variety of operant responses. Some of the characteristics of performance generated by each schedule are noted below. These descriptions are of behaviour once it reaches a steady state and will not change significantly with extended further exposure to the same conditions. It is then that schedule-controlled behaviour can be used as a baseline for investigating the effects of drugs or other interventions in the central nervous system.

- Fixed ratio schedule (FR): a high rate of response is sustained until reinforcement occurs. This is followed by a relatively lengthy *post-reinforcement pause* before the high rate of responding is resumed. The post-reinforcement pause increases with the ratio of responses required for reinforcements, and can occupy the greater part of the experimental participant's time.
- Variable ratio schedule (VR): in common with the fixed ratio schedule, this procedure generates a high rate of response, but regular pausing for any length of time is very uncommon. Instead, a high rate of responding for prolonged periods is seen.
- Fixed interval schedule (FI): like the fixed ratio schedule, this procedure also produces a post-reinforcement pause, but responding at other times occurs at a lower rate than on ratio schedules, except towards the end of the interval, where it accelerates to meet the reinforcer. The characteristic positively accelerated curve seen on the cumulative record is called a 'scallop'. In general, longer fixed intervals produce lower rates of responding.
- Variable interval (VI): as with the variable ratio schedule, consistent pauses of any length are rare. However, response rates are moderate to low, depending on the mean interval, with longer mean intervals producing lower response rates. Because this schedule tends to produce a steady, intermediate rate of operant responding, the behaviour generated by it has often been used as a baseline for the investigation of other variables.

Intermittent schedule performances cannot, in general, be explained as the experimental participant adopting the optimal strategy: they do not appear to learn to do what would benefit them most. For instance, treating operant responding as analogous to working (perhaps as a labourer), we would expect response rates on fixed interval schedules to fall until only one response per reinforcer occurred, emitted at precisely the end of the interval. Indeed, several early theorists suggested that the number of responses made on what we now call a schedule of reinforcement would be the least required to obtain all the reinforcers: this notion has not stood the test of time as many schedules generate numbers of responses that greatly exceed the minimum required. Furthermore, on fixed ratio schedules we might expect a maximum rate of operant responding to be continuously sustained for as long as possible, because that would maximize the rate of reinforcement, but long pauses occur. Finally, there seems to be no simple reason why response rates under variable interval schedules should fluctuate systematically with the mean interval. Clearly then, schedule phenomena go beyond, and sometimes even contradict, 'common sense'.

Behaviour analysts have carried out much research to identify basic processes that generate these characteristic, but not immediately obvious, schedule-controlled performances (see Leslie, 1996, Chapter 4, for a review of this research). Not surprisingly, a number of behavioural processes can be identified that combine in different ways on these different schedules to produce these characteristic performances. From the point of view of behaviour pharmacology, schedules of intermittent reinforcement offer a number of different baselines that may be useful in assessing many types of behavioural effects of drugs.

Earlier, in Chapter 4, we saw that the amount of responding in extinction was affected by the number of reinforcers, and the effortfulness of the response during the previous period of reinforcement. As noted there, an even more powerful influence on resistance to extinction is the schedule on which reinforcers were previously delivered. Indeed, the fact that any type of intermittent reinforcement increases *resistance to extinction* has generated a large research area of its own. This phenomenon, termed the *partial reinforcement extinction effect*, has been used as a baseline to study the effects of drugs and physiological manipulations believed to affect emotional processes taking place during extinction (note that 'partial' here means the same as 'intermittent'). We noted in Section 4.7 that extinction can result in aggression, and we will see in Section 5.6 that there is other evidence that emotional processes occur during extinction.

From a purely behavioural standpoint, the introduction of extinction, once a schedule-controlled performance has been established, provides further evidence of the powerful control of behaviour by schedules, because the pattern of behaviour in extinction depends on the nature of the preceding schedule. For example, extinction following exposure to a VI schedule produces what might be described as an 'extinction curve' (see Chapter 3), but a large number of responses may be emitted. In one study (Skinner, 1950), a pigeon emitted over 3000 responses in more than 8 hours. Behaviour in extinction following training on each basic schedule is distinctive, and reflects a gradual breakdown of the schedule-controlled behaviour. From the point of view of behaviour pharmacology, the pattern of behaviour in extinction may be an additional baseline upon which to assess drug effects, and this is also a feature of the procedure discussed in Section 5.6.

# 5.4  USE OF OPERANT TECHNIQUES IN BEHAVIOUR PHARMACOLOGY

The main strategy of behaviour pharmacology is to use a behavioural method that has some 'face validity' in relation to the possible mode of action of the drug, and to compare what happens when the drug has been administered with behaviour in the absence of the drug. A method will have face validity if the situation in the experiment appears to resemble the clinical condition that it is planned the drug will affect. Behaviour maintained by schedules of reinforcement is particularly useful because of the reliability and persistence of the patterns of behaviour generated. To explain how this works, we will first examine a hypothetical study (which is somewhat simpler than those actually carried out, but otherwise identical to many published studies). In subsequent sections, we will outline a number of more complex research techniques.

The purpose of this study is to assess the sedative and locomotor effects of a drug, and to see whether these are changed by the presence of another agent that is believed to antagonize (and thus prevent) the action of the drug in the brain. As indicated in Figure 5.1, variable-interval schedules of reinforcement generate intermediate, steady rates of responding. For this reason, they have often been used when the plan is to maintain behaviour over a long period and measure how it is disrupted by some experimental intervention. In our hypothetical study, food-deprived rats are trained to lever press in a Skinner box and are then given a 1-hour session every day with a variable-interval 60-second schedule of reinforcement with small pellets of food (the intervals between opportunities for reinforcement of lever pressing will vary unpredictably, but average out at 60 seconds). Once behaviour has stabilized, in that roughly the same number (plus or minus 10%) of responses are made in each session, a small number of sessions are immediately preceded by administration of saline at the same concentration at which it naturally occurs in the blood supply (which should have no effect on the central nervous system), the drug, or a combination of the drug and the antagonist. The order of injections would be 'controlled for' by varying it across experimental participants.

Figure 5.2 shows what might be found in this hypothetical but realistic experiment. The rate of response on 'saline sessions' does not change much across 10-minute periods during the session. When the drug has been administered immediately before the session, there is a low rate of responding in the 10- to 20-minute period, followed by a recovery of response rate. When the antagonist has also been administered, the rate of responding is little different from that under saline (the 'control condition'). Because data from a group of eight rats have been (hypothetically) aggregated to produce the data in Figure 5.2, we would only be justified in making these summary statements if statistical analysis of the average data in the figure supported them.

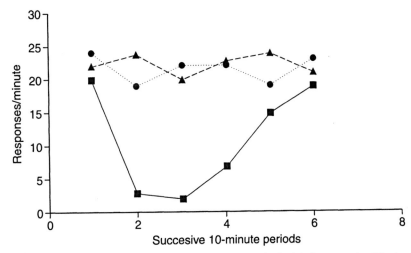

**Figure 5.2** Response rates maintained by a variable-interval schedule in successive 10-minute periods following administration of a drug (squares), drug plus antagonist (circles) or saline (triangles) (see text for details)

Such a study provides much useful information about drug action. The drug in question did produce an effect on lever pressing that is consistent with a brief period of partial sedation or locomotor impairment – this is a common effect of many 'anxiolytics' (drugs used to reduce anxiety) – but, after an hour, the effect seems to be disappearing. When the antagonist was also administered, behaviour returned to the normal pattern seen with saline. This is strong evidence for the mechanism of action of this putative drug. If the effect had not been reversed by the antagonist, this would have indicated that perhaps some 'non-specific' effect of the drug was involved – it made the rats feel very sick, say – and this could not be reversed by the antagonist.

The particular research technique in this hypothetical study – operant behaviour maintained over a period of 1 hour – had face validity for this type of investigation because it clearly could be disrupted by sedation or locomotor impairment and, as we have seen, it might be possible to distinguish effects that were due to specific effects in the central nervous system from other non-specific effects. In subsequent parts of this chapter several other behavioural procedures will be examined, which can be said to model other human psychological processes.

## 5.5 CONDITIONED SUPPRESSION

This technique involves a combination of operant conditioning and classical conditioning procedures. In a typical experiment, liquid-deprived rats were trained to press a lever for water reinforcement on a variable-interval schedule. When response rates on this schedule had become stable, a clicker-noise, CS, was presented periodically for 5 minutes, and immediately followed by a brief electric shock, US, to the rat's feet. Some of the typical behavioural changes that ensued are shown in the cumulative lever-pressing records in Figure 5.3. The first CS presentation had little discernible effect. but the accompanying US (denoted by S in Fig. 5.3b) temporarily slowed the response rate. After a

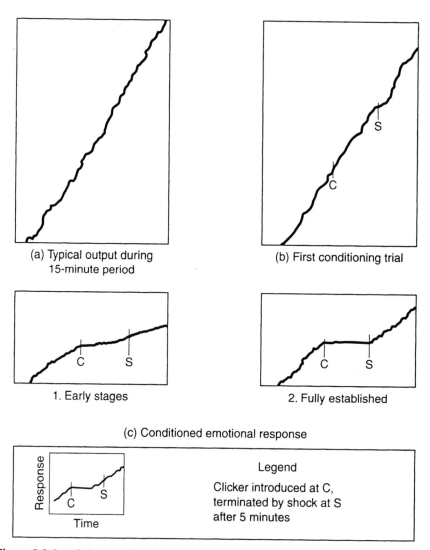

(a) Typical output during
15-minute period

(b) First conditioning trial

1. Early stages

2. Fully established

(c) Conditioned emotional response

Legend

Clicker introduced at C,
terminated by shock at S
after 5 minutes

**Figure 5.3** Cumulative records showing development of conditioned suppression in a rat lever pressing for water reinforcement on a variable-interval schedule (Hunt and Brady, 1951)

number of CS–US pairings, the CS suppressed responding almost totally, but responding recovered as soon as the US had been delivered. Because suppression of responding during the CS is dependent on a conditioning history, it is called *conditioned suppression*.

The conditioned-suppression procedure has proved to be a very sensitive behavioural technique. The effect of the CS is usually described in terms of the degree of suppression of the positively reinforced operant behaviour relative to the rate of the operant response during the non-CS periods. Measured in this way, conditioned suppression increases with magnitude of the US, decreases with length of the CS and is, in general, such a sensitive indicator of classical conditioning parameters that it has often been treated as the best method of studying classical conditioning effects, although it actually measures the reduction in, or disruption of, operant responding.

The sensitivity of the conditioned-suppression technique has led to its widespread use in the evaluation of drug effects. It is often found that anxiolytic drugs reduce conditioned suppression. That is, responding on the operant reinforcement schedule is not much affected by the drug, but when the CS is presented there is now little reduction of responding. The drugs tested have mostly been those known clinically to reduce anxiety, because conditioned suppression has often been treated as a model of fear or anxiety. Recent studies have demonstrated that conditioned suppression can be used to disentangle neuropharmacological mechanisms. For example, the conditioned suppression-reducing effects of some anxiety-reducing drugs, or *anxiolytics*, can be selectively reversed by another drug with a known effect in the brain. From this evidence we can deduce much about the pharmacological action of the anxiolytic agent.

Those working as behaviour pharmacologists in the development and testing of drugs wish to use techniques with the following features: a technique should have some *face validity* as a measurement of the psychological phenomenon of interest; it should reliably *detect* existing drugs that are known to be effective clinically with that psychological phenomenon; and it should also detect *novel compounds* that turn out in due course to be effective clinically. Conditioned suppression has good face validity as a measure of anxiety, because the procedure in which ongoing positively reinforced operant behaviour is disrupted by a fear-inducing stimulus looks like many of the real-life situations in which we know that fear and anxiety occur. Also, as indicated, it has a good 'track record' in showing that known anxiolytics reduce conditioned suppression and in aiding the evaluation of new compounds. Despite this, some scientists have suggested that it should not be used because there are a small number of published studies in which anxiolytic drugs did not have the predicted effects.

Because of the many positive results, the existence of some 'negative results' does not mean that the technique should not be used, but it does bring out two important points. The first is that techniques of behaviour pharmacology are complex – they have many parameters, features that have to be correctly 'set' for the procedure to work properly – and if mistakes are made the technique will become insensitive. The second point is that a range of behavioural techniques should be used in the assessment of any drug. Because of the many differences between a non-human animal experimental procedure and a human clinical situation, it is best to use a range of behavioural procedures and examine the 'batting average' or typical effect of the drug.

## 5.6 RESISTANCE TO EXTINCTION AFTER FIXED-RATIO TRAINING

As noted earlier, the partial reinforcement extinction effect has been used as a baseline to study the effects of drugs and physiological manipulations believed to affect emotional processes taking place during extinction. In Section 4.7, it was reported that the onset of extinction produces aggression and emotional responses. A series of experiments using a simple piece of apparatus called an *alley-way* showed that there was link between those effects and the effects of intermittent reinforcement.

An alley-way (or runway) is simply a long thin box. The rat (this is the species that has usually been studied) is put in at one end and allowed to run to the other end, where a food reinforcer is delivered. As in Thorndike's early experiments with cats in a puzzle box, it is found that over a number of trials the time taken to complete the task greatly decreases. Initially the rat takes a very long time to get to the 'goal box' where the food is, but this latency decreases to a few seconds as the rat learns to run to the far end. The partial reinforcement extinction effect can be demonstrated by giving a group of rats food on only half the trials in the alley-way. Although they run more slowly in initial training, after a number of trials they will run as fast as rats given food on every trial. More interestingly, when extinction is introduced for both groups, and alley-way trials are continued but there is no food in the goal box, they will continue to run for longer (Gray, 1975).

It has been known for a long time that emotional responses are involved in the partial reinforcement extinction effect, because administration of anxiolytic drugs interferes with the effect. This is a valuable finding because it enables us to study the behavioural effects of anxiolytic drugs in a procedure that involves only reinforcement and extinction, whereas in conditioned suppression, electric shocks or other painful stimuli have to be administered. However, alley-way experiments are slow and inefficient (they take a long time and a lot of animals to demonstrate any behavioural effects), so it would be useful to have a procedure using a Skinner box where the same effects can be studied.

Williams *et al.* (1990) produced such a procedure. They trained rats in a discrete-trial fixed-ratio procedure, which has some face validity as an analogue of the alley-way training experiments. In this procedure, the rat is in an empty Skinner box and there is an inter-trial interval of 1 minute – this is a time in an experiment in which nothing happens before the next important event, or *trial* – and then the lever is presented. That is, a motor is operated that moves the lever into the box where the rat can reach it. If the lever is pressed five times, it is withdrawn and a food is presented. The 1-minute inter-trial interval then starts before the next lever presentation. A daily session consists of six trials with lever presentations, each of which ends once the required five responses have been made. This procedure is called a discrete-trial fixed ratio schedule of food reinforcement. It resembles an alley-way experiment because it has the following features. There is an inter-trial interval, corresponding to times when the rat is not in the alley-way, followed by a small 'work requirement' of pressing the lever five times, corresponding to traversing the alley, followed by food reinforcement. Importantly, Williams *et al.* found it also resembled the alley-way experiments in that a number of treatments that affected the partial reinforcement extinction effect seen there also had an effect on behaviour on the discrete-trial fixed ratio schedule of food reinforcement.

In particular, they found an effect with chlordiazepoxide. This drug, which is marketed as Librium, was the first of a large group of drugs called the benzodiazepines to be shown to be effective in reducing human anxiety. The benzodiazepines act at a type of receptor in the brain called the GABA-benzodiazepine receptor complex, and facilitate the effects of GABA. In turn, GABA (or gamma-aminobutyric acid) acts to inhibit neural activity at widespread sites in the brain. In Williams *et al.*'s study, chlordiazepoxide was administered to the rats on the last two days of training with the discrete-trial fixed ratio procedure, and then on a number of subsequent days when an extinction procedure was in effect. The rats given chlordiazepoxide showed less resistance to extinction. That is, they tended to stop responding quicker in extinction sessions than those rats not given a drug.

Although rats and pigeons have been widely used in behaviour pharmacology studies, there is currently much interest in studying mice as well. This is because mice have been the primary species used in the development of *transgenic techniques*. It is now possible to alter the genetics of mice in very specific ways, and this gives us new ways to investigate theories as to how behavioural processes affect the brain. For example, if we believe that some anxiolytic drugs have their clinically important effect through activating certain receptors in the GABA-benzodiazepine receptor complex, we may be able to test this theory through examining the behaviour of a type of 'knockout mouse'. This term refers to a mouse in which a very specific region of genetic material, known to produce the receptors in question, has been knocked out or made ineffective. This genetically modified mouse can be compared with other mice from the same

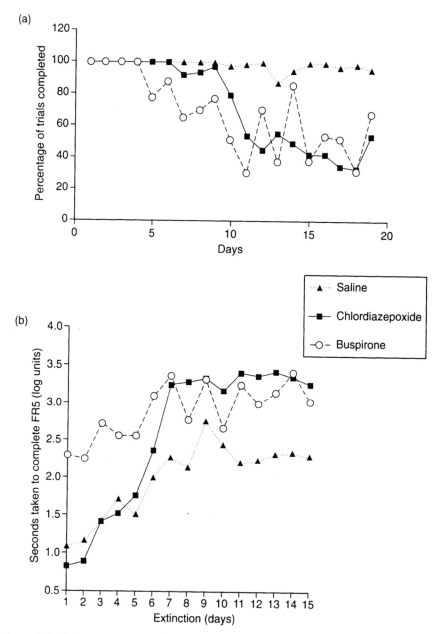

**Figure 5.4** (a) shows percentages of trials completed by groups of mice given saline (dark triangles), chlordiazepoxide (dark squares), or buspirone (open circles) over the last four days of discrete-trial FR5 reinforcement followed by 15 days of extinction; (b) shows average time to complete FR5 requirement in log units over 15 days of extinction for the three groups of mice (McCabe and Leslie, unpublished data)

strain that have not had this small genetic modification. This new research strategy will provide stronger evidence than most other methods of the putative role of certain receptors in important behavioural processes. However, in order to evaluate the effect of changes in receptor systems in the brain, we need to know how unmodified mice behave in the behavioural procedures that may be used to assess those changes.

For these reasons, the discrete-trial fixed ratio schedule experiment was repeated in our laboratory with an inbred strain of laboratory mice called the C57 Black 6 strain. This strain is often used as the 'genetic background' on which specific types of knockout mouse are developed. The procedure used closely resembled the one used by Williams *et al.* (1990) with rats, and the effects of both chlordiazepoxide and buspirone, another clinically important anxiolytic, are shown in Figure 5.4. A 'control' group of mice was given injections only of isotonic saline, which should not have affected the central nervous system, and the behaviour of this group provides a baseline against which the effects of the two drugs used can be measured. Because a between-group design was used, the results described below are based on a statistical analysis of between-group differences and only those differences that reached statistical significance are reported.

One measure used was the percentage of trials completed (if a mouse paused between lever presses for 10 minutes at any time, that session ended and no more trials could be completed). Prior to extinction, all three groups of mice completed 100% of trials, and this continued for a while during extinction. That is, although no food reinforcements were occurring, all the mice were still completing the fixed ratio requirement on all six trials in the session. This is evidence that this procedure generates a lot of resistance to extinction and thus could be a useful baseline for the investigation of drug effects and other interventions. On later extinction sessions, the score for the saline control group remains close to 100%, but the scores for the other two groups, which were being given anxiolytic drugs, fell to a much lower level (and the differences from the saline scores are statistically significant). This replicates Williams *et al.*'s finding that an anxiolytic drug reduced resistance to extinction in this procedure with a different species.

The other measure used was the average time to make each response. As Figure 5.4 shows, there is now an effect for all three groups across the days of extinction, but the behaviour of each group is quite different. For the saline control group, there is a steady increase in the average time taken to make a response across the days of extinction (note that a log scale is used, which means that a value of 1.0 corresponds to an average time of 10 seconds, and a value of 2.0 corresponds to 100 seconds). This indicates that there is a tendency towards extinction of responding in this group, even though it was not evident in the less sensitive measure shown in the other half of the figure. With chlordiazepoxide, the mice actually respond faster for the first two extinction days, but in later extinction sessions they respond considerably more slowly. With buspirone, the mice respond more slowly throughout the extinction sessions.

What this tells us is that chlordiazepoxide led to less resistance to extinction, replicating Williams *et al.*'s finding with rats. This suggests that this procedure would provide a good baseline for investigation of mice with genetic changes in the GABA-benzodiazepine receptor complex, or of drugs with a specific action at that site. The results with buspirone were less helpful. Buspirone is a more recently introduced drug for the clinical management of anxiety, and it affects a different receptor system in the brain, the serotonergic system. Although it has been shown to have the same effects of chlordiazepoxide in some procedures (for example, on unconditioned measures of fear when naïve rats are 'stressed' by being placed in an open, noisy and brightly lit environment), its effects on operant behaviour are often hard to interpret. In this case, the problem is that, unlike chlordiazepoxide, buspirone produced a marked slowing down of responding *before* extinction was introduced, and this makes the further slowing in extinction hard to interpret. The drug may have had a motivational or locomotor effect that concealed any specific effect on resistance to extinction.

## 5.7 BEHAVIOURAL EFFECTS OF AMPHETAMINES

A major theme of this chapter is that operant procedures can generate a behavioural baseline upon which the effects of a drug or other intervention in the nervous system can be assessed. This idea was taken further in the rate-dependency hypothesis, which proposed that it was the current rate of an operant response that may determine the behavioural effect of a drug. A number of studies conducted with schedules of intermittent reinforcement in the 1960s and 1970s appeared to demonstrate 'rate-dependent' effects of drugs, which could be seen with behaviour maintained by a number of different schedules of reinforcement. This means that the drug effect depends on the pre-existing rate of the operant response maintained by the reinforcement schedule, with low rates being increased by the drug and high rates being decreased. If this rate-dependency hypothesis had been sustained, it might provide a very simple (and thus parsimonious) characterization of the effects of many drugs that might be acting on different brain mechanisms.

One drug for which rate-dependent effects were reported is *d*-amphetamine. The amphetamines are a group of 'stimulant' drugs of social significance because they have been widely abused and are the subject of restrictive legislation in many countries. If the effects of *d*-amphetamine were invariably rate-dependent, this would be a different characterization of its behavioural effects than that implied by the earlier term 'stimulant'. Rather, it would be the case that low-rate activities were increased, while high-rate activities were decreased, or depressed. More recent studies of the behavioural effects of this drug have, however, shown that while rate-dependency is a good description of its action in some cases (and is thus a better label than 'stimulant'), it is not the full story. McAuley and Leslie (1986) studied the effects of various doses of *d*-amphetamine on the behaviour of rats on fixed-interval schedules where the interval between reinforcements was 30, 60 or 120 seconds. We saw in Section 5.1 that behaviour under fixed-interval schedules generally consists of a post-reinforcement pause followed by responding that accelerates towards the end of the interval. For all three schedules, McAuley and Leslie found that drug administration had three effects: (i) responding started earlier in the interval; (ii) acceleration of responding through the interval was reduced; (iii) the high rate of responding at the end of the interval was reduced. (To understand all these effects, look again at the cumulative records in Figure 5.1.) All these effects increased as the dose of the drug administered increased.

These results are best characterized as an effect of *d*-amphetamine on temporal discrimination. That is, behaviour on the fixed-interval schedule shows evidence of temporal discrimination, with a post-reinforcement pause giving way to responding that tends to accelerate when the next reinforcer is 'due', and both aspects of behaviour are disrupted by the drug. Other procedures have found that, following treatment with amphetamines, rats 'overestimate' elapsed time (for example, in a completely different procedure in which the required response was to choose to press the left lever in a Skinner box following presentation of a short 2-second stimulus or the right lever after a long 8-second stimulus). Following amphetamine administration, the 'long' response was selected by rats more often than it should have been (Maricq and Church, 1983).

This brief 'case study' of our knowledge of the behavioural effects of amphetamines is typical of what has been found with many groups of drugs. It points up the importance of using a range of behavioural procedures, because an erroneous conclusion that rate-dependency was crucial was reached when only a limited range of procedures had been investigated. Studies of the effects of drugs on behaviour maintained by a wide range of schedules of reinforcement are gradually refining our accounts of their behavioural effects. Very often, similarities and differences between the effects of different groups of drugs have been revealed, which were not suspected from their previous clinical use or from neuropharmacological studies. Such discoveries may enhance the clinical effectiveness of drug treatment.

## 5.8 ANIMAL MODELS OF PSYCHIATRIC AND NEUROLOGICAL DISORDERS

We have described the use of a behavioural procedure, such as a reinforcement schedule, to assess the effect of a drug that is intended to reduce a psychological problem. When the technique also has face validity as a measurement of the human psychological phenomenon, the behavioural procedure is termed an *animal model* of the human psychological problem. Animal models are also useful in trying to provide therapy for those people who suffer from a number of other psychiatric or neurological disorders, and one of these will be discussed here.

Because of the rapidly increasing numbers of older people in many countries, the prevalence of intellectual and psychological deterioration, or dementia, is also increasing. The most common type of dementia is Alzheimer's disease; this has become the fourth major cause of death in modern society, after heart disease, stroke and cancer. Even though Alzheimer's disease is so prevalent, there is still no reliable way of confirming that someone has been suffering from the disease until that person has died, and there are as yet no effective pharmacological interventions. For all these reasons it is particularly important that valid animal models are developed.

Alzheimer's disease is characterized by two distinctive types of damage to the brain (these are seen when a post-mortem examination is carried out on a sufferer). These are known as neurofibrillary tangles and neuritic plaques. Neuritic plaques are primarily composed of extra-cellular aggregates of β-amyloid protein. Since the primary symptoms of Alzheimer's disease are memory loss and learning difficulties, any valid animal model should have these features along with the two main brain changes found in Alzheimer's patients.

Recently, a means has been developed by which β-amyloid protein can be injected into the brain in an aggregated form that resembles the neuritic plaques seen, post-mortem, in the brains of people who have had Alzheimer's disease. If this type of β-amyloid protein is injected into the brains of rats and then the rats are sacrificed some weeks later, a series of brain changes are found to have taken place that resemble those that occur in brains of people who have had Alzheimer's disease. It is therefore possible that this injection of β-amyloid protein produces the same series of events in the rat brain that leads to Alzheimer's disease in humans.

The behavioural effects of injecting β-amyloid protein into the hippocampus have been assessed, because the hippocampus is a subcortical brain structure that is very closely involved in learning and memory processes. In one experiment, rats were trained to lever press for food reinforcement, and then placed on a complex schedule of reinforcement. In a Skinner box with two levers available, they were required to press one lever a specified number of times. Once reinforcement had been delivered, they were then required to press the other lever a different number of times until reinforced, and so on. In this schedule, called an 'alternating lever cyclic ratio schedule', the ratio requirement changes from reinforcer to reinforcer, but in a fixed cycle. (An example of a cycle is 2, 4, 8, 16, 32, 32, 16, 8, 4, 2, which would then be repeated.) From approximately 30 days following aggregated β-amyloid

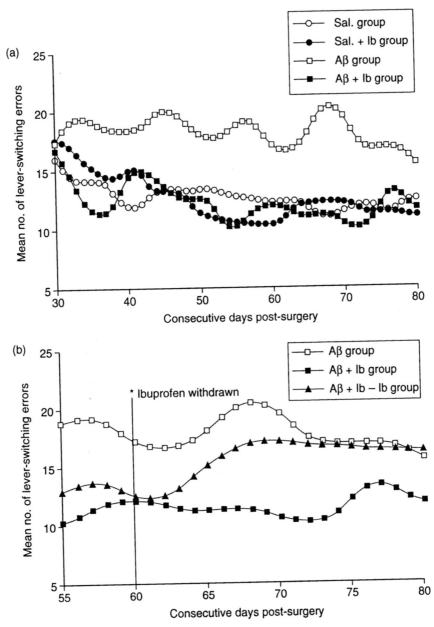

**Figure 5.5** (a) shows average number of switching errors in groups of rats given b amyloid (Aβ) or saline (Sal.) injections in the hippocampus followed for two groups by daily treatment with ibuprofen (Ib) – data shown are from 30 to 80 days post-surgery; (b) shows similar data for Aβ and Aβ+Ib groups and for a group where the daily Ib treatment was withdrawn after 60 days (Aβ+Ib-Ib) group – data shown are from 55 to 80 days post-surgery (Richardson *et al.*, 2000)

injection, rats had impaired ability to track the changing parameters of the schedule and a decrease in the efficiency by which they obtained reinforcers. These rats tended to go to the 'wrong' lever more often following a reinforcer, and then persist longer before switching back to the lever that was currently 'correct'. These effects appeared to be a disruption of learning and memory processes, rather than merely a reflection of general malaise, as β-amyloid injection did not decrease overall operant response rates under the schedule (O'Hare et al., 1999).

A further study showed that daily treatments with an anti-inflammatory drug, ibuprofen, affords protection against learning and memory deficits in the same operant task following aggregated β-amyloid injection into the hippocampus of the rat. Furthermore, when ibuprofen administration was withdrawn 60 days after β-amyloid injection, learning and memory deficits began to develop at that stage. The results are shown in Figure 5.5. These were interesting findings, particularly as several epidemiological studies have reported a reduced incidence of Alzheimer's disease in populations exposed to chronic usage of anti-inflammatory drugs (e.g., those suffering from arthritis). It is possible that anti-inflammatory drugs could also become the drug therapy of choice for Alzheimer's disease.

## 5.9 THE NEW GENETICS AND THE USE OF 'TRANSGENIC ANIMALS' IN BEHAVIOURAL STUDIES

The huge progress that has been made in molecular biology has led to the so-called new genetics, where DNA can be studied and manipulated directly. As mentioned earlier, this opens up some completely new research strategies for behavioural neuroscience. One of the first lines of research of this type to be developed also concerns Alzheimer's disease.

Several research groups have produced genetically modified or transgenic mice that over-express amyloid precursor protein (the most studied type of mouse is the TG2576 mouse, first described by Hsiao et al., 1996). The gene involved is one that occurs in some human families with a very high incidence of Alzheimer's disease. As the mice with the gene develop, far more amyloid precursor protein is produced in their brains than in mice of the same strain that do not have this gene. Post-mortem, these mice have very large amounts of β-amyloid in their brains, suggesting that this is a plausible model of Alzheimer's disease. This suggestion would be greatly strengthened, however, if it was shown that the mice had deficits in learning and memory that are similar to those seen in Alzheimer's disease.

Behavioural studies have been carried out with amyloid precursor protein over-expressing mice. Most of these have used the Morris water maze. (As with the Skinner box, this piece of apparatus is given the name of the researcher who developed it. In this case it was R.G.M. Morris; see Morris, 1984.) In the maze, which was developed initially for rats, the experimental participant is required to swim in a circular pool of water until it finds a submerged platform, on which it can rest and escape from the requirement to swim. It is thus an escape learning procedure. The maze is surrounded by distinctive 'extra-maze cues'. These are distinctive visual stimuli, such as posters showing large black and white geometric figures or brightly coloured objects. Over a series of trials, the animal learns to go to the platform more and more quickly. This occurs even if the animal is required to start from a different point of the periphery of the water maze on each trial. This means that 'spatial learning' occurs in which a particular location is found more and more quickly on later trials. A schematic diagram of the apparatus is shown in Figure 5.6.

Rats rapidly reach an asymptotic performance on this task. That is, their speed increases over several trials and then remains constant on later trials.

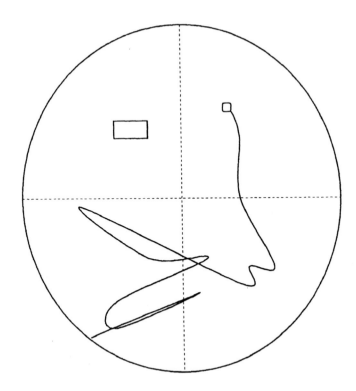

**Figure 5.6** A schematic view from above of a Morris water maze; a track towards the submerged platform is shown

Interventions that disrupt the functioning of the hippocampus, a sub-cortical brain structure that is involved in learning and memory, impair performance on this task. Because of its good 'track record' with rats, this task has often been used to examine the behaviour of transgenic mice, and was indeed used by Hsiao *et al.* (1996) to evaluate their amyloid precursor protein over-expressing mouse. However, some researchers have questioned the results of these studies. Although differences between transgenic and 'normal' wild-type mice (similar mice that do not have the genetic modification are called wild-type mice) are sometimes found, the inbred mouse strains used as the genetic background on which these transgenic mice are developed are often not very good at the water maze task. That is, they do not show a clear learning curve of gradual improvement in performance on the basic spatial learning task, but tend to continue to swim around erratically in the pool even after many training trials (if an animal does this, it will still find the submerged platform eventually and be able to escape from the water). This does not mean that there is no 'learning deficit' in these mice; it suggests instead that other training procedures should be used. This has happened in recent research, and transgenic mice with large amounts of β-amyloid in their brains have indeed been found to have deficits in avoidance learning and object-recognition tasks.

There are many potential benefits from using transgenic techniques in behavioural neuroscience, and these are currently being investigated. The most useful one at this stage is the gene knockout that was briefly described in Section 5.6. It is evident from the research reviewed in this section that, in order to fully utilize these techniques, the behaviour of the mouse strain in the absence of the genetic change needs to be well understood.

## 5.10 COMPLETING THE CIRCLE: EFFECTS OF ENVIRONMENTAL ENRICHMENT

In this chapter, various research strategies have been described in which some intervention in the central system changes behaviour. This indicates that the brain affects behaviour in a variety of ways. There is a tendency to assume that the brain is 'fixed' in its structures and that these will then determine behaviour. This is not correct: although the current structure and function of the brain determines behaviour, the brain changes over time through the interaction between behaviour and the environment. There is a lot of current interest in these changes, which are called *neuronal plasticity*. This plasticity has a role to play in major human medical problems, such as recovery from strokes.

The long-term effects on the brain of interactions between behaviour and the environment can be seen in *environmental enrichment* studies.

Laboratory animals tend to be kept in very clean but boring environments in which there is little to do until the next meal arrives. Starting in the 1960s, Rosenzweig (see Rosenzweig, 1984; Rosenzweig and Bennett, 1996) showed that putting laboratory rats into much more stimulating environments, which included a range of daily activities appropriate for the species, produced big changes in their brains. These included changes in neurochemistry, and increases in weight and thickness of regions in the cerebral cortex of the rat. Enriched early experience also improved performance on several tests of learning. A clear implication is that sufficiently rich experience may be necessary for full growth of the brain and corresponding behavioural potential.

The development of neuroscience techniques has made it possible to show more specific changes in neuronal function and structure resulting from interaction with the environment. For example, Chen *et al.* (1998) found that prolonged physical training, involving the opportunity to 'work out' through 1 hour per day access to a running wheel for 5 days a week, initiated at 3 months of age with C57 Black 6 mice had pronounced effects in their brains. After 21 months of training, the brains of these mice were compared with those of mice who were put in an immobilized wheel on the same number of occasions, and with the brains of young (3 month old) mice. The unexercised older mice showed a significant reduction in the amounts of chemical indicators of nerve growth and development in the hippocampus, compared with the young mice. However, the older mice given the exercise programme had higher levels of these chemical indicators in the hippocampus than did the age-matched unexercised mice. This supports the saying 'Use it or lose it!' – that is, this experimental evidence favours the idea that if you continue to use your brain throughout life it will continue to function well, whereas lack of use will lead to deterioration of function.

These research findings have implications for the treatment of stroke victims. A stroke is a disorder of blood vessels in the brain, either a blockage or a rupture of a vessel, which destroys part of the brain. Stroke victims do receive rehabilitative physiotherapy if, for example, they have lost the use of a limb following a stroke. However, this experimental research with non-human animals, and evidence of neural growth from human brain imaging techniques, have led to the development of more intensive techniques that produce better recovery of function (Robertson, 1999). Neural plasticity, resulting from interaction between the individual and the environment is now an accepted fact that is revolutionizing treatment of serious neurological problems.

In the previous section, we discussed transgenic techniques that are aimed at modelling human neurological disorders. One of these is a transgenic mouse model of the progressive and devastating human disease, Huntington's chorea. Recent research has shown that if transgenic mice with the Huntington's gene are kept in an enriched environment, the deterioration in their behaviour can be greatly reduced (van Dellen *et al.*, 2000).

This section is entitled 'completing the circle' because the evidence reviewed indicates that the life-long interaction between the behaviour of the individual and the environment produces continuing changes in the brain. These, of course, change behaviour in turn. The central notion is one of *interaction*, rather than a one-way casual chain. This means that attempts to deal with a human behavioural problem can involve attempts to change the nervous system, the behaviour or the environment, or any combination of the three. Whichever element is changed will, in due course, have the effect of changing the other two as well.

## 5.11 SUMMARY

Behavioural neuroscience is an interdisciplinary field of study, using behavioural techniques to understand brain function and neuroscience techniques to elucidate behavioural processes. While there is a tendency to believe that behavioural processes can be reduced to, and thus explained by, brain processes, the material reviewed in this chapter shows that each is dependent on the other.

The second half of the twentieth century saw very rapid growth in the pharmaceutical industry, and a corresponding need to assess the behavioural effects of new compounds. Along with this came the extensive use of schedules of reinforcement in the allied discipline of behaviour pharmacology. There are a number of simple schedules of intermittent reinforcement; among them the fixed ratio, fixed interval, variable ratio and variable interval schedules, which each produce a distinctive and reliable pattern of operant behaviour. These are useful behavioural baselines for assessing the effects of drugs that modify central nervous system activity. Particularly important features are the long periods over which consistent patterns of behaviour can be seen, and the high level of resistance to extinction of operant behaviour following exposure to a variety of schedules.

Conditioned suppression, which involves both operant and classical conditioning, is a valuable and sensitive technique. It is sensitive to variables of both operant and classical conditioning and has face validity as a measure of anxiety. More importantly, it has very often been found to be affected in a systematic and predictable way by drugs known to be clinically effective in reducing human anxiety. A Skinner box version of the partial reinforcement extinction effect has also been found to be a useful model for the study of anxiolytic drugs, with both rats and mice. This is significant, because it will facilitate the use of transgenic mice in the development of new anxiolytic agents.

A number of early findings in behaviour pharmacology were interpreted in terms of the rate-dependency hypothesis, which states that the behavioural effect of the drug will depend only on the rate of the operant response in the absence of the drug. Use of a wide range of behavioural procedures with amphetamines has shown that the hypothesis is only supportable with certain procedures. None the less, it was an early illustration of the fact that many behavioural effects of drugs are determined as much by the current behaviour and reinforcement contingencies as by effects in the central nervous system.

Animal models of neurological disorders are important, especially in view of the increasing clinical significance of these disorders. Some complex reinforcement schedules provide a useful model in which to examine aspects of Alzheimer's disease. Support for this approach comes from multidisciplinary studies in which it is shown that injections of β-amyloid into the hippocampus of the rat brain are followed by impairments in learning and memory, but that these impairments can be deferred if anti-inflammatory drugs are constantly administered after the injections.

Alzheimer's disease has also been studied by producing a transgenic mouse that over-expresses β-amyloid, leading to very high levels in the brain. These mice also show impairments in learning and memory tasks. More generally, transgenic and knockout mouse models raise the possibility of answering very specific questions about the neural correlates of behavioural processes, but good data from mouse behavioural procedures will also be required.

Environmental enrichment studies are producing much evidence of neuronal plasticity. Older studies produced evidence of gross changes in the brain, such as increased size of the cortex, while recent ones show more specific changes, such as increased evidence of chemical factors in the hippocampus that promote neural development. It is the interaction between the behaviour of the organism and the enriched environment that produces these changes. These findings have exciting implications for the treatment of strokes, and other conditions where the human central nervous system has been damaged.

The life-long interaction between the behaviour of the individual and the environment produces changes in the brain. This in turn changes behaviour, and so the interaction goes on. Any attempt to deal with a human behavioural problem can involve changes to the nervous system, behaviour or the environment.

## Study question for Chapter 5

As mentioned early in this chapter, there is a tendency to assume that a psychological problem is either due to environmental factors or to biological ones, but not both. An objective of this chapter has been to explain that such an idea is illogical, and that there is much evidence of the interplay of biological, behavioural and environmental factors in relation to many psychological and psychiatric problems.

A useful exercise in this context is to find a psychological problem that has an 'obvious' environmental cause and to suggest a biological treatment. This exercise can also be repeated the other way round: find a psychological problem that appears to have a biological origin and suggest an environmental intervention that may remove the problem.

*Now check your answer with my suggestion in the 'Possible answers to study questions' section, see pages 221–2.*

# 6

# Applied Behaviour Analysis

- Assessing behaviour in applied settings
- Functional assessment and functional analysis
- Methods of functional analysis
- Single-case experimental designs
- Withdrawal or ABAB designs
- Multiple baseline designs
- Increasing adaptive behaviour in applied settings
- Using reinforcement to decrease maladaptive behaviour
- Establishing new behavioural repertoires: prompting, shaping and chaining
- Ensuring generalization of newly acquired skills
- Extinction in applied settings
- Punishment in applied settings
- Ethical guidelines for the use of behavioural treatment
- Summary

So far, this book has been concerned with putting across the main message of behaviour analysis (Chapter 1), providing a general introduction (Chapter 2), setting out the basic principles (Chapter 3), giving an account of some further principles required to deal with later material in the book (Chapter 4) and outlining the contribution of behaviour analysis to behavioural neuroscience (Chapter 5). This chapter takes a different tack and introduces the applications of behaviour analysis to human behaviour problems. These applications began as an aspect of one type of professional practice, that of *clinical psychology*, but they now make a contribution to *education*, *social work* and many other areas where human behaviour is a central concern. As will become clear, the methods used are strongly derived from experimental methods even though they are used in the world outside the laboratory.

In health care there has been much concern in recent years about evidence-based practice. That is, it is now believed that medical and other types of treatment should be based on evidence of effectiveness with the medical or other problem under treatment. This idea is not new in applied behaviour analysis, in fact it has been central since applied behaviour analysis was first developed in the 1960s. It was success in demonstrating progress with conditions that had seemed intractable when approached from other medical, psychiatric or clinical-psychological perspectives that led to applied behaviour analysis being more widely used.

In applied behaviour analysis, 'evidence' is collected throughout, in the form of behavioural measurements. The first type of evidence comes from a *behavioural assessment* of the nature of the problem. The treatment or intervention is derived from that assessment and, across the period of the intervention and after that time, further evidence about the behaviour in question is collected. Only if there has been significant change in the required direction is the intervention said to have been effective. Because there has been continual monitoring, a different intervention strategy may have even been adopted during the course of the intervention, if evidence had accumulated that the first strategy was not in fact producing the required change in behaviour.

Applied behaviour analysis is based on the assumption that reinforcement contingencies, similar to those described in Chapters 3 and 4, are responsible for the behaviour in question. The 'problem' now, however, is that all elements of the contingency have to be discovered in a real-life context rather being implemented by an experimenter. Because antecedents, behaviours and consequences are all functionally defined, they can only be identified through a careful scrutiny of the situation. This is the first stage of applied behaviour analysis.

# 6.1 ASSESSING BEHAVIOUR IN APPLIED SETTINGS

Behavioural assessment involves selecting and defining the behaviour to be changed. This behaviour is typically referred to as the target behaviour. Additionally, the context or environment in which the behaviour occurs must also be clearly identified.

In Figure 6.1 the well-known three-term relationship – of $S^D$, R and S+ (or A, B and C) – is augmented by the addition of establishing operations. Establishing operations are social or biological conditions of satiation or deprivation that may affect the power of a discriminative stimulus or the reinforcing power of a consequence. For example, sweets or candies may be powerful reinforcers for increasing appropriate behaviour (such as cleaning up the play room) with some children, but the effectiveness of such a reinforcer may be related to the level of food deprivation at any given point in time. Hence, presentation of sweets made contingent upon appropriate behaviour may be effective and produce high levels of room cleaning prior to a mealtime, but be ineffective in increasing room cleaning following a meal. Establishing operations include all the social and biological conditions necessary for the three-term relationship of $S^D$, R and S+ to be effective.

$$\text{EOs:} \quad (\ S^D : R \longrightarrow S+)$$

| Establishing operations | Antecedent | Behaviour | Consequence |

**Figure 6.1** A model of the behaviour and environmental conditions to be assessed: the three-term relation of operant conditioning is augmented with establishing operations (see text)

The formal definitions of the three elements of the three-term contingency are, of course, the same as those encountered in previous chapters. Antecedent stimuli are those environmental conditions that occur prior to the performance of a behaviour and predict specific consequences of the behaviour. Much of our everyday behaviour is under the control of antecedent stimuli. A knock at the door or a telephone ring predicts that opening the door or answering the telephone will reveal a person or a voice at the other end. In our earlier example, the presence of a parent may predict that cleaning the room will result in a sweet for the child. Cleaning the play room in the presence of the babysitter will not result in a similar reinforcer and therefore the room remains untidy. The presence of a parent is therefore an antecedent or discriminative stimulus for room cleaning.

Behaviour refers to the responses of an individual or group. These responses must be observable by at least one individual. Behaviours in our previous examples include picking up toys and placing them in appropriate containers, answering the telephone and answering the door.

Finally, consequences or reinforcing stimuli are those events that follow the performance of the behaviour and affect its future probability. They are also contingent upon the performance of the behaviour. In other words, these consequences are only available to the person following the performance of that behaviour and are otherwise not available. Contingent consequences can either increase (reinforce) or decrease (punish) the probability of a behaviour.

In summary, a comprehensive behavioural assessment must provide unambiguous and measurable information about the behaviour to be decreased or increased, and the context in which the behaviour occurs. The context is operationalized in terms of how establishing operations, antecedent stimuli, and consequence stimuli enter into a functional relationship with the behaviour of interest.

A number of questions should be asked about the proposed target behaviours before a formal assessment. These include the following.

- Will increasing and/or decreasing this behaviour result in positive outcomes for the person concerned?
- Who will be the primary beneficiary of this programme?
- Is the behaviour appropriate or typical for somebody of that age?

These and other possible questions concern the rights of individuals concerned and the *social validity* of the proposed intervention. Interventions are not 'value free' and everyone concerned must always be alert to this. Interventions are said to be socially valid when there is a consensus (in the family or in the wider community) that the planned behaviour change that the intervention should produce is appropriate.

Once there is agreement regarding the need for a behavioural intervention, the target behaviour must be carefully defined. Initially, the presenting behaviour is typically defined in general terms such as personality characteristics, and summary labels in the form of statements such as 'I want to lose weight', 'my child is too aggressive' or 'this student is withdrawn'. These global terms must be translated into *operational definitions*. That is, the behaviour in question must be described in a way that makes reliable measurement possible.

An example of an operational definition of behaviour arising from the statement 'my child is too aggressive' might be the behaviour category 'striking siblings in a forceful manner with an open hand or closed fist but excluding touching siblings with tips of fingers or with an open hand in a non-forceful manner'. This operational definition identifies the problematic behaviours in objective terms and delineates examples of behaviour to be included and excluded from the definition. In the case of the withdrawn student in the example cited at the beginning of this section, it is most probable that the target of the intervention will be to increase appropriate social interactions in the school setting. One potential target behaviour might be to increase verbal interactions and might be defined as 'a verbal statement that begins a conversation, changes a topic, or provides instruction to take some action'.

If an intervention is to be designed to develop a complex sequence of behaviours, it may not be possible to produce a simple operational definition. Such complex behaviours must be broken down into their component parts. Each component behaviour must be discrete and essential for completing the task sequence. The process by which a complex sequence of behaviours is broken down and the outcome of such a process (that is, the set of behaviours) is called a *task analysis*.

Once the target behaviour has been identified, the next step is to select a sensitive and practical measurement strategy for that behaviour. A sensitive measurement system is one that produces an accurate and complete picture of the target behaviour, and a practical measurement system is one that is usable from the point of view of the observer. Whether a measurement system is usable depends on the context. For example, it would be difficult for a teacher with a normal classroom responsibility of some 30 students to record the amount of time spent 'out of seat' (that is, time spent away from the seat the student should be occupying) for an individual student, because of the need to attend to all the other students.

Some of the most common measurement methods used include frequency or event recording, duration and latency, and time sampling methods. Further information about how to implement such methods is available in more extended accounts of applied behaviour analysis (see, for example, Leslie and O'Reilly, 1999).

Behaviour typically fluctuates over time, and this must be taken into account when designing observation sessions, so that a representative sample of the target behaviour is obtained. Additionally, the strategy for conducting observations will also be influenced by the overall goal of the proposed intervention. Factors to be considered when conducting observations include: the number of times that observations are made; the length of observation sessions; the time of day of sessions. All these decisions should be informed by knowledge of the behaviour already available (e.g., that the tantrums usually occur at bedtime) and by practical limitations (e.g., rarely is a great deal of observation possible in an applied setting such as home or school).

The target behaviour must be reliably assessed. Reliability generally means that two observers can concurrently, but independently, observe the target behaviour and agree on its occurrence and non-occurrence. Reliability or inter-observer agreement is therefore an assessment of the consistency and accuracy with which the target behaviour is measured before, during and after the intervention. High levels of inter-observer agreement allow the behaviour analyst to conclude that patterns of responding (e.g., percentage of intervals that the target behaviour occurs across days) reflect actual performance of the target behaviour. Low levels of inter-observer agreement may reflect observation biases and not actual performance. An acceptable level of agreement between observers typically ranges between 80 and 100%. This can be accomplished by conducting reliability observations and checking agreement levels on the target behaviour before formal baseline observations. There should be training of all observers before any measurements are conducted. If the obtained levels of inter-observer agreement are too low when first calculated, then further training should be implemented.

## 6.2 FUNCTIONAL ASSESSMENT AND FUNCTIONAL ANALYSIS

Until recently, applied behaviour analysts have primarily been interested in isolating target behaviours and selecting interventions to increase or decrease the frequency of these behaviours. This led to a concern with the form or topography of the target behaviours rather than by the operant function of these behaviours. For example, in a child with learning disabilities who showed self-injurious behaviour, the target behaviour might be described as 'eye gouging', without reference to its function for the individual. This approach contradicted a fundamental premise of behaviour analysis, which describes behaviour primarily in terms of its function (see Chapter 1). However, in recent years many researchers and therapists have conducted a *functional assessment* or *functional analysis* of the environmental determinants of target behaviours and subsequently matched a treatment to the function the target behaviour currently has for the individual concerned.

Functional assessment describes a variety of systematic procedures to determine antecedent and consequent variables that produce and maintain the target behaviour. Typically, behaviours are defined by interviewing significant others and are subsequently observed in those contexts where the behaviour has been described as being problematic. This form of assessment reveals *correlational information* regarding establishing operations, antecedents and consequences for the target behaviour. When assessment procedures go further and also involve the systematic manipulation of hypothesized controlling variables (that is, reinforcement contingencies) this is called a functional analysis. As will become clear in Section 6.3, functional analysis comes closer to providing a causal explanation of the behavioural problem.

The first stage of functional assessment is usually a *behavioural interview*. There are three main objectives of a behavioural interview.

1. Operationalize the behaviour(s): *what is it?*
2. Identification of those physical and environmental factor(s) predictive of the target behaviour(s): *when does it occur?*
3. Identification of the potential functions of behaviour(s) in terms of their maintaining consequences: *what reinforces it?*

Those who are interviewed (such as parents, teachers and others) should be in daily contact with the individual showing the target behaviour and therefore be in a position to describe events as they have witnessed them in the past and to draw conclusions about the causes of an individual's behaviour. A complete interview should include questions that probe the informant about the topography of the behaviour, the situations in which it does and does not occur, and the typical reactions of others in response to the behaviour. In essence, the behavioural interview attempts to review a large number of potential variables and narrow the focus to those that appear to be of some importance in generating and maintaining the target behaviour.

There are a number of advantages to the interview approach, including ease of application, cost and efficiency (the interview takes only a brief period), but there are also a number of inherent difficulties. Interviews and other discussions do not allow for direct access to the relevant behaviours and their controlling variables, and there may be faulty recollection of events, informant bias, informant expectation etc. We can never assume that verbal reports give us direct evidence as to the 'truth'. Our informant may wish to appear knowledgeable, or to present him/herself in a good light. For these reasons, information gained through these methods may provide unreliable estimates of behaviour and may lead to invalid conclusions about its controlling variables.

A more objective and systematic approach to assessment involves first-hand observation of an individual's behaviour in environmental contexts that are relevant to the problem. In a typical method, the individual may be observed in their usual daily routine in as many settings and across as much time per day as is possible for a minimum period of three to five days. Little control may be exerted over the environmental conditions during this form of assessment. Details of such direct observations should be based on information gleaned from the interview process (i.e., behaviours and situations that have been identified as problematic are observed). The method is usually carried out by those parents, teachers and support staff who already work with the individual, and is conducted in a manner that does not require extensive time or training on their part. Two general classes of descriptive analysis will be outlined.

1. The *Antecedent–Behaviour–Consequence (ABC) Assessment* method attempts to evaluate the immediate antecedent and consequent events surrounding the target behaviour and assess the extent to which these specific events may be related to the occurrence of behaviour. This assessment usually entails a narrative account of directly observed behaviour and the environment in which it occurs. Those working with the individual exhibiting the problem behaviour are asked to write brief descriptors of what occurs immediately before (A) and after (C) the target behaviour (B). Such accounts can be recorded on an ABC, or sequence analysis, chart. Although the procedure is relatively easy to learn, it requires extensive effort to implement and may still lead to subjective interpretation of events rather than objective descriptions. This problem can be reduced by further instruction and training of informants. This, of course, increases the costs.

2. *Scatterplot Assessment* is a simple direct observation method that records temporal distributions of behaviour. Observers are trained to record the time of day of the occurrence of each instance of the target behaviour on a grid that identifies time of day on the ordinate (usually in 30-minute segments) and consecutive days on the abscissa. As the behaviours are repeatedly observed and plotted, correlations between particular times of day and differential rates of behaviour usually become evident. These data allow for more detailed observational analyses (such as ABC assessments) during those time periods in which the behaviour has been identified as most probable. An example of a scatterplot data sheet used by staff in a residential setting to identify the temporal distribution of 'scratching other clients' by an adult with severe learning disabilities in a group home is presented in Figure 6.2. This scatterplot shows that the target behaviour clusters around certain time periods during the day when the client was required to engage in task-related activities. These results would imply that the aggressive scratching behaviour might be maintained by negative reinforcement contingencies (i.e., escape from demanding activities).

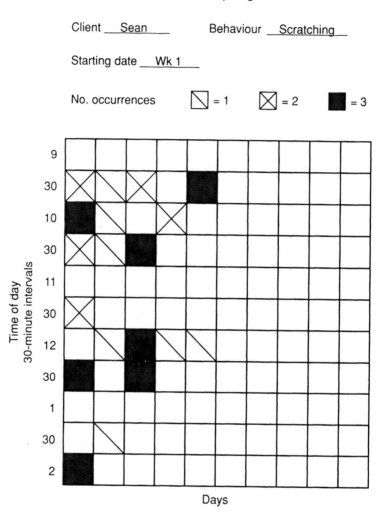

**Figure 6.2** Example of a scatterplot grid over a five-day period

In summary, direct observation methods have a number of advantages. They allow direct access to problem behaviour in the natural environment and therefore are more objective in that they reflect current behaviour and not recall of past observations. Like most procedures, direct observations also have a number of limitations. Relative to indirect methods, such procedures are time consuming. More importantly, these procedures do not necessarily reveal functional relationships. This issue is discussed in the next section.

# 6.3 METHODS OF FUNCTIONAL ANALYSIS

The methods of functional assessment seek to identify contingencies of reinforcement, but it will be evident from earlier chapters that contingencies are known to be in effect only when they actually change behaviour. That is, in an experiment we introduce a contingency, see the behaviour change and attribute that change in behaviour to the introduced reinforcement contingency. We may then test this conclusion by withdrawing or reversing the reinforcement contingency to see whether the behaviour change that had occurred is now reversed. The 'static' and correlational methods of functional assessment cannot provide this type of information. Methods that go beyond those, and do attempt to vary the contingencies in some way, are called functional analysis.

Functional analysis has been tried in various ways (Sturmey, 1996). Here we will describe the methods that go to the greatest lengths to change the contingencies that may be maintaining the behaviour and thus provide the 'best quality' information. The most important feature of this approach is its direct and systematic manipulation of variables that potentially maintain the target behaviour. This form of analysis is important for many reasons. First, it emphasizes the importance of gaining information about the contingencies maintaining behaviour rather than merely describing the topographical features (e.g., crying, biting or hitting). It also explains how topographically similar behaviours can serve different functions for a given individual. For example, one individual may engage in self-injurious behaviour to gain access to attention and their behaviour may be maintained by attention functioning as positive reinforcement. On the other hand, another individual's self-injury may be negatively reinforced and serve to escape from an aversive situation. Through identification of these different functions of topographically similar behaviours, researchers have recognized the need to develop *highly individualized treatment programmes* that are tailored to the specific function of the problem behaviour.

The control necessary to demonstrate functional relationships in an experimental analysis is often difficult to obtain in the natural environment. Functional relationships are therefore often assessed in an *analogue setting* that approximates the natural environment. An example of how this is done is given below. Once the conditions that control the behaviour are identified, these contingencies can be manipulated in the natural environment.

The classic study of functional analysis was published in 1982, but attracted so much interest a few years later that it was re-issued in 1994 in a more widely read journal (Iwata *et al.*, 1982 and 1994). The idea of this study (and some earlier ones that use somewhat simpler designs) was that the effectiveness of interventions with people who show self-injurious behaviour might be improved if the contingency maintaining this distressing behaviour was successfully identified for each person before any intervention was attempted. It was hypothesized that in a group of people with this problem, there might be at least three different reasons why they do it: they might be seeking attention from care-givers and others (self-injurious behaviour certainly often generates attention); they might be seeking to escape from the demands of an educational or other task; or they might be doing it because of its sensory or self-stimulatory effects.

Within the study, each person with self-injurious behaviour was exposed several times to each of four conditions for brief sessions of a few minutes each. The first of these assessed the impact of positive reinforcement, because a person was with them and had been told to give them attention contingent on self-injury. The second condition assessed the role of negative reinforcement, because the person with them asked them to engage in a task, but they could escape from these demands if they showed self-injury. The third condition allowed for only sensory reinforcement, because they were placed in a barren environment with no access to either attention or toys, and the final condition was a control procedure where there was no attention for self-injury, no demands were made, play materials were available and attention was given contingent on the absence of self-injury. These procedures are termed a *multi-element* or *reversal design* (more information on experimental designs is given in the next section).

Two hypothetical examples of analogue analyses for self-injury using multi-element designs in an analogue assessment are presented in Figure 6.3. For the Person 1 graph in the figure, there are higher levels of self-injury in the attention condition relative to the other conditions. These results imply that self-injury for this individual is maintained by social positive reinforcement. In the graph for Person 2 we see higher levels of self-injury in the demand condition relative to the other conditions. The results in this second graph imply that self-injury for Person 2 is maintained by escape from task demands, or social negative reinforcement.

The initial study (Iwata *et al.*, 1982 and 1994) with nine persons produced results of the type shown in Figure 6.3. That is, self-injurious behaviour was indeed found to be maintained by different reinforcers in different individuals in the analogue assessment. In fact, four of the nine persons showed most self-injury with sensory reinforcement, two with escape from task demands, and the other three showed different individual patterns across the multi-element assessment. In a further 1994 report, Iwata *et al.* were able to show that using this type of assessment with 152 people had shown specific functions of these various sources of reinforcement for 145 of the cases, with one of three types of reinforcement listed earlier being clearly crucial in over 90% of cases. These assessment findings were very good predictors of effective treatment. For example, in self-injury motivated by social positive reinforcement, attention extinction was an effective intervention in almost all cases.

This represents a very high success rate with a type of problem with which,

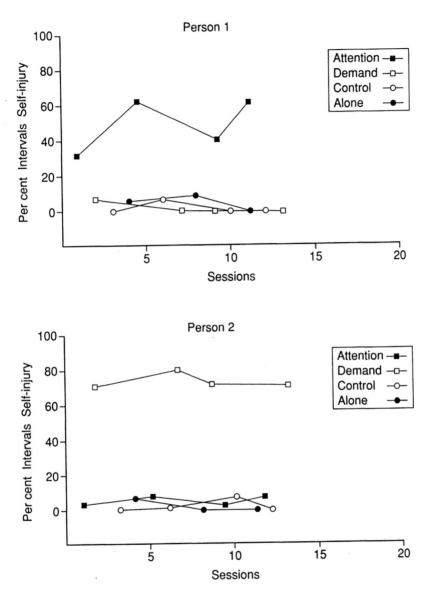

**Figure 6.3** Results from a functional analysis of two individuals who were successively tested in four conditions (attention, demand, control, alone) with each condition occurring at least three times; in these hypothetical data, each person showed a high rate of self-injury in only one condition

prior to the use of applied behaviour analysis, success was very rare. In the absence of successful intervention the people showing self-injurious behaviour are often put into restraints or given sedating medication indefinitely. Following successful application of applied behaviour analysis, on the other hand, they may have a much better quality of life.

One potential disadvantage in conducting this type of functional analysis is that it may be difficult or impractical for use in many applied settings due to the stringent control necessary and also the limitations of staff, time and facilities. This is probably not a legitimate objection, however, in cases such as self-injurious behaviour where much time and effort are often spent even on ineffective strategies. In any case, it has now been shown that brief 60- or 90-minute sessions may be sufficient to complete a functional analysis (see, for example, Northup *et al.*, 1991; O'Reilly *et al.*, 1996).

Another potential disadvantage is that the analogue analysis may not be ecologically valid, and for accidental reasons may not mirror exactly the variables operating in the natural environment. This is a potentially serious problem, but it has been overcome in studies where experimental analyses have been conducted successfully with parents in 'natural' settings such as classrooms and outpatient clinics. Functional analysis, sometimes in less well-controlled forms, has also been shown to be useful with a wide range of clinical problems.

## 6.4 SINGLE-CASE EXPERIMENTAL DESIGNS

Applied behaviour analysis generally uses *single-case designs*. These experimental techniques, which resemble those used in laboratory studies of operant conditioning, are used to determine if changes in the target behaviour can be attributed to the treatment or intervention. These experimental techniques examine the *functional relationships* between changes in the environment and changes in the target behaviour.

Single-case research designs typically use graphic display to present visually each assessment session. Graphic display is a simple method for organizing, interpreting and communicating findings of this type. While many forms of graphic display can be used, simple line graphs or 'frequency polygons' are most often used in applied behaviour analysis. The line graph represents changes in the dependent variable, which is a measure of the target behaviour, relative to a specific point in time or treatment, which is the independent variable.

An example of a line graph is presented in Figure 6.4. The major features of this graph include the horizontal and vertical axes, condition change lines, condition labels, data points and data paths. The horizontal axis represents the passage of time (consecutive sessions) and the different levels of the

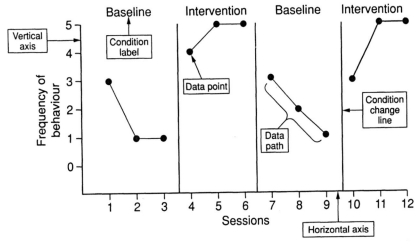

**Figure 6.4** Hypothetical example of a single-case design graph depicting the major features of graphic display (illustration courtesy of Mark O'Reilly)

independent variable (baseline and intervention). The vertical axis represents values of the dependent variable, which will be a measure of behaviour. The condition change lines represent that point in time when the levels of the independent variable were systematically changed. Condition labels are brief descriptions of the experimental conditions in effect during each phase of the study. Each data point represents the occurrence of the target behaviour during a session under a given experimental condition. Connecting the data points with a straight line under a given experimental condition creates a data path. A data path represents the relationship between the independent and dependent variables and is of primary interest when interpreting graphed data.

The primary method of analysis with all single-case research designs is a *visual interpretation of graphic displays*. It is important to collect a sufficient number of data points in order to provide a reliable estimate of the performance of the target behaviour under a given experimental condition. There are no hard-and-fast rules about the number of data points that should be collected under a given experimental condition. Sidman (1960) suggests that at least three measures of the target behaviour should be collected per experimental condition. This is an optimal suggestion if the data path is stable (see below), and the nature of the target behaviour allows for multiple assessments under baseline and intervention conditions. For example, if the target behaviour is dangerous to the individual or others (for example, when it involves aggression) it may be unethical to conduct extended assessments under *baseline conditions* when the treatment has not been applied.

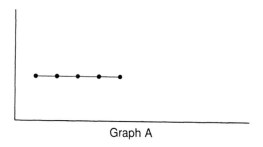

Graph A

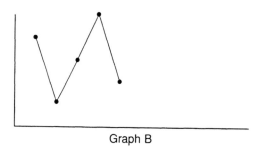

Graph B

**Figure 6.5** Data plots for successive sessions showing a stable data path (Graph A) and an unstable data path (Graph B)

Stability refers to a lack of variability in the data under a given experimental condition. In Figure 6.5 it is clear that Graph A presents a stable data path, whereas the data in Graph B are variable. It is, however, unusual in applied research to achieve perfect stability of data as illustrated in Graph A. If stability is not obvious from a visual examination of the data then it may be prudent to identify those environmental stimuli that are causing such variability.

Stability of data within a given experimental condition is also important because the data path serves a predictive function for interpreting data within the subsequent experimental condition. A stable data path within a given experimental condition allows the behaviour analyst to infer that if that experimental condition was continued over time, a similar data pattern would emerge. In Figure 6.6 the predicted data paths for a stable data set (Graph A) and a variable data set (Graph B) are plotted. It is obvious that the effects of the intervention can be more clearly interpreted by comparing predicted with observed data for Graph A than for Graph B.

*Level* can be defined as the value of a behavioural measure or group of measures on the vertical axis of a line graph. Level can be used to describe overall performance within an experimental condition or between experimental conditions. Typically, the levels of performance within and between conditions are analysed visually by the behaviour analyst. However, a mean level can also be calculated for each condition. Stability and level are

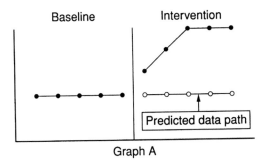

Graph A

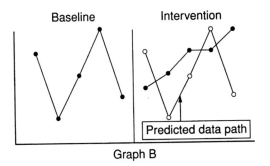

Graph B

**Figure 6.6** Data plots for successive sessions showing a stable data path during baseline followed by an intervention (Graph A) or an unstable data path (Graph B) followed by an intervention

inextricably linked in the visual analysis of data. If extreme variability exists in the data paths, then an examination of level within and between conditions may be impossible. In Figure 6.7 (Graph A) there is an obvious level change between conditions when the intervention is implemented. In Graph B the level change during the intervention phase does not occur until the third data point. It may be the case for Graph B that something other than, or in addition to, the intervention causes a level change in behaviour from the third data point onwards.

*Trend* can be defined as the overall direction taken by a data path. Trends can be described as increasing, decreasing or zero. A stable data path represents a zero trend. Increasing and decreasing trends can be problematic for interpreting data. If, for example, the plan is to increase frequency of the target behaviour, an increasing trend in the baseline data path may make interpretation of the effects of the intervention difficult (see Figure 6.8, Graph A). This logic also holds for decreasing trends (see Figure 6.8, Graph B). It is advisable in such cases to withhold the intervention until the data path stabilizes under baseline conditions or until the behaviour reaches the desired goal. In some applied situations it may be impractical (the intervention may be time-limited) or unethical (the behaviour may be dangerous to self or others)

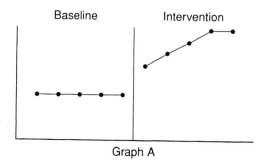

Graph A

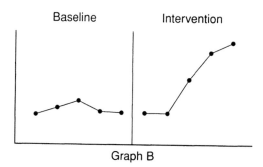

Graph B

**Figure 6.7** Data plots for successive sessions showing a stable data path during baseline followed by an intervention which has an immediate effect (Graph A) or a stable data path followed by an intervention which has a delayed effect (Graph B)

to withhold treatment for extended periods. In these situations experimental control may need to be sacrificed in order to achieve the desired behavioural outcomes. Under some circumstances a trend in data may not interfere with the interpretation of the subsequent experimental condition. This is true for situations where the trend under a given experimental condition is going in the opposite direction than would be predicted when the subsequent experimental condition is implemented (see Figure 6.8, Graph C).

## 6.5 WITHDRAWAL OR ABAB DESIGNS

*Withdrawal* or *ABAB* designs represent a series of experimental arrangements whereby selected conditions are systematically presented and withdrawn over time. This design typically consists of two phases, a baseline or A phase and an intervention or B phase, which are repeated or *replicated* (hence the ABAB notation). The design begins with an assessment of behaviour under baseline conditions. Once the target behaviour stabilizes under baseline conditions the intervention condition is implemented. The intervention condition is continued until the target behaviour reaches a stable level. At this point the intervention is withdrawn and the baseline condition is replicated until stability is again

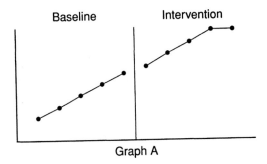

Graph A

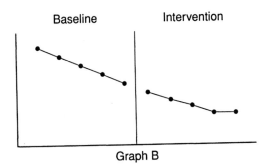

Graph B

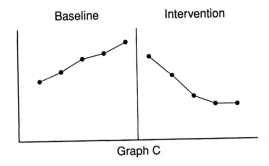

Graph C

**Figure 6.8** Data plots for successive sessions showing a trend during baseline which persists following the intervention (Graphs A and B) or a trend during baseline which is reversed following the intervention (Graph C)

achieved. Finally, the intervention condition is once again implemented. Experimental control is achieved when there is a visible difference between the data paths in the A and B phases, and this difference is again achieved in the A and B phase replications. Examples of the use of ABAB designs abound in the applied literature, and some will be discussed later in this chapter. An important feature of the ABAB design is that the final stage is a B phase, which is the intervention to produce the required behaviour change.

The withdrawal or ABAB design is a very effective means of examining the effects of a treatment on selected target behaviours. There are several issues that must be considered, however, before deciding to use it. It demonstrates experimental control by systematically applying and removing the treatment variables. The purposeful withdrawal of treatment is seldom desirable in clinical practice. There may therefore be ethical reasons (for example, with behaviour that is dangerous to self or others) for not using an ABAB design. A different type of problem arises with types of behaviours (e.g., social skills) that might be expected to remain at high frequency or at least to continue to be performed above initial baseline levels after the intervention is withdrawn. If the target behaviour does not revert to the initial baseline levels with the withdrawal of treatment (i.e., second A phase) then experimental control is lost. It is therefore important to consider whether the target behaviour would be sensitive to the changing contingencies of an ABAB design. Where there are ethical, practical or other problems with an ABAB design, additional designs are available. The most important of these is discussed in the next section.

# 6.6 MULTIPLE BASELINE DESIGNS

The multiple baseline design is a procedure whereby the independent variable is sequentially applied to a minimum of two levels of a dependent variable. There are three important types: the *multiple baseline across behaviours* design examines behaviour change across two or more behaviours of a particular individual; the *multiple baseline across settings* design examines changes in the same behaviour of the same individual across two or more different settings; and *the multiple baseline across participants* design examines changes in the same behaviour across two or more individuals. These designs do not include a withdrawal or reversal to the baseline, pre-intervention, condition. They are thus particularly useful where such a return would be undesirable or impractical.

These are extremely powerful techniques. The key idea with all of these types of design is that an intervention (the independent variable) is applied at a certain stage to one category (a behaviour, a setting, or an individual) but not to one or more others. This enables the effect of the intervention to be seen by comparison across categories. Put more formally, experimental control is demonstrated by sequentially applying the treatment variable across behaviours, settings or persons. In a multiple baseline across persons design, baseline data on a target behaviour are collected across two or more individuals. Once baseline reaches stability for all individuals then the intervention is implemented with the first individual. Baseline assessment is continued with the other individuals while the intervention is implemented with the first individual. The behaviour of the first individual is expected to change while the other individuals should continue to show stable baseline responding. The intervention is continued with the first individual until the target behaviour reaches a stable level or diverges from the level predicted from the baseline data. At this point the intervention is implemented with the second individual while the third individual continues to remain under baseline conditions. This procedure is continued until all individuals are exposed to the intervention. Experimental control is demonstrated if baseline responding changes at that point in time when the treatment variable is applied to each person. Typically, three or more behaviours, persons or settings are used in a multiple baseline design.

In this design, a confident interpretation of the effects of the independent variable can be made if there are visible changes in the data paths *when, and only when,* the independent variable is applied across the separate baselines. The multiple baseline design, therefore, does not require a withdrawal of treatment in order to demonstrate experimental control. This design option should be considered when it is expected that a withdrawal of treatment might not result in a return of behaviour to previous baseline levels. Multiple baseline designs are often employed to examine the effectiveness of teaching strategies on the acquisition of skills, as such skills are expected to continue once instruction is withdrawn.

## 6.7 INCREASING ADAPTIVE BEHAVIOUR IN APPLIED SETTINGS

Many behavioural interventions are designed to increase adaptive responding. In such cases, individuals may possess appropriate behavioural repertoires but not perform them frequently. For example, someone who is described as being socially withdrawn may possess the appropriate social skills for initiating interactions with others but may not use them when in the presence of other people. In a similar vein, community behavioural interventions often seek to increase adaptive community behaviours, such as healthy lifestyles, safe use of working and leisure environments etc. In other instances, individuals may not possess the targeted skills. For example, people with developmental disabilities sometimes exhibit deficits in various social, daily living and academic skills. In these cases, behavioural techniques can be used to establish or teach these new skills.

Positive reinforcement is the most frequently used intervention by applied behaviour analysts. To recap, it can be defined as the contingent application of consequences that increase the probability of behaviours. The process of positive reinforcement requires several necessary conditions. First, a consequence must be contingent on responding. Second, the response must increase in probability when the consequence is made contingent on responding. Finally, the application of the consequence must be a necessary and sufficient condition to explain the increase in probability of responding.

Empirical methods can be used to assess the reinforcing effectiveness of various contingent consequences. This may seem strange; why not just ask the person what they would like, and then devise the reinforcing consequence? There are several reasons why this may not be sufficient: the person may be very young, or have learning disabilities, or their verbal statements may not be a highly reliable indicator of their choices. Various preference and forced-choice methods have consequently been used to choose reinforcers for particular programmes, and these have been found to be more useful than verbal reports of preferences. Ultimately, the reinforcing effectiveness of a contingent stimulus can only be determined by causally examining its influence on the probability of the target behaviour.

Given that a reinforcer has been decided upon, there are a number of other factors to be taken into account. Early in the programme, the reinforcer should be delivered very soon after the target behaviour to ensure its effectiveness. Otherwise, the 'wrong' behaviour may accidentally be reinforced. A child may complete an educational target behaviour, for example, and then immediately switch to playing with toys. It is important that the reinforcer is delivered after the first behaviour, not the second. Once the contingency between the target behaviour and reinforcing consequence has been firmly established through immediate reinforcement, then the delay may be systematically lengthened. Indeed, this may then be desirable, because in 'real-life contingencies' the reinforcement is often delayed. Providing an intermittent schedule of reinforcement is also a tactic for guarding against rapid extinction of the target behaviour once the behaviour change programme is removed.

The level of satiation or deprivation of the reinforcer further influences responding. In the terms of Figure 6.1, these variables are classified as establishing operations. Through understanding these contextual influences on the power of reinforcement the behaviour analyst may be able to identify optimal times and conditions to conduct training. For example, attractive food can be used as a reinforcer before mealtimes, but not immediately afterwards. Relatedly, the amount of a reinforcer that an individual receives over the course of a given training session can also affect performance. For a reinforcer to be effective, the individual must remain deprived of it during the session, and if the amount delivered is too great the deprivation will be reduced too much. However, conditioned reinforcers such as social attention and generalized conditioned reinforcers such as money may be more resistant to satiation within training sessions.

The *token economy* is an applied example of the use of a generalized conditioned reinforcer to modify behaviour (look back at Section 4.5 for a description of conditioned reinforcement). The participant in a token economy is required to perform certain target behaviours at predefined levels in order to receive a particular number of tokens. *Tokens* typically consist of coins, check marks, stars or 'smiley faces'. In and of themselves, these tokens have no inherent reinforcing value, but within the token economy system they can be used to purchase *back-up reinforcers*. Back-up reinforcers are consequences of known reinforcing value to those participating in the token system. Back-up reinforcers can consist of anything from food and other consumables, to activities and outings. Each back-up reinforcer can be purchased by a specific number of tokens. Because tokens can allow the participant to access various reinforcers they are defined as generalized conditioned reinforcers.

Token economy systems have proved successful in increasing appropriate behaviour for many populations (developmentally disabled, psychiatric,

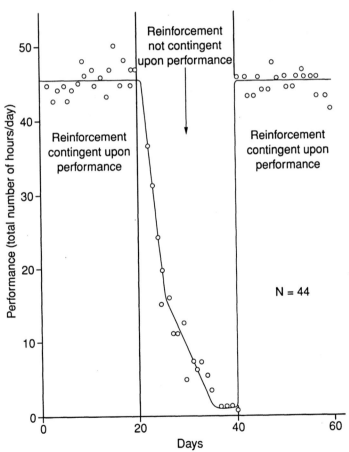

**Figure 6.9** Total number of hours each day a group of 44 clients participated in rehabilitative activities under reinforcement with tokens (B), independent or noncontingent presentation of tokens (A) and reinstatement of reinforcement with tokens (B)

children etc.) and across many settings (hospitals, institutions, the home etc.). In the classic evaluations of the token economy system, Ayllon and Azrin (1965, 1968) developed such a system to increase appropriate responding in hospitalized psychiatric patients. High-frequency activities such as going for walks, privacy and religious services were identified as back-up reinforcers for participants. Participants earned tokens from ward staff for engaging in a number of targeted work activities around the hospital. The findings of this intervention are presented in Figure 6.9. In this study, the token system was implemented for an entire ward of 44 clients. The effectiveness of the token system was evaluated using a BAB design. In the reversal or A phase, access to tokens and reinforcers was not contingent on occurrence of the target work activities. When the token system was made contingent on performance there was a dramatic increase in work activity in both B phases.

The use of tokens as a generalized conditioned reinforcer has a number of inherent advantages over using single conditioned or primary reinforcers within an intervention programme. First, because the participant has access to a set of back-up reinforcers the problem of satiation on any one reinforcer is reduced. Also, additional back-up reinforcers can be identified and added to the token economy during the intervention. Second, because of the nature of tokens themselves, they can be presented immediately following the performance of the target behaviour. This overcomes the potential problem of delaying access to reinforcers. Third, token delivery does not interfere with ongoing activities. Of course, staff must also be trained to administer the token system consistently. In fact, a token system can be seen as an intervention to change the behaviour of those who work with the participants, as well as that of the 'participants' themselves. For example, a token system can be used to establish positive interactions between parents and their children. Similarly, in psychiatric contexts, staff must be aware that they should attend to positive behaviour and not selectively respond to disruptive behaviour by individuals. Ironically, a 'caring orientation' in staff often means that they react to, and thus often unknowingly reinforce, disruptive or disturbed behaviour, and ignore, and thus sometimes extinguish, 'good' behaviour.

## 6.8  USING REINFORCEMENT TO DECREASE MALADAPTIVE BEHAVIOUR

Positive reinforcement strategies can be used to decrease maladaptive or unwanted behaviour. These strategies are based on the idea that if behaviour other than maladaptive responding is reinforced and thus increased in frequency, there will be a corresponding decrease in maladaptive behaviour. These techniques are therefore described as *differential reinforcement* strategies because selected responses or levels of responding are reinforced while other responses are not. (Differential reinforcement schedules were briefly introduced in Section 4.11.)

For this strategy to work in an applied setting, it is essential to identify the reinforcers that are maintaining the maladaptive behaviour. Differential reinforcement is based on two behavioural processes: extinction and reinforcement. In extinction, the reinforcers that maintain the unwanted behaviour must be withheld from that behaviour, and can be delivered contingent on other more appropriate responses. The behaviour analyst should therefore conduct a functional analysis of the maladaptive behaviour prior to developing the intervention. Reinforcing stimuli must also be selected and applied contingent on appropriate responding. These reinforcing consequences should themselves be systematically identified through empirical tests, or the reinforcers that previously maintained the unwanted behaviour can be used to increase adaptive responding.

There are a number of differential reinforcement schedules. For example, *differential reinforcement of incompatible behaviour* (DRI) is a technique whereby reinforcement is delivered contingent on the occurrence of a behaviour that is topographically incompatible with the targeted maladaptive behaviour. The increase in frequency of the incompatible behaviour thus results in a decrease in the frequency of the maladaptive behaviour, as both behaviours cannot be performed simultaneously. Deitz *et al.* (1976) used a DRI intervention to decrease episodes of in-class sleeping for a student with mild disabilities. The intervention consisted of teacher-delivered praise for appropriate academic activity approximately every 5 minutes. Academic performance is directly incompatible with sleeping. The effectiveness of the intervention was evaluated using an ABAB design. The results of this intervention are presented in Figure 6.10 and demonstrate the effectiveness of the DRI intervention.

*Differential reinforcement of alternative behaviour* (DRA) is a similar procedure to DRI. In this case, however, the behaviour chosen for reinforcement is not topographically incompatible with the maladaptive behaviour. The DRA schedule is based on the premise that increasing the frequency of alternative behaviours will decrease the frequency of the undesired behaviour. For example, reinforcing academic activity may decrease maladaptive behaviour in the classroom such as talking inappropriately, or leaving one's seat.

A functional analysis can allow the behaviour analyst to tailor an intervention to the function of the behaviour. For example, a functional analysis may demonstrate that a person with learning disabilities who engages in hand biting does this to gain attention from staff. This information allows the behaviour analyst to identify an alternative behaviour (such as raising of a hand) that the person can be taught to use to access the same reinforcer (in this case, staff attention). This alternative behaviour is therefore functionally equivalent to the challenging behaviour. The differential reinforcement

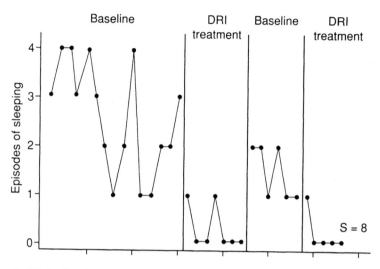

**Figure 6.10** Episodes of sleeping in class under baseline conditions and DRI contingencies (Deitz *et al.*, 1976)

programme therefore consists of withholding the reinforcer for the maladaptive behaviour and making the same reinforcer available for the functionally equivalent behaviour. This type of intervention is described as *functional communication training* because more appropriate behaviour now has a communicative function for the person.

The *noncontingent delivery of a reinforcing stimulus* (NCR) can result in a rapid reduction in operant responding in experimental studies, because the response-reinforcer contingency no longer exists if the reinforcing stimulus is now delivered independently from the response. This technique has also been shown to be effective in reducing the frequency of unwanted behaviour in applied settings. In such cases, as with so many others, it is crucial first to carry out a functional analysis to identify what the reinforcer actually is.

## 6.9 ESTABLISHING NEW BEHAVIOURAL REPERTOIRES: PROMPTING, SHAPING AND CHAINING

In the previous sections, strategies to increase or decrease the current frequency of responding have been outlined, but behavioural strategies can also be used to establish or develop new behaviours, which can be either specific individual skills or complex sequences of skills. One way of doing this is through the use of *prompts*.

Prompts are antecedent stimuli that are used to evoke the desired response, they are thus *stimulus control* techniques. These antecedent stimuli are typically supplementary stimuli that can be removed once the target behaviour is performed appropriately in the presence of the more natural discriminative stimuli. Prompts are of two general types: *response prompts* describe or demonstrate the new desired response; *stimulus prompts* highlight the natural discriminative stimuli in the environment.

There are several types of response prompts, including verbal, modelling, picture and physical prompts. *Verbal response prompts* are the most commonly and widely used instructional prompts in educational and applied settings. An *indirect verbal prompt* is used to cue the person that some behaviour needs to be performed, but it does not describe what the target behaviour is. For example, 'What do you need to do next?' is an indirect verbal prompt, for it indicates that the person needs to perform but it does not indicate what the person needs to do. A *direct verbal prompt* specifies the behaviour that the person should perform. For example, 'Open your book' clearly identifies what needs to be performed. Written instructions can also be used to prompt performance.

A *picture response prompt* is a visual representation of the behaviour to be performed. Behaviours can be illustrated using drawings, photographs, paintings etc. Picture prompts can be used to illustrate single behaviours or many pictures can be used to illustrate complete sequences of behaviours. Picture prompt systems have been used to teach complex daily living and vocational skills to people with intellectual disabilities.

A *modelling response prompt* involves the therapist or teacher demonstrating the desired behaviour so that it can be imitated by the person. Modelling can be a very effective response prompt as it allows the therapist to show the person what is to be performed. (An account of the functional properties of modelling was presented in Chapter 4.) Modelling is frequently used in applied interventions to promote appropriate responding – for example, to teach social skills.

*Physical response prompts* produce correct responding by manually guiding the person through the appropriate response. Physical prompting is obviously a very intrusive way to teach somebody to respond correctly. However, in cases where the response is very difficult for the learner to perform it may be the only option. Physical prompting can consist of manually guiding the person through the entire sequence of steps of a task. For example, in teaching tooth brushing to a child with severe learning disabilities, the therapist may place his hands on top of the child's and guide the child to open the toothpaste, reach for the toothbrush, place toothpaste on the toothbrush, replace the cap on the toothpaste and so on.

*Stimulus prompts* are additional stimuli that are used to highlight the natural discriminative stimulus or the stimulus that is to become the discriminative stimulus with training. They are used to increase the evocative effectiveness of the discriminative stimulus. When teaching cooking skills to persons with intellectual disabilities the teacher may attach a card to the temperature dial of the oven, which indicates the appropriate oven temperature for the meal. The participant need only attend to the information on the card and not the range of temperatures on the dial when setting the oven. Another example of a stimulus cue is a point prompt. The therapist may point to the relevant stimulus during training. In teaching time a teacher may ask 'What time is it?' and then point to the hour hand and the minute hand on the clock.

Response and stimulus prompts are supplementary or additional instructional procedures that must eventually be removed. The goal of any instructional programme is that the participant will eventually be able to perform the skills independent of these additional prompts. In other words, the natural or normal discriminative stimuli must eventually come to control responding. Once the participant performs the new skill at an appropriate level for a predetermined period of time, the prompting conditions are then gradually faded. *Fading* is a procedure in which the discriminative stimuli for the response are gradually changed so that they become increasingly similar to the natural discriminative stimuli. In other words, fading is a gradual process by which stimulus control is transferred from the prompts to the natural stimulus in a manner that reduces the probability of error responses in the presence of the natural stimulus. Fading is therefore sometimes called *errorless learning*, because the intention is to keep correct responding occurring as the discriminative stimulus changes. Minimizing errors during instruction and fading is highly desirable, mainly because if an incorrect response occurs it tends to be repeated and must be unlearned. This can substantially delay the overall goals of a training programme.

*Least-to-most prompting* is a prompt fading sequence that has been used to teach a large variety of skills. The participant is given the opportunity to perform a response with a minimum amount of assistance, usually a direct verbal prompt, during each training trial. If the participant does not respond appropriately with minimal assistance, then more intrusive response prompts are systematically introduced.

*Most-to-least prompt sequences* have also been used. These employ the alternative logic to the least-to-most prompt strategy. With most-to-least prompts the most intrusive prompt is employed initially, gradually faded to the least intrusive prompt, and eventually to the natural discriminative stimulus. Once the participant has performed the responses without error under the current prompt system for a number of trials, then the next level of less intrusive prompt is initiated. This procedure continues until the participant performs the behaviour under the control of the natural discriminative stimuli.

Stimulus prompts can also be faded systematically. Again, the goal of such procedures is to evoke the target response in the presence of the natural discriminative stimulus. In stimulus fading, an exaggerated or highlighted

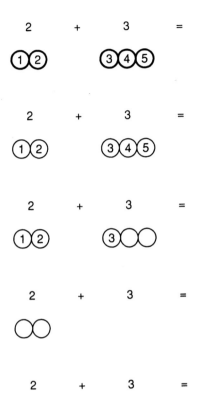

**Figure 6.11** An example of stimulus fading in which additional stimulus prompts are superimposed on the natural discriminative stimuli and gradually faded out

dimension of the natural discriminative stimulus is systematically removed. In Figure 6.11 we see an example of stimulus fading in maths education. In this example, the stimulus prompt is gradually faded out. Finally, *stimulus shaping* is a stimulus prompting strategy in which the topography of the stimulus is changed. Again, it is necessary to select an initial stimulus that will prompt the correct response. The shape of the stimulus prompt is then changed gradually so that the person continues to respond correctly. An example of stimulus shaping to teach word identification is presented in Figure 6.12.

*Shaping* involves the differential reinforcement of successive approximations to the final or goal response. As discussed in Section 3.7, this procedure is particularly valuable when the component behaviours of a target response are not currently in the repertoire of the individual. Shaping involves two basic processes. First, responses that resemble the final response, or include components of the final response, are reinforced. Second, as responses occur that are more similar to the target response, these are reinforced while the original (less similar) responses are no longer reinforced. The process of reinforcing successive approximations to the target response while

**Figure 6.12** An example of stimulus shaping to teach identification of the word 'cat'

extinguishing earlier responses continues until the target response occurs. At this point in the intervention the target response alone is reinforced. Shaping is an important strategy for teaching behaviours that cannot easily be learned through the use of response and stimulus prompts alone.

Examples of shaping are common in everyday situations. For instance, when infants begin to babble this behaviour is enthusiastically reinforced by parents. As time progresses the parents attend to vocalizations that more closely approximate words and ignore the babbling. Initially the tennis coach may prompt and reinforce merely getting the ball over the net with a novice. Over time, the coach will eventually require appropriate stance and stroke from the student.

Shaping is a particularly effective applied strategy for developing social and language responses. For example, children with autism often do not possess rudimentary social or language skills. To develop eye contact with another person, a therapist may begin by reinforcing the general orientation of the child with autism towards the other person. The therapist may then reinforce facial orientation towards the other person. Eventually, the therapist will only reinforce eye contact with the other person. The final goal of the programme may then be to shape eye contact over the period of an entire interaction with another person. Longer and longer periods of eye contact may therefore be reinforced.

Chaining is a process whereby a series of discrete behaviours are linked together to achieve some reinforcing outcome. Many everyday tasks consist of a sequence or chain of several responses. The final response of this sequence produces some form of reinforcement and this reinforcement signals the end of the chain. Each discrete behaviour in the chain acts as a conditioned reinforcer for the previous step and simultaneously acts as a discriminative stimulus for the upcoming step. (As noted in Section 4.5, a stimulus that is discriminative or predicts that responding will be reinforced also gains reinforcing value itself through pairing with a reinforcer.) For example, in brushing teeth, accessing the toothbrush and toothpaste is the first response; this acts as a discriminative stimulus for putting the toothpaste on the toothbrush, which in turn is a discriminative stimulus for brushing teeth. Brushing teeth is a discriminative stimulus for rinsing teeth, which is a discriminative stimulus for restoring the environment (i.e., putting away materials and turning off the tap). Eventually, the stimulus-response chain ends in the desired outcome of clean teeth.

The ability to identify and teach chains is an important skill for the behaviour analyst. For example, when working with people with developmental disabilities, much of the effort of the behaviour analyst involves developing and teaching curricula to promote independence. Daily living skills such as grooming and meal preparation are broken down into teachable component behaviours. In other words, the first step of the teaching process is to develop a task analysis of the behaviours involved in the chain. The next step is to select prompting procedures and reinforcing consequences that will be used to teach each component behaviour of the chain. Finally, the therapist must choose a strategy by which to link each discrete behaviour during training so that each behaviour is a conditioned reinforcer for the previous response and a discriminative stimulus for the subsequent response. The strategies used to develop a behavioural chain during training include forward chaining and backward chaining.

In *forward chaining*, training begins with the first step of the task. Training continues on this first step until a predetermined criterion of responding is achieved. At this point the participant is then trained on the first and second steps of the chain. Once the training criterion is achieved with these two steps, then the third step is included in training and so on. Each successive step trained involves cumulative practice on all previous steps.

When using a *backward chaining* procedure, the therapist begins with training the final step of the task sequence. Reinforcement is delivered once the participant performs the last step appropriately. When the participant achieves the criterion for responding on the final step of the task analysis then the second last step of the chain is added to the training. Once the last two steps of the chain are completed to criterion then the third last step is added to the training sequence, and so on.

# 6.10 ENSURING GENERALIZATION OF NEWLY ACQUIRED SKILLS

An effective behavioural intervention must do more than change behaviour, it must produce behaviour that has generality. That is, we are almost invariably concerned to change behaviour in such a way that the change will be evident over a long period of time and in many situations. In the basic experimental paradigm, as outlined in Chapter 4, generalization can be defined as a lack of stimulus control over responding, and this lack disappears with appropriate discrimination training. In other words, discrimination training is an active process with generalization being no more than a demonstration of a lack of tight stimulus control. In applied work, the focus is somewhat different, and what in a sense is required is a 'lack of control' by the specific training situation. In the simplest case, there is no point in training apparently appropriate behaviour if this behaviour is only ever seen at the health centre where the training took place. There are a number of training strategies that can be used to avoid this problem.

One method is to introduce *natural maintaining contingencies.* This strategy involves selecting target behaviours that will produce reinforcement for the individual after the intervention ceases. For example, as well as teaching children appropriate classroom skills, such as working consistently and quietly, they can be taught to prompt the teacher to deliver reinforcement for quality performance ('How is this work?' 'Have I been working carefully?'). Another technique is to select discriminative stimuli for in the training setting that will be present in important natural settings. These discriminative stimuli might, for example, be people such as classmates, who can be present in both contexts.

Another important strategy is *multiple exemplar training.* That is, several variants of the response are trained during the acquisition phase of training. This has proved to be an effective strategy for teaching generalized independent living skills, such as vending machine usage, to persons with severe learning disabilities. Research findings suggest the more generalization strategies that are included in training the greater the chances of achieving generalized responding. The use of multiple exemplar training is a major improvement in behaviour analysis programmes. The improvement occurs because, when multiple exemplars are used, the participant in the training eventually 'learns the right thing', rather than learning about some irrelevant features of the situation. We will see in Chapter 7 that multiple exemplar training is an important feature of early language learning in young children.

## 6.11 EXTINCTION IN APPLIED SETTINGS

In many applied and clinical situations the behaviour analyst is faced with the task of decreasing behaviours that may be maladaptive or inappropriate for the setting in which they occur. In such situations there should, of course, be a very clear rationale for the need to reduce behaviours. Maladaptive behaviours may generally be defined as behaviours that result in some form of negative outcome for the person or for others. For example, a child's aggression towards other classroom students may result in physical harm to those students, or harm to the aggressive child through retaliation. The aggressive child might also be removed from the classroom setting, thereby losing access to educational opportunities. Again, the behaviour analyst must conduct a rigorous assessment of the function of the behaviour and establish a firm rationale for reducing such behaviour prior to any intervention.

Behaviour change programmes are rarely designed exclusively to reduce maladaptive behaviours. Typically, interventions consist of a combination of strategies designed to decrease maladaptive responding while simultaneously increasing appropriate responding. These programmes ideally consist of a three-stage process: (i) a functional analysis to identify the maintaining contingencies; (ii) elimination of those maintaining contingencies for the maladaptive behaviour (through extinction); and (iii) presentation of the reinforcer that previously maintained the maladaptive behaviour, now contingent upon appropriate alternative behaviours. Such programmes thus include the use of positive reinforcement to enhance appropriate behaviour. However, in some situations it may simply not be possible to use this three-stage process to develop interventions to reduce maladaptive behaviour. For example, in some cases a functional analysis may not be successful in revealing maintaining contingencies, and if these contingencies remain unknown then it is technically impossible to place the behaviour on extinction. In such circumstances, punishment strategies may be required to achieve behaviour change, and these are discussed in the next section. In other circumstances, although the function of the maladaptive behaviour is clear, it may not be possible or desirable to replace the maladaptive behaviour with alternative behaviours, and *extinction* will be the preferred strategy. For example, if a child's night-time wakings are maintained by parent attention (that is, the parent enters the child's bedroom and comforts the child when crying begins or continues), then the intervention of choice may be to place the child's crying on extinction (that is, the parent should no longer enter the child's bedroom contingent upon crying). In this situation it would not be appropriate to replace the child's crying with a functionally equivalent alternative behaviour.

Extinction was defined in Chapter 4 as a procedure in which the contingency between the reinforcer and response is removed. The eventual outcome of this process is a reduction of the rate of the behaviour towards its operant level. Other properties of behaviour during the extinction process include topographical changes in responding, extinction bursts, extinction-induced aggression and spontaneous recovery. Extinction can be accomplished in two ways: first, the reinforcer can be removed or eliminated completely; and, second, the reinforcer can be delivered but in a noncontingent manner. While both of these procedures effectively extinguish behaviour there may be distinct applied advantages for using noncontingent delivery of reinforcing stimuli (NCR) rather than eliminating the reinforcer entirely in many instances. This option will be discussed in detail later in this section. Obviously, for extinction to be effective, the reinforcer for the maladaptive behaviour must be clearly identified prior to the intervention.

An *extinction burst* has been defined as a transitory increase in responding almost immediately after shift to an extinction procedure when reinforcers are no longer forthcoming for that response (see Section 4.6). This effect has been reported in several applied behaviour analysis studies. In one study of this type, Neisworth and Moore (1972) trained parents to ignore the asthmatic behaviour of their child. In this particular example of extinction, the reinforcer was eliminated completely. The child's asthmatic behaviour, which consisted of coughing, wheezing and gasping, usually occurred in the evenings around bedtime. During the extinction procedure, the parents did not attend to his asthmatic attacks once the boy was put to bed. Additionally, the boy received a monetary reward contingent on reductions in asthmatic behaviour. The duration of coughing and wheezing was measured once the child was placed in bed. The results of the intervention are displayed in Figure 6.13. The effectiveness of this intervention was evaluated using a reversal design. It is clear from the data that there is an immediate increase in the duration of asthmatic behaviour once the intervention is implemented. Asthmatic behaviour then decreases dramatically under the intervention condition. A return to baseline results in an increase in asthmatic behaviour and once again we see an extinction burst when the intervention is applied for the second time.

It may be difficult for staff or parents to tolerate an initial increase in responding, and there would be obvious ethical problems with using extinction in cases where the behaviour was of danger to the individual under treatment or others. Additionally, parents or staff may interpret the increase in intensity of the behaviour as a failure of the behavioural programme and may therefore revert to reinforcing the behaviour. However, the extinction burst has not been reported in many applied studies.

The extinction burst seems to occur when the reinforcer is no longer available, and not under the alternative extinction operation where the contingency between the behaviour and the reinforcer is broken but the reinforcer continues to be delivered in a noncontingent manner. In Section 6.8 we noted that *the noncontingent delivery of reinforcing stimuli (NCR) can be*

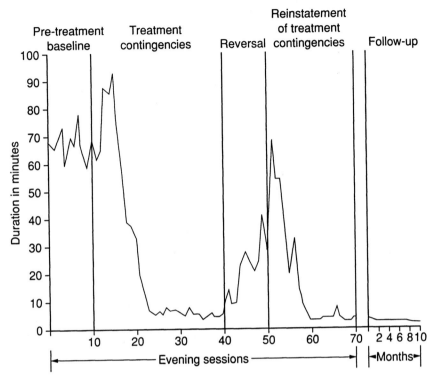

**Figure 6.13** Duration of asthmatic responding at bedtime during baseline and extinction phases (Neisworth and Moore, 1972)

an effective method to rapidly decrease unwanted behaviour. During NCR interventions, reinforcement is typically delivered on a fixed time schedule and is not influenced by the individual's behaviour. In a *fixed time schedule of reinforcement*, the reinforcer is delivered after a fixed period of time, regardless of whether or not a response occurs; delivery of the reinforcer is thus not contingent on the behaviour.

Figure 6.14 illustrates the effects of delivering attention on this noncontingent schedule for self-injurious behaviour that is maintained by attention. Self-injury for Brenda consisted of banging her head on solid stationary objects and hitting her head with her fist; a functional analysis had identified social attention as the maintaining contingency for self-injury. The results of the NCR intervention demonstrate an almost immediate elimination of self-injurious behaviour, and no extinction burst or gradual reduction in self-injurious behaviour occurred.

Another behavioural phenomenon associated with the process of eliminating reinforcement is that of *spontaneous recovery*. As noted in

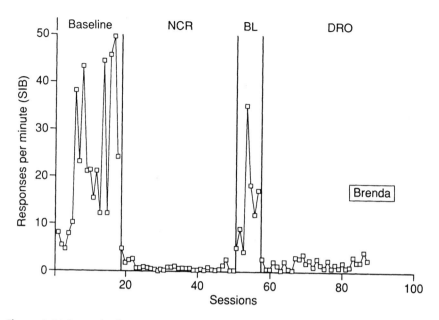

**Figure 6.14** Rates of self-injurious behaviour during baseline, noncontingent reinforcement (NCR) and return to baseline (BL) phases (Vollmer *et al.*, 1993)

Chapter 4, spontaneous recovery means that there is a temporary recurrence of the behaviour under the extinction condition. Under experimental conditions, it is typically found that recovery of responding is typically not as strong as original responding prior to the extinction programme. The danger with spontaneous recovery during applied interventions is that the behaviour may unwittingly be reinforced by those care-givers who are implementing the extinction programme. Reinforcement during spontaneous recovery could place the behaviour on an intermittent schedule of reinforcement and thus make it more difficult to eliminate.

Spontaneous recovery was clearly illustrated in an applied intervention to decrease night-time waking in young children through extinction (France and Hudson, 1990). Night-time waking, which occurs with approximately 20% of children, can cause severe disruption for parents. In this study the parents of seven children were trained to ignore night-time wakings. Night-time waking was operationally defined as sustained noise for more than 1 minute from the onset of sleep until an agreed waking time for the child the next morning. The effectiveness of the intervention was examined using a multiple-baseline design across children (see Figure 6.15). The frequency of night wakings each week was plotted during baseline, intervention and follow-up assessments. These results clearly illustrate gradual decreases in the frequency of night wakings

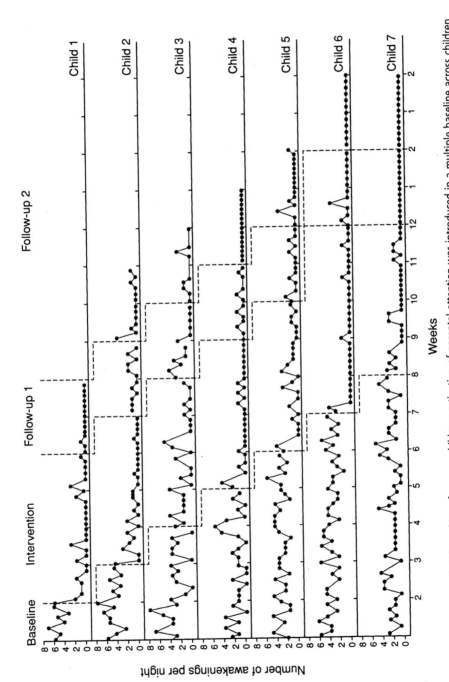

**Figure 6.15** Frequency of night wakings for seven children; extinction of parental attention was introduced in a multiple baseline across children design; the large solid dots indicate nights on which a child was ill (France and Hudson, 1990)

once the intervention had been implemented. Additionally, there are clear instances of spontaneous recovery with all children during the intervention phase.

One of the most frequently described side-effects of placing behaviour on extinction in experimental studies is the occurrence of extinction-induced aggression. Breaking the contingency between behaviour and reinforcement seems to constitute an aversive event that results in aggression and other forms of emotional behaviour, and there is ample evidence from experimental studies to document this effect (see Chapter 4). Extinction-induced aggression has not often been reported in applied research. However, Goh and Iwata (1994) carried out a rigorous assessment of extinction-induced aggression for a man with severe disabilities who engaged in self-injurious behaviour in order to escape from demanding tasks. During the extinction condition, self-injurious behaviour did not result in escape from tasks. An evaluation of the escape extinction intervention was conducted using a withdrawal design (see Figure 6.16). In the baseline phases of the design, self-injurious behaviour produced escape from demanding tasks. This data set demonstrates some of the fundamental properties of extinction such as the extinction burst, a gradual reduction of behaviour during extinction and a more rapid extinction process

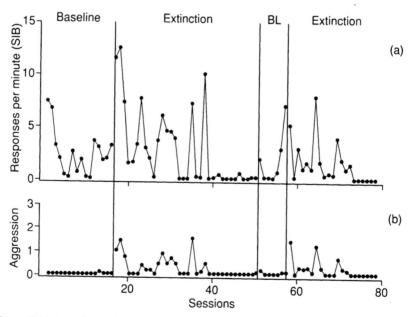

**Figure 6.16** Rate of self-injurious behaviour (a) and aggressive responses (b) for one individual under baseline and extinction conditions in an ABAB design (Goh and Iwata, 1994)

during the second application of extinction. Additionally, the presence of aggression is also clearly documented when the extinction process is implemented on both occasions.

## 6.12 PUNISHMENT IN APPLIED SETTINGS

Chapter 4 outlined the basic properties of punishment as demonstrated by experimental research. In this section of the current chapter, the use of punishment in applied settings will be examined. Punishment can be defined as the application or removal of a stimulus contingent on responding that decreases the probability of responding. As discussed in Chapter 4, it is important to remember that punishment is defined functionally in terms of changes in responding. Punishment in behaviour analysis is therefore different from some of the ways in which the term is used in everyday language. In everyday use punishment is typically equated with an aversive consequence for engaging or not engaging in an activity. For example, a student may be expelled from school for fighting, or a person may be fined or imprisoned for driving a car without insurance. These procedures are described as punishment whether or not the so-called punished behaviour actually decreases. Nevertheless, the expectation is that the behaviour will not recur.

Do we normally punish each other? Yes, at least using mild punishment, we do it all the time. That is, we arrange consequences for the behaviour of others that reduce classes of their behaviour. For example, we may adopt a critical tone or raise our voice in protest when the other person says something we disagree with; we may glare at people who arrive late at meetings; we may complain when service is slow in a restaurant, and so on. We may also sometimes engage in the more controversial activities often called 'physical punishment'. In many cultures, young children are frequently subjected to physical punishments by parents when they engage in unacceptable behaviour. In other cultures, this is not regarded as acceptable and children are verbally reprimanded instead. In all cases, the intended outcome of punishment practices is a reduction in certain classes of behaviour, although this reduction does not always occur.

Punishment procedures are sometimes used by behaviour analysts to decrease maladaptive behaviour, but punishment is the last resort for the behaviour analyst, and should only be used in cases where positive and less intrusive alternatives (e.g., differential reinforcement strategies, functional communication training etc.) have been considered or tried, and have failed to reduce the behaviour. As evidence of the importance and controversy surrounding the use of punishment techniques the US National Institutes of Health (NIH) convened a consensus development conference to discuss the use of such techniques. This conference concluded that:

Behaviour reductive procedures should be selected for their rapid effectiveness only if the exigencies of the clinical situation require such restrictive interventions and only after appropriate review. These interventions should only be used in the context of a comprehensive and individualised behaviour enhancement treatment package (NIH, 1989: 13).

In practice, punishment techniques are only considered for use when those conditions are met, and the consequences of not intervening are severe and may involve immediate danger to the individual (e.g., through self-injurious behaviour) or others (e.g., through high levels of aggression). Punishment techniques can be divided into three general categories: the presentation of aversive events contingent on responding; the removal of positive events contingent on responding; and, finally, techniques that require the person to engage in activities contingent on performance of the target behaviour. With all these techniques, the events used can only be defined as punishers if their contingent application reduces the probability of the target behaviour.

Aversive consequences, when made contingent upon performance of maladaptive behaviour, can rapidly reduce that behaviour. Aversive consequences can either be unconditioned (i.e., inherently aversive) or conditioned (i.e., learned) stimuli. Unconditioned aversive stimuli such as water misting or electric shock have been demonstrated to produce rapid and long-lasting reductions with very severe behaviour problems. When using conditioned aversive stimuli such as verbal reprimands it is important to establish that such stimuli are in fact aversive for the person concerned. Under those rare and extreme situations where aversive stimuli are selected for use they should be embedded within a more general behavioural programme to increase adaptive responding in the individual.

The removal of positive events contingent on responding can also be used to decrease maladaptive behaviour. Two general techniques have typically been used by behaviour analysts to remove positive events contingent on maladaptive responding. These techniques are called *time out* from positive reinforcement and *response cost*. Time out from positive reinforcement can involve various procedures whereby the person is removed from all positively reinforcing events for a brief period of time. Time out can be either exclusionary or non-exclusionary (both types were described in Chapter 4). While sometimes effective, removing someone from a situation or from access to reinforcers in a situation is not always practical and thus the use of these techniques has been limited.

Response cost is another punishment technique that involves the removal of positive events contingent on responding. This type of punishment can be shown to have reliable and orderly effects in experiments with adult humans. In applied contexts, response cost is a form of penalty that is imposed on the individual for engaging in a particular maladaptive behaviour. This type of technique is readily recognizable to the general public (e.g., fines for late payment of domestic charges or for parking a car inappropriately) and is viewed as an acceptable method to reduce maladaptive behaviours. It thus has social validity (see Section 6.1). Response cost differs from time out in a number of ways. With response cost, the reinforcer may be permanently withdrawn (as when somebody is fined for a motoring offence), while with time out the reinforcers are withdrawn only for a brief period of time. Additionally, with time out all opportunities for reinforcement are removed for a period of time, but with a response cost intervention all other positive events continue to be available apart from the fine itself. A response cost system can be used as part of a token economy to increase adaptive responding of psychiatric patients in a hospital ward. If patients are fined (in tokens) for such behaviours as sleeping late, public undressing and aggressive outbursts, there can be dramatic reductions of these antisocial behaviours.

A variety of punishment procedures employ the performance of activities contingent on maladaptive behaviour. In other words the person must perform aversive activities after they engage in the targeted behaviour. The most frequently described technique using 'activity punishers' is that of *overcorrection* (Foxx and Azrin, 1972; Foxx and Bechtel, 1983). Overcorrection typically consists of two components: restitution and positive practice. Initially the individual is required to restore any items in the environment that have been damaged as a result of the maladaptive behaviour. For example, if an individual engaged in an aggressive outburst overturned a chair, then the individual would be required to replace the chair in its original position. The positive practice component involves repeated practice of a behaviour that is an appropriate alternative to the maladaptive behaviour. In the overturned chair example, the individual might then be required to straighten all the chairs in the room.

As mentioned earlier, these punishment techniques are best reserved for the treatment of behaviour that is of danger to the person or others. Punishment is usually considered in situations where other less intrusive interventions (e.g., differential reinforcement strategies) have been tried and have failed to reduce maladaptive responding. Punishment interventions are not typically used in isolation but are combined with interventions to increase appropriate alternative behaviours. In addition to a knowledge of the various punishment techniques described here, the behaviour analyst should be aware of some of the likely advantages and disadvantages.

One of the major advantages of using punishment is that it can often produce an almost immediate reduction or elimination of the maladaptive response. This is particularly true with unconditioned aversive stimuli such as electric shock. In such procedures the reduction in maladaptive responding is often quite dramatic and the treatment gains generally last for extended periods of time after the intervention is removed. The unwanted behaviour may, however, re-emerge following the removal of some punishment techniques. If punishment does not quickly produce the desired reduction in responding following several applications, then alternative protocol should be considered again, as it is not appropriate to expose an individual to extended periods of aversive contingencies if these contingencies do not have the desired functional effect.

In addition to eliminating maladaptive responding, punishment may also result in positive side-effects. For example, some of the positive side-effects in studies with people with learning disabilities have included weight gain, increased social behaviour, decreased crying and tantrums, improved self-feeding, and overall increases in activity levels. These improvements probably came about simply because the maladaptive behaviour, which previously was at a high frequency, was not now occurring. Thus there was more time available for other more appropriate behaviour.

There are also several disadvantages associated with using punishment techniques in applied settings, most of which have already been alluded to in this section. Punishment procedures can produce negative side-effects such as crying, tantrums, soiling, wetting and general agitation. Many of these negative side-effects occur when punishment is first implemented and tend to decrease as the intervention is continued. It is important to note that these emotional side-effects have been reported relatively infrequently. Interestingly, it is also commonly observed that in experimental studies with non-human animals, punishment does not persistently produce emotional behaviour.

Punishment can produce avoidance behaviour in applied settings because the use of punishment with an individual could result in many aspects of an environment such as a school setting becoming aversive for that individual. As we noted in Chapter 4, this would be predicted from a theoretical consideration of the effects of using aversive stimuli. Relatedly, an individual may show aggression towards a therapist in order to escape from a punishment procedure. When this happens, the therapist may unwittingly reinforce escape-maintained aggression if the individual is allowed to escape from treatment. Alternative treatments to punishment should obviously be considered in such situations.

When a therapist, parent or other care provider uses punishment they are in effect providing examples of how to control another individual's behaviour. Through this modelled punishment, those who observe such practices can learn that such techniques can be used to control the behaviour of others (see Sections 4.17 to 4.20 for other aspects of modelling). Children who are referred to clinicians for severe aggression usually come from homes where physical aggression is used by parents to control their children. In such home environments, children learn that physical aggression is an acceptable and powerful tool for controlling the behaviour of others.

For all the reasons outlined here, the use of punishment techniques with humans, especially individuals with developmental disabilities who may be unable to give informed consent, has been the source of much public controversy in the last decade. Many parent support groups have taken stances against the use of punishment. Indeed several states in the USA have banned the use of punishment techniques in treatment. Much of this debate has been confused by a lack of understanding of the technical meaning of the term 'punishment' in behaviour analysis. Many of the position statements from interest groups equate punishment with the more everyday uses of the term, and punishment is sometimes equated with such notions as cruelty, revenge and harm. Despite the confusion, these debates highlight the need to use punishment only as a treatment of last resort, with very clear guidelines for its use, and within the context of a more general behavioural programme to teach adaptive skills to the person. In the next section, we will relate these issues to the human rights of individuals in treatment.

## 6.13 ETHICAL GUIDELINES FOR THE USE OF BEHAVIOURAL TREATMENT

Applied behavioural scientists have amassed a wealth of data that demonstrates the effectiveness of behavioural procedures for increasing appropriate behaviour and decreasing inappropriate behaviour. These techniques have been used in a variety of applied settings (including the community, the clinic and in education) and with many behavioural problems. However, those who advocate the use of applied behavioural techniques have not been without their critics. It was noted in the previous section that some audiences have misconstrued punishment procedures in particular. In fact, some individuals have gone so far as to describe behaviour analysis and those who practise behaviour analysis as evil and controlling (McGee et al., 1987). Such conclusions are based in part on misinformation about applied behaviour analysis, in part on a small number of cases of abuse and in part on ideological objections to all scientific accounts of human behaviour. None the less, this only strengthens the need for behaviour analysts to explain how and why their practices are ethical.

While no professional group can exert total control over the practices of each individual member, applied behaviour analysts have developed a set of guidelines designed to guide their professional practices (Van Houten et al., 1988). These guidelines for the practice of applied behaviour analysis are described as a set of six fundamental rights of individuals for whom behavioural interventions are provided.

1. *An individual has a right to a therapeutic environment:* the social environment should be pleasant; social interaction should be frequent; leisure activities should be available; restrictions on choices of activity should be minimized.
2. *An individual has a right to services whose overriding goal is personal welfare:* the individual or their legal guardian should be actively involved in

selecting target behaviours and intervention methods, and identifying goals
of treatment.
3. *An individual has a right to treatment by a competent behaviour analyst:*
persons who develop, implement and supervise behavioural programmes
should be trained to the highest standard.
4. *An individual has a right to programmes that teach functional skills:* the aim
should be to enable full participation in every aspect of community life, and
the goals of intervention should not be based on assumptions about an
individual's potential or limitations.
5. *An individual has a right to behavioural assessment and ongoing evaluation:*
the selection of any behaviour-change strategy should be based on an
assessment of the environmental determinants of that behaviour. Once the
intervention is implemented it should be continuously evaluated. This will
allow the behaviour analyst to determine if the treatment is effective and to
modify the intervention if it is not achieving the desired objectives.
6. *An individual has a right to the most effective treatment procedures
available:* treatments that have been scientifically validated should only be
selected for use. Exposure of individuals to restrictive treatments (including
punishment) is unacceptable unless these treatments are essential to produce
clinically significant behaviour change. Alternatively, exposure to less
restrictive interventions may be equally unacceptable if they produce
gradual change with behaviour that may be of immediate danger to the
individual or other individuals in that person's environment.

As these guidelines indicate, professionals who practise applied behaviour
analysis are fundamentally interested in improving the lives of the people they
work with and of society in general. Regrettably, there will, from time to time,
be individuals in any discipline who will violate professional guidelines, and
such individuals should not be allowed to practise behaviour analysis.

## 6.14 SUMMARY

Applied behaviour analysis deals with human behavioural problems by
drawing on the principles of behaviour analysis established in experimental
studies. It also includes strategies derived from experimental methods to
demonstrate when and why behaviour change has occurred.

Behavioural assessment seeks to establish the three-term relationship
between antecedent, the behaviour of interest and consequence, along with
establishing operations that may have a major influence on whether the
behaviour occurs. Prior to any further steps, the social validity of any proposed
intervention with the identified target behaviour should be established. The
target behaviour should be operationally defined, and an appropriate method

of measurement should be selected. The main strategies of a full behavioural assessment are functional assessment, where descriptive or correlational techniques are used to identify antecedent, behaviour and consequence, and functional analysis, where the effects of contingencies are directly assessed. Techniques of functional assessment include ABC assessment and scatterplot assessment. The most thoroughgoing form of functional analysis is the multi-element analogue method, where several contingencies are tested out under analogue conditions to see which is most likely to engender the target behaviour. Functional analysis takes behavioural assessment further than other techniques because it makes it possible to plan an intervention based on a knowledge of why the behaviour was occurring prior to any intervention.

Single-case designs are typically used in applied behaviour analysis. These allow functional relationships between the target behaviour and environmental variables to be established. The usual data analysis method is the interpretation of graphic displays. In these, stability, level and trend are critical features.

The most powerful single-case design is the withdrawal or ABAB design, where the baseline condition (A) is alternated with the intervention condition (B). Control by the procedure is demonstrated if a change from baseline occurs with the intervention, and if the reversal to baseline produces a change back to the baseline level of the behaviour, and a repeat of the intervention again changes the behaviour in the expected direction. Where this is impractical or unethical, a multiple baseline design may be used. In this, a baseline is established for several measures. These may be several behaviours in one individual, the same behaviour in several individuals, or one behaviour in several settings. Following this, the intervention is introduced at different times for each behaviour. Control by the intervention is demonstrated if a change from baseline occurs when, and only when, the intervention occurs for that behaviour. This design has the benefit of not requiring a return, or reversal, to the baseline condition.

Many behavioural interventions can increase adaptive responding. Positive reinforcement can be used, provided an effective reinforcer is available. It may be necessary to use a reinforcer assessment technique to identify one. Once selected, the reinforcer is effective at the time of use. Token economies are useful in many contexts. Because they use a generalized conditioned reinforcer, supported by back-up reinforcers, satiation is unlikely to be a problem. They have worked well in many institutional settings, but staff training is a major part of successful implementation.

Positive reinforcement can also be used to decrease target behaviours with differential reinforcement strategies. Differential reinforcement of incompatible behaviour, or of alternative behaviour can be effective. An important version of the latter is functional communication training. This can be used where a maladaptive behaviour has been evident because it enables the individual to communicate to some extent with others. They are taught an alternative, more socially acceptable, behaviour that is now followed by social attention. Noncontingent delivery of a reinforcer can also be effective in reducing maladaptive behaviour.

New behaviour, not currently in the individual's repertoire, can be developed through the use of antecedent stimuli that evoke the desired response; these are called prompts. Response prompts include direct and indirect verbal response prompts, and picture, modelling and physical response prompts. Stimulus prompts are ways of highlighting discriminative stimuli that are already present. Any instructional programme that initially includes prompts will proceed to fade out the prompts at a later stage.

Shaping is an important technique when the component behaviours of a target response are not currently occurring. Successive approximations to the target response are reinforced, until the target response itself occurs and can be reinforced. This technique is important where prompts are not adequate. Chaining is a process whereby a series of behaviours are performed in sequence and followed by a reinforcer. Both forward chaining and backward chaining techniques can be used, and are important in establishing extended sequences of behaviour.

Behavioural interventions are much more useful if the behaviour that has been established is shown under 'real life' conditions, rather than simply under the restricted training conditions. This can be achieved by introducing the natural maintaining contingencies into the training situation, and by using multiple exemplar training.

Extinction is used in behaviour change programmes, but usually as part of a package that also includes positive reinforcement for appropriate behaviour. Extinction can have unwanted aspects – such as the extinction burst, extinction-induced aggression and spontaneous recovery – but these have not often been reported as problems in applied studies.

Punishment is 'normal' in that people seek to modify each others' behaviour by providing mildly aversive consequences for unwanted or socially unacceptable behaviour. However, the use of punishment in applied settings is controversial. It can be effective and may be indicated through the lack of effective alternatives. Nevertheless, it should be a technique of last resort, both because the situation in which it occurs may become aversive and lead to escape or aggression, and because of the public debate that surrounds its use. Other techniques will invariably have greater social validity. As well as procedures in which an aversive consequence follows an operant response, punishment can also involve the procedures of time out, response cost, or overcorrection.

Ethical guidelines for the use of behavioural treatment have been developed. These should be used by professionals at all times, and are primarily intended to protect the human rights of individuals taking part in intervention programmes.

## Study question for Chapter 6

Most of the studies that have been reported in scientific journals, and that have formed the literature on which Chapter 6 is based, concern the types of problem that are taken to clinical psychologists or special education professionals. However, the techniques reviewed here can readily be applied in exactly the same form to everyday behaviour problems. A useful exercise would be to identify something that is a problem for you, such as some aspect of the behaviour of some (or all!) of the people with whom you share your living space or working space. Have selected this target behaviour, try to write a complete research protocol. This might involve: an account of why the behaviour is a problem; suggestions as to how the behaviour can be operationally defined; an account of an appropriate behavioural assessment strategy; an indication of what intervention might be appropriate; along with an account of how the behaviour will be monitored during the intervention.

*Now check your answer with my suggestion in the 'Possible answers to study questions' section, see page 222.*

# 7

# Language and Cognition

We noted in Chapter 2 that there has been resistance to the notion that psychological processes might be scientifically analysed, or analysable, despite progress in many other sciences, most notably in the biological sciences. An aim of this book has been to sketch a pathway between, at one end, those relatively simple types of animal behaviour that have been the subject of scientific analysis for a long time and, at the other end, those processes that lie in the heartland of human psychology. It is when this pathway reaches human language that the going gets difficult, and the main objective of this chapter is to indicate how language and cognition can be conceptualized in the same terms as other behaviour, and then explained using the same principles that have been shown to be effective throughout the rest of the book.

## 7.1 BEING PARSIMONIOUS: OCCAM'S RAZOR AND LLOYD MORGAN'S CANON

At the outset, it may help to consider again the reasons why we try to explain human psychology with principles that were initially developed for the explanation of behaviour in smaller-brained animals that do not appear to use language.

The *principle of parsimony* (or 'fewness') has been debated by philosophers, and applied by scientists, as best they can, for many generations. The argument is that explanations should use as few and as simple principles as will meet the case; it is sometimes called 'Occam's razor'. Occam's razor is a logical principle attributed to the mediaeval philosopher William of Occam (or Ockham). William, born in the village of Ockham in Surrey about 1285, was an influential philosopher of the fourteenth century. He entered the Franciscan order at an early age and took the traditional course of theological studies at Merton College, Oxford. The principle states that one should not make more assumptions than the minimum needed. This principle is important in all scientific modelling and theory building. It tells us to choose the simplest one from a set of otherwise equivalent models of a given phenomenon. In any given model, Occam's razor helps us to 'shave off' those concepts that are not really needed to explain the phenomenon. For a given set of observations or data, there is always an infinite number of possible models explaining those same data, and Occam's razor helps us select the more effective theories and to discard unnecessarily elaborate ones.

Early in the history of psychology, C. Lloyd Morgan recognized the applicability of Occam's razor to the developing study of animal behaviour. As noted in Chapter 2, Darwin's theory of evolution had led to renewed interest in animal behaviour in the late nineteenth century. However, there was a tendency both to accept anecdotes of 'clever' animal behaviour at face value and to attribute complex intellectual abilities to animals based on this 'evidence'. Consider the following example. A report that a horse pulling a cart had learned to traverse a sloping field on the diagonal, thus lessening the angle of slope up which the cart had to be pulled, was interpreted as evidence of the horse's ability to understand geometry!

To guard against such obvious over-interpretation of the facts, C. Lloyd Morgan proposed the following principle, which is an application of the principle of parsimony: 'In no case may we interpret an action as the outcome of the exercise of a higher psychic faculty, if it can be interpreted as the outcome of one that stands lower in the psychological scale' (Morgan, 1894). This principle, known as 'Lloyd Morgan's canon' (where 'canon' means 'rule'), urges us to not adopt additional principles of explanation of animal behaviour if our well-established principles will suffice.

These two historic figures, William of Occam and C. Lloyd Morgan, have been important in the development of behaviour analysis. Their ideas, along with the behaviourism proposed by J.B. Watson and developed by B.F. Skinner, have suggested that we seriously consider the following argument.

- Much apparently complex animal behaviour can be shown, through experiment, to depend on a small number of behavioural principles.
- Humans are also animals, and perhaps much apparently complex human behaviour can also be explained with these principles.

- Given that simple behaviour principles provide an explanation of some human behaviour, we should therefore assess whether they can be used to explain all human behaviour before deciding to use additional explanatory principles.
- If we do decide that additional explanatory principles are necessary, then we should try to use the simplest and fewest number of additional principles that will enable us to explain the phenomena in which we are interested.

## COULD THIS WORK? THE 'CASE OF THE EYE' PROVIDES INSPIRATION FROM EVOLUTIONARY THEORY

Despite the successes in accounting for some types of human behaviour reported in Chapter 6, the principles that have been introduced so far to account for the phenomena of classical and operant conditioning might seem unlikely candidates to explain the wonderful complexities of human language and cognition. However, the history of science is very much one of relatively simple principles being used with ingenuity to explain complex events. It may be helpful to consider a case in evolution where a similar scepticism has been expressed about the possibility of using simple principles to explain the existence of a complex entity.

All science and speculation by scientists is checked in the first instance against common sense: non-scientists pass comment on whether, from their perspective, the proposed explanation is reasonable. All the most famous 'breakthroughs' in science have provoked controversy in this way, and so did Darwin's ideas. He proposed that evolution came about through natural selection of small variations in characteristics of a species.

Darwin realized that what he called 'organs of extreme perfection and complication' were most likely to provoke the response that it is highly implausible that they evolved gradually from very primitive beginnings. But, he argued, the same explanation can be offered for their evolution as for apparently simpler features of organisms:

> To suppose that the eye, with all its inimitable contrivances for adjusting the focus to different distances, for admitting different amounts of light, and for the correction of spherical and chromatic aberration, could have been formed by natural selection, seems, I freely confess, absurd in the highest possible degree. Yet reason tells me, that if numerous gradations from a perfect and complex eye to one very imperfect and simple, each grade being useful to its possessor can be shown to exist; if further, the eye does vary ever so slightly, and the variations be inherited, which is certainly the case; and if any variation or modification in the organ be ever useful to an animal under changing conditions of life, then the difficulty of believing that a perfect and complex eye could be formed by natural selection ... can hardly be considered real (Darwin, 1859: 217).

Darwin argued that the basic explanatory 'tool kit' he used to account for the evolution of any feature might also do the job here. About 140 years later, Dawkins (1996) was able to spell out in some detail how the simple-to-complex route may proceed, and also was able to estimate how long the evolution of the main features of a 'camera eye', which admits light through a lens to an enclosed area containing an inner surface of light-sensitive cells, actually took. Using pessimistic (slow) assumptions about the probable rate of change, the estimated time is around half a million years. This is a very small fraction of the time in which animals have been on the planet and have, Darwinian theory claims, been evolving in response to their interactions with the environment. Consequently, Dawkins argued that the common-sense assumption that these simple mechanisms could not have generated such complexity as seen in the eye in the time available, was simply wrong.

The purpose of this example is to give us confidence that simple behavioural processes may yet be shown to be able to generate behavioural processes of 'extreme perfection and complication' as evidenced in language and cognition. This assumes, of course, that the behavioural processes that we have identified are the right ones. In the rest of this chapter, the ways in which behaviour analysts have begun to use their 'tool kit' to attempt to explain complex processes will be outlined.

## 7.3 CONCEPT FORMATION AND RELATIONAL LEARNING

The investigation of concept formation provides a link between the simple processes of discrimination learning discussed earlier and some more complex forms of human behaviour. A young child may find herself in a certain situation, and hear something that is present called 'dog'. On another occasion she is in a somewhat different situation, and again hears something called 'dog'. Later, she is in a different situation again, and hears something there called 'dog' also. As a result of a string of such experiences, a time arrives when the child is said to 'have the concept of dog'. We could hypothesize that there are some common features of 'dogginess' that now produce the spoken response 'dog' in the child. However, these are not simple physical properties (for example, all dogs are not the same colour or the same size). Instead, it is probable that concept formation in general would seem to involve a response under the control of *relationships* common to a group of stimulus patterns.

Consider, for example, the elements of Figure 7.1. All the elements in the left-hand box are members of the stimulus class named 'dax', while none of the figures in the right-hand box is a 'dax' figure. The rule for 'dax' is a circle and two dots; one dot being inside the circle, the other outside it. In an experiment, adult participants readily acquired the behaviour of categorizing separately 'daxes' from other patterns, even though their only prior 'discrimination

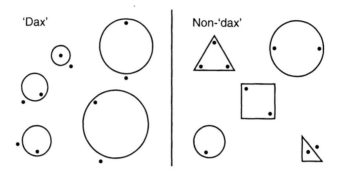

**Figure 7.1** Examples of 'Dax' S^Ds and Non-'dax' S^Δs.

training' was a presentation of some appropriately labelled 'daxes' and non-'daxes', with instructions to note the differences. Though they were frequently unable to verbalize the rule given above for class inclusion, participants could still correctly identify new instances of 'dax' that they had never seen before.

The word 'concept' denotes the behavioural fact that a given response is under the control of a class of related antecedent stimuli, or S^Ds. How, then, does a concept differ from a discrimination? Sometimes the difference is one only of degree; our word usage in a particular case can be determined merely by the broadness of the class of controlling S^Ds. If the class of S^Ds seems relatively narrow, we call the behaviour a discrimination, if it seems relatively wide or broad, we are more likely to call the behaviour a concept. It is plausible to speak either of the concept of yellow, or of the discrimination of yellow if either a broad range or a narrow range of stimuli is involved. However, the class of stimuli involved in a concept can also be of various other more complex types.

First of all, we may have 'polymorphous concepts'. This means that a member of the stimulus class must have some but not all features of a longer list. Most of our 'real world' or natural concepts, including the apparently straightforward ones mentioned earlier, are actually of this type. For example, a tree will have many features common to trees in general, but no one feature is necessary. This idea has formed the basis of some experiments with humans involved in learning artificial concepts. In one of these, college students were asked to sort packs of cards showing either rows of shapes (see the examples in Figure 7.2), typewritten letters, or random shapes into two piles (A and B). After each response, the experimenter told them whether their allocation of a card to a pile was right or wrong. On different trials, the participants were required to sort the cards by one of two types of relatively simple rules, such as the conjunctive rule, 'A's are black and composed of circles', or the disjunctive rule, 'A's are black or composed of triangles', or a more complex

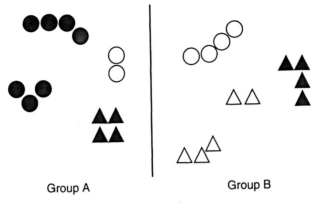

Group A                    Group B

**Figure 7.2** Examples of patterns used in a card-sorting task by Dennis *et al.* (1973)

polymorphous rule such as 'A's must possess at least two out of three of the properties of being symmetrical, black and circular'. Participants had to sort a pack of 48 cards into piles of A's and B's, and the response measured was the number of cards sorted before the last error, where an error is putting a card in the wrong pile. It was found that the median number of cards sorted was 9, 28 and 40 for the conjunctive, disjunctive and polymorphous rules, respectively. This shows that the polymorphous concept was the most difficult to acquire. A related experiment with the same material showed that participants could not state the polymorphous verbal rule within the 10 minutes they were allowed, even though they could rapidly work out what the rule was in the other two cases.

This type of learning is not uniquely human, because pigeons can also show polymorphous conceptual behaviour. Using food reinforcement for key pecking, pigeons have been trained to discriminate successfully between colour slides with and without people in them, although the people were in all sorts of positions, at different angles, distances and so forth (the classic study in this area is that of Herrnstein and Loveland, 1964). 'Person' is clearly a polymorphous natural concept as previously defined. Furthermore, pigeons (and other species we would expect to be 'more intelligent', such as monkeys) have also been trained to discriminate on the basis of a two-out-of-three polymorphous artificial concept, similar to the ones used in the human learning experiments described above.

It appears, then, that much learning is relational. That is, the members of the antecedent stimulus class are relations between stimuli, or aspects of stimuli, rather than individual stimuli. This is evident from studies showing that many species can learn to pick the bigger or brighter of two stimuli, as well as in the more complex studies described in this section. The facts of relational learning illustrate both the continuity between psychological processes in humans and other species, and also the differences. Many species have the capacity to respond to relations between stimuli and this is probably essential in order to identify natural concepts. However, human beings show greater facility on all relational learning tasks, and have the additional capacity to form stimulus equivalence classes.

In Section 4.16, we described how a set of unrelated stimuli come to be treated as equivalent to each other and how, once the *equivalence class* is established, there is *transfer of function*. This means that a response established to one member of the class will transfer to, and thus be shown in the presence of, other members of the class. In the terms we are using here, this is a type of conceptual behaviour, or we could say that a concept had been formed. The special feature is that there need be no physical relationship between the class members. We noted in Section 4.16 that this is a type of learning and behaviour that is strongly linked to human language. That is, verbally competent humans (ones with a certain amount of language, including most children over the age of three years) are 'very good at it', while it has been difficult to find any evidence of it in well-controlled studies with other species. Because the failure to find a phenomenon rightly makes scientists try harder to obtain it, research with other species is continuing. The main point is that there seems to be a link between 'equivalencing', which can be described as an extension of simple discrimination learning or 'discriminating', and human language.

## 7.4 LEARNING BASED ON ARBITRARY RELATIONS

The ideas to be developed in this section and later are as follows. The human capacity to learn to respond (through operant conditioning) to relations between events includes a capacity (apparently not shared with other animals) to respond to arbitrary relations between events. This capacity, in turn, is the basis of human language and of what is distinctive about human cognition.

Simple discrimination learning involves the three terms of antecedent, behaviour and consequence. Let us apply this to aspects of interaction between an adult and a language-learning young child. Here are two likely sequences where the antecedent or discriminative stimulus is provided by the adult, the behaviour or operant response is carried out by the child, and the consequence or reinforcing stimulus is again provided by the adult.

| $S^D$ : | R → | S+ |
|---|---|---|
| Adult holds Teddy, says 'What's this?' | Child says 'Teddy' | Adult says 'Good girl!' |

And:

| $S^D$ | : | R | $\rightarrow$ | S+ |
|-------|---|---|----|-----|
| Adult | | Child points | | Adult says |
| says 'Where's | | at Teddy | | 'Good girl!' |
| Teddy?' | | | | |

These two normal events (observational studies show that sequences such as these often occur) are called *bidirectional object-name training*, because, given the object, the child is reinforced for naming it and, given the name, the child is reinforced for finding the object. This is an example of *learning based on an arbitrary relation between stimuli* because, in contrast to most of the relations discussed in the previous section, there is no formal or physical relation between the two stimulus events: the spoken word 'Teddy' has nothing in common with an actual teddy.

A similar process occurs with action-name training.

| $S^D$ | : | R | $\rightarrow$ | S+ |
|-------|---|---|----|-----|
| Adult waves | | Child says | | Adult says |
| and says | | 'Waving' | | 'Good girl!' |
| 'What's this?' | | | | |

And:

| $S^D$ | : | R | $\rightarrow$ | S+ |
|-------|---|---|----|-----|
| Adult | | Child | | Adult says |
| says 'You | | waves | | 'Good girl!' |
| wave' | | | | |

Given the action, the child is reinforced for naming it and, given the name, the child is reinforced for carrying out the action. Again, this is an example of learning an arbitrary relation because there is no formal or physical relation between the two events: the spoken word 'waving' has nothing in common with waving movements.

Another ingredient in a language learning situation for a child is *multiple exemplar training*. That is, bidirectional training will occur with very many objects and actions, and the outcome of this is another generalized form of behaviour or skill. After experience with many examples, the child starts to treat the name and the object, or the name and the action, as *equivalent without explicit training*. When they are later given what we called in Section 4.16 a stimulus equivalence training task with novel and physically unrelated stimuli, they behave in a predictable way. That is they learn 'given A1, pick B1' and 'given B1, pick C1' and this leads to all three stimuli being treated as equivalent. That is, given any one of the three, they may match it to either of the other two. As explained in Section 4.16, this class of stimuli can come to include many stimuli, which may all then have the same function.

The behaviour or skill of being able pick B1 given A1, when the only directly relevant training has been to pick A1 given B1, is called *deriving relations*. That is, we are taught one relation C (e.g., the A1–B1 relation between two stimuli) and we derive another (e.g., the B1–A1 relation) without further teaching. This type of learning is extremely productive of new behaviour, because we only have to be taught 'given A1, pick B1' and 'given B1, pick C1', and we can derive the following relations:

given B1, pick A1
given A1, pick C1
given C1, pick B1
given C1, pick A1.

And verbally competent humans (but not necessarily other species), will also perform correctly on the corresponding identity matches:

given A1, pick A1
given B1, pick B1
given C1, pick C1.

Training only two relations and setting up a three-member stimulus class generates all this behaviour. But if nine relations are trained to form a 10-member class, 91 additional two-stimulus relations will emerge without further training! (The formula is $n^2-n+1$, where n is the number of stimuli in the class.)

This learning is always context-dependent. That is, we learn that A1, B1 and C1 are equivalent in a certain context. We might learn that the spoken word 'shoe', a picture of a shoe and the written word 'shoe' – three events or objects with very different physical characteristics – are equivalent in certain contexts. When asked what we want, we could respond with any one of the three in, for example, the context of a shoe shop and be responded to in the same way.

The shoe shop example is, of course, one concerned with verbal interaction, and what has been outlined here is the beginning of a theory of word meanings or, more technically, of word-referent relations. Clearly, being able to relate a spoken word to the written word, to a picture and to the actual object is a large part of what we mean by understanding the meaning of a word.

The type of arbitrary relation that we have discussed could be called 'sameness' or 'sameness-in-this-context', because it results in members of the stimulus class being treated as equivalent, and the functions of one member of the class being transferred to other members. Thus if someone has an extreme fear or phobia of snakes, we find that he not only runs away from a snake, but also refuses to open a book entitled *Snakes*, does not wish to visit a zoo, and so on. This is because responses involved in fear of snakes transfer to all members of the stimulus class.

What about other types of arbitrary relation? Hayes and others (see, for example, Hayes *et al.*, 2001) have argued that what we have just described is only one (albeit the most important one) of a number of types of arbitrary relational learning that underpin human language. Consider the 'more than/less than' relation. This has different properties from the 'sameness' relation. For example, if A1 is more than B1, and B1 is more than C1, then A1 is more than C1. This is an example of transitivity, as described for equivalence relations earlier (see Section 4.16), but the symmetry relations do not hold for this different type of relation. That is, B1 is less than A1, rather than more than A1, and C1 is less than B1, rather than more than C1.

A further complication is that with non-symmetrical relations, such as 'more than/less than', functions do not simply transfer between class members. For example, using coins with monetary values we might teach a child that 'Coin A1 is worth more than coin B1' and 'Coin A1 is worth more than coin C1'. Following this, if the child is asked 'Which coin will buy more sweets?' we expect the child to pick A1 in preference to B1, and to pick A1 in preference to C1. However, if we now offer them a choice between B1 and C1, the choice is undetermined by their previous training. Knowing that A1 is worth more than B1 or C1, does not specify whether B1 or C1 is worth more than the other. For these reasons, Hayes (e.g., Hayes and Hayes, 1992) prefers the term *transformation of function* for stimulus relations. That is, the relation between A1 and B1 (which may be 'sameness', 'more than/less than' or another relation) results in the transformation of stimulus functions from A1 to B1. The nature of the stimulus relation determines the type of transformation.

This may all seem esoteric, but of course young children learn to deal with the arbitrary relation of 'more than/less than'. For example, they learn that 'four cats are more than two cats' entails the relation 'two cats are less than four cats'. Even more practically, they learn in the UK that a 2-pence coin is worth less than a 5-pence coin, even though the 2-pence coin is the larger. Similarly, young children in the USA learn that a dime is worth more than a nickel, even though the nickel is larger. Indeed, many of our so-called cognitive skills involve the learning of relations which, as well as 'sameness' and 'more than/less than', include 'same/opposite', 'same/different' and many more. All these can be investigated experimentally.

## 7.5 VERBAL BEHAVIOUR

In the previous two sections, we have moved from a consideration of simple and then complex examples of discrimination learning, to a discussion of a type of human learning that, among other things, provides an account of meanings of some words. We will return to consider further the implications of learning arbitrary relations, but this is an appropriate point to give a general account of language, or verbal behaviour as behaviour analysts prefer to call it.

Throughout this book so far, animal behaviour has been discussed, and human behaviour has been treated as a section of that broader class. The general approach has been to identify behavioural processes that can be seen under well-controlled, and thus simple, circumstances, and then to see how effectively these processes can be deployed to explain or interpret human behaviour in more complex situations. For these purposes, 'human behaviour' has mostly been regarded as a single category. This is, of course, an unconventional approach. It is more usual to reserve the term human behaviour for visible actions, while also using the terms speech (or language) and thought to describe other parts of the domain of human psychology. This section will deal with the approach of behaviour analysis to speech and language. Later in the chapter, thinking and cognition will be discussed.

Almost 50 years ago, B.F. Skinner set out a general approach to speech and language in his book, *Verbal Behavior* (Skinner, 1957). That volume was extremely radical – that is, it looked at these aspects of human behaviour very differently than is usual – and it was several decades before the scientific community was able to take it seriously. Only recently has research from this perspective begun to gain momentum.

We will only mention some of Skinner's key concepts here. The one that linguists and others have found most surprising is that he provides a functional, and not a structural, account of language. He also assumed that speech and language, in its various forms, is often operant behaviour. He thus proposed to treat these human activities in terms of *functionally defined operant behaviour*, which is of course the approach we have taken to all behaviour throughout this volume. The reader will probably find it more difficult to accept this move away from a formal or structural account than with other types of human behaviour. If you like, we assume that two statements that look different, are different. But, on the other hand, we are also very aware of the function of speech and other language. If one child says to another in the playground, 'You are stupid' or 'That bike is useless', we may guess (or know from knowledge of the context), that these structurally different statements have the same function of humiliating the child spoken to.

Talking is the most obvious and important type of verbal behaviour and it should be seen as the emission of various types of operant that have different functions. For example, a person might emit a *mand* (this term is derived from 'demand'), which is reinforced by the removal of a cold draught from a door. That is its function, its *form* might be to say 'Shut the door!', or 'It is draughty in here', or even to gesture at the person standing nearest the door that they should close it. Skinner saw this as strictly analogous to the various response topographies that might occur when a rat presses a lever: a paw, the nose or even the tail might be used, but these members of the operant response class all have the common effect on the environment of depressing the lever. Another type of verbal operant is the *tact* (a descriptive act) where a person might say 'What a beautiful day', or 'It has turned out nice again'; or the person may simply smile with pleasure as they emerge from a building into the sunshine. Sources of reinforcement for this type are not specified by the operant itself, as they are with mands, but usually involve eliciting social approval or conversation from other people.

Dialogue or conversation is crucial to the behaviour analysis approach to verbal behaviour. Key concepts here are *the speaker* and *the listener*, who are both part of a *verbal community*. In a normal conversation, two people repeatedly swap the roles of speaker and listener, or 'take turns'. A hypothetical example is given in Figure 7.3. As conversation progresses, an utterance (an element of verbal behaviour) by one person may act as the discriminative stimulus for the next utterance by the other person, which may in turn act both as a reinforcer for the previous utterance and a discriminative stimulus for the next utterance by the first person. This analysis is complex, but it is entirely consistent with the treatment of other behavioural processes within behavioural analysis in that the function of a feature of behaviour or of the environment is not fixed, but depends on the context in which it occurs.

Verbal behaviour takes place within a verbal community. Being members of a verbal community simply means being part of a group of people who routinely talk to each and reinforce each others' verbal behaviour. Most of us are extremely sensitive to how our verbal behaviour is reacted to by the verbal community: our enjoyment of many social occasions, for example, is critically dependent on the occurrence of 'good' conversation. The social practice of shunning, or 'being sent to Coventry', where at school or work no one speaks or replies to the victim, is rightly seen as a severe and cruel punishment.

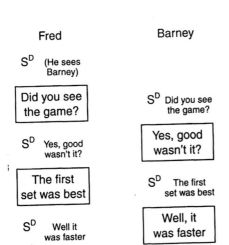

**Figure 7.3** In conversation, Fred and Barney repeatedly swap the roles of speaker and listener, each utterance is shown as a response (in a box) but when it is heard it becomes the S$^D$ for the next utterance; in this fictitious example, the first S$^D$ is a visual one

What is the relationship between verbal behaviour and language? Baum (1994) suggests that while verbal behaviour is actual human activity (and thus an appropriate subject matter for psychology), language is an abstraction:

> The English language, as set of words and grammatical rules for combining them, is a rough description of verbal behavior. It summarizes the way a lot of people talk. It is rough because people often use poor English. Neither the explanations in a dictionary nor the rules in a book of grammar exactly coincide with the utterances of English speakers (Baum, 1994: 111).

## 7.6 TEACHING VERBAL BEHAVIOUR TO CHILDREN

Section 7.4 outlined the elements of bidirectional training that are crucial in the earliest stages of the acquisition of verbal behaviour by children. At later stages, several aspects of verbal behaviour are more readily described in terms of modelling than in terms of the other behavioural processes we have introduced. In particular, the rapid acquisition of language by children and the speedy adoption of new accents, mannerisms and slang by adults depend primarily on modelling.

Observation by children of adults using either simple or complex sentences can be sufficient to induce the children to shorten or lengthen their own sentences correspondingly. In one study, a child (observer) and an adult (model) sat together and were asked to make up sentences about simple pictures presented on cards. In different phases of the study, the model used long sentences (more than 10 words) or short sentences (fewer than five words) for the descriptions. For boys and girls of two different ages (second and fourth grades), speaking in Spanish or English, the sentence length was greater when the model used longer and more complex sentences. This study is important because no explicit reinforcement was provided, but systematic modelling effects were still obtained.

There has been much debate as to the role of reinforcement and modelling in language acquisition by very young children; it has even been claimed that these strategies of 'training by parents', which all parents engage in at a high level, are not very relevant to children's acquisition of these crucial verbal behavioural skills (most notably by Chomsky, 1959). However, there are strong, but complex, relationships between modelling of verbal behaviour by mothers and the development of verbal competence in children. For example, from early on (perhaps when the child is 18 months old), the child imitates labels (names given to objects by the mother), and the mother may then selectively imitate the child's utterance by expanding it into a sentence. After weeks or months where this pattern of interaction is typical, the child develops the capacity to produce tacts, as defined in the previous section. As illustrated in that section, these tacts will be regularly reinforced when they occur, and the frequency of them will therefore increase.

Another type of study has provided compelling evidence that children benefit directly from the amount talk of directed to them, and this is reflected in their vocabulary at any age and in their later educational achievement. The most important research in this area found effects that were very striking, and in some ways alarming. It is worth describing in some detail.

Hart and Risley (1995) began their work after experience working with 'Headstart' programmes in the USA in the 1960s. These were early intervention programmes that were intended to compensate for the educational difficulties of young people from socially disadvantaged backgrounds. The programmes began when the children were four years old, and at the beginning of the programmes there appeared to be very big differences in the spontaneous use of speech between these children and children from 'advantaged' backgrounds. These differences made success in the programme very hard to achieve, because this would entail bringing the lower-achieving group up to the level of educational attainment of the other group within a few months. Consequently, they decided to investigate this topic directly and in due course completed two separate studies.

In the first study, they made recordings every week for a year of spontaneous speech from a group of disadvantaged children and a group of children in a university child-care facility (whose parents mostly taught in the university). Both groups of children asked questions, made demands and described what they were doing, but the 'university children' talked at least twice as much as the other children. They also asked more questions about how things worked and why. These differences were so pronounced that Hart and Risley embarked on a wider-ranging study of vocabulary growth starting with much younger children.

This programme focused on the everyday language of children; 1-hour recordings in children's homes were made monthly for two and a half years, with 42 children aged 7–11 months at the time of the first session. The researchers tried to record all behaviour of anyone present that was likely to contribute to vocabulary growth in a child. This was a group of 42 families that were prepared to contribute to the study, and was by no means a random sample of the population. None the less, Hart and Risley found a very wide range of rates of interaction with the children and, as in the first study, a wide range of vocabulary at any particular age. The children were from 13 professional families, 23 working-class families and 6 families on welfare benefits. As in the earlier study, socio-economic status was a strong predictor of the amount of interaction with the young child.

Figure 7.4a shows that, for the three groups, the estimated total number of words spoken to a child in his or her life so far (estimated from the monthly samples) varied a great deal. As an example, look at the projected totals for children at the age of four. These are roughly 13 million words for a child in a welfare family, 28 million words for a child in a working-class family (although this estimated average conceals a huge range in this group), and 47 million words for a child in a professional family. Figure 7.4b gives the average number of words in the current vocabulary for each group of children. At the age of three years, these are roughly 500 for the welfare children, 700 for the working-class children and 1100 for the children of professional families. Note that in both parts of Figure 7.4 (a and b), the graphs for each group become roughly linear and thus diverge from each other as the children get older.

The two parts of Figure 7.4 taken together show remarkably strong effects of family environment. There is a huge range in the amount of talk received by a child, and a related large amount of variation in the rate of vocabulary growth up to the age of three years. The strength of this relationship was confirmed by further analyses. A 'parenting' measure was constructed that combined five aspects of family experience (language diversity, feedback tone, symbolic richness of utterances, guidance style and parental responsiveness; see Hart and Risley, 1995, for details). Parenting correlated very highly with vocabulary growth and vocabulary use at three years of age (for 41 and 42 children respectively, Pearson's $r=0.78$ in both cases). For some of the children (29 in all), Hart and Risley were able to obtain measures six years later of performance on two tests of language skill that are good measures of educational achievement. These were the Peabody Picture Vocabulary Test-Revised, and the Test of Language Development-2: Intermediate. At ages 9 to 10, the measure of parenting in early years obtained six years earlier correlated with these current measures of language skill just as well as it had with vocabulary growth and use at age three years (for 29 children, Pearson's $r=0.78$ for each language skill test).

Overall, these findings illustrate the huge influence of the family environment, probably through modelling and positive reinforcement of utterances by parents and others, on the verbal behaviour of the developing child. What they also appear to show is that patterns of interactions with a child from when it is a few months old have a cumulative effect on vocabulary growth and later educational achievement. This means that any attempt to change the family environment must start really from the time the child is born. This would be 'intervention' at an earlier stage, and probably in a more comprehensive style than anything attempted so far in programmes like Headstart, which attempt to raise the educational level of disadvantaged children.

One would speculate that a child in institutional care would be in a more impoverished environment with regard to what have been shown to be the key factors for verbal development, than any of the children in Hart and Risley's study. Consequently, a radical change in their social environment would be required to give them a chance of educational attainment equal to that of a child in an 'ordinary family'.

In summary, there is a variety of sources of evidence of typical interactions

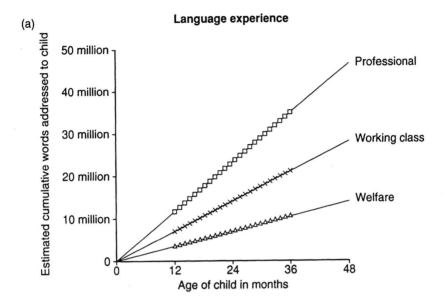

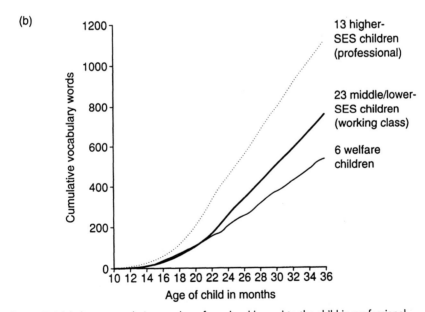

**Figure 7.4** (a) shows cumulative number of words addressed to the child in professional, working-class, or welfare families extrapolated from birth to 48 months of age; (b) shows average number of vocabulary words in that and all previous months for the three groups of children recorded from 10 to 36 months of age (Hart and Risley, 1995)

between the behaviour of the developing child and his or her social environment that produce, over several years, a huge growth in vocabulary and other linguistic skills. What about children who have learning disabilities? One of the most obvious, and concerning, differences between these children and others is their poor speech and generally slower acquisition of verbal behaviour. We noted earlier that, when applied to the written word, the spoken word and the corresponding object, stimulus equivalence provides an account of word meaning. That is, when these stimuli are all in the same class we can say that the word is known and the written word is understood. This suggests that stimulus equivalence training procedures can be used to enhance verbal behaviour. They have been used effectively in this way; indeed, they were actually developed initially by Sidman (1971, 1994) for the particular purpose of enhancing verbal behaviour in children with deficits in this area.

## 7.7 RULE-GOVERNED BEHAVIOUR

We have said something about the nature and origins of human verbal behaviour. This allows us to address one of the most difficult questions in psychology: 'How does verbal behaviour, or language, interact with other forms of human behaviour?' The short answer is that while some human behaviour is *contingency shaped*, much of it is *rule governed*. By contingency-shaped behaviour, we mean that reinforcement contingencies modify the behaviour, as is seen in the experimental studies of contingencies that we have outlined throughout this book. Rule-governed behaviour, on the other hand, is the general name for those occasions where verbal behaviour, in the form of a rule, is acquired either through verbal instruction or through direct experience of some reinforcement contingencies, and then determines other behaviour. We should note that while 'having a concept' and 'following a verbal rule' are related they are not the same thing. As discussed earlier in this chapter (Section 7.3), animals that do not appear to have verbal abilities, such as pigeons, can show some evidence of conceptual behaviour, and humans can solve complex problems even on occasions when they prove unable to verbalize the correct rule.

These complexities can be clarified by distinguishing between 'following the rule', and 'stating the rule'. Skinner (1969) defined a rule as a verbal discriminative stimulus that points to a contingency, and for any contingency it is possible to state a verbal rule but, as we have seen with various types of example, observation that behaviour consistent with the verbal rule is occurring does not prove that it is rule-governed – it may be contingency-shaped. With verbally competent humans, these two types of influence on behaviour interact in complex ways. A vehicle driver, for example, cannot readily provide verbal statements about the adjustments he or she makes to the controls of the car in response to changes in the road surface, but he or she will be able to describe what they decided to do once they realized that they had taken the wrong turning.

The most straightforward way in which verbal rules affect human behaviour is through *verbal instruction*. Very often, we act because we are told what to do. The statement 'Drive to the end of the street, turn left, go as far as the car park, park there, go into the adjacent restaurant, have a drink and wait for me there' may generate a long and complex sequence of behaviour in the listener. Verbal instruction is thus a powerful method of producing behavioural variation. As has been said several times in this book, there are a number of sources of variation or 'new' behaviour, and verbal instruction is probably the most important of these for adult humans. Ironically, a further feature of verbal rules, or instructions, is that the powerful effects on behaviour they exert may restrict behavioural variation that would otherwise occur. Many older people in urban areas, for example, have been given messages such as 'You will be attacked if you go out at night' or 'Your home will be robbed'. Under these influences, but without suffering any crime themselves, they may then lead very restricted lives with much time spent barricaded into their homes. Their behaviour may or may not be appropriate, depending on the local level of crime, but it has not been shaped directly by the contingencies.

A general feature of human behaviour is that it is more influenced by *short-term* rather than *long-term consequences* or contingencies. Many everyday phenomena fit in with this 'rule of thumb': we eat sweets (followed by short-term positive consequences) and fail to clean our teeth adequately (avoiding short-term negative consequences) and thus incur the long-term negative consequences of tooth decay and aversive dental treatment. We stay up late having a good time at the party (short-term positive consequences) and are unable to complete our work requirements the following day (long-term negative consequences), and so on. Our tendency to follow rules, rather than allowing contingencies to shape our behaviour can be seen as a further instance. Rule following is generally itself followed by immediate positive social consequences, while the contingency indicated by the rule may be very far off. An example of the two contingencies – the 'real' contingency and the contingency involving following the corresponding rule – is shown in Figure 7.5.

We each have an extended personal history of being reinforced for complying with rules. Although it may not always be possible to identify reinforcing consequences for a particular instance of rule following, we also engage in a great many social practices that offer generalized support for rule-following behaviour. These range from children's games that reward rule following *per se*, such as 'Simon says', to using negative labels, such as 'psychopath', for adults who fail to obey rules.

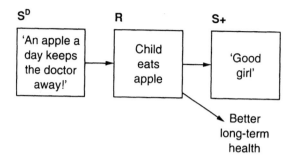

**Figure 7.5** An example of rule following: the rule-following response receives short-term social reinforcement and also results in long-term benefit for the child

Our history of reinforcement for rule following results in generalized rule following even when we 'make up' our own rules. That is, human beings tend to formulate verbal statements of rules in certain types of problem-solving situations. This may make the 'real' contingencies ineffective, in just the same way as in the example of older people being told of the dangers of crime. This phenomenon has often been observed in laboratory studies of reinforcement schedules with adult humans. While many species show the patterns of behaviour typical of each schedule of reinforcement described in Chapter 5 (and see Figure 5.1), verbally competent humans usually do not. Extensive investigation of this discrepancy between the behaviour of humans and that of other species in these operant conditioning situations has shown that the difference arises through verbal rule following. Given a very simple task and a schedule of reinforcement for performance of the task, a person may verbalize a rule such as, 'I will win a point sooner if I press the button very fast.' This rule will then determine the pattern of operant behaviour, even when the rule is incorrect, in that it does not correctly describe the reinforcement contingency, or when the contingency has changed (to extinction, for example). Following rules has great value – as shown, for example, by the many dangers children can avoid by following rules given to them by adults. This overall value is presumably the reason why we persist in following rules, even when we have made them up ourselves and they happen to be wrong!

If the discrepancy between the rule and the contingency is great enough, human behaviour will switch from being rule-governed to being contingency-shaped. This effect is seen in experiments where the participant is told to respond in a particular way but, in parts of the experiment, this pattern of operant behaviour produces a lower rate of reinforcement than an alternative pattern of behaviour (see Leslie, 1996, Section 10.5, for an example of this). Eventually, the behaviour switches to another pattern that 'breaks the rule' but produces more reinforcement. This is analogous to many social situations where the child (or adult) has often been told not to do something (e.g., smoke a cigarette), but eventually the 'temptation becomes too great' and they switch to the immediately reinforced behaviour.

## 7.8 THOUGHTS AND FEELINGS

This book has tried to introduce the approach to human psychology from behaviour analysis in a systematic fashion. After dealing at some length with behavioural processes that can be seen in many species, we have dealt with human verbal behaviour. Verbal behaviour is typically human, but it is not usually private. That is, it is behaviour that can be observed and recorded by other people. Thoughts and feelings, however, are important in any account of human psychology, and they do seem to be private. I cannot read your thoughts or feel your pain.

B.F. Skinner often argued (for example, in Skinner, 1974) that this 'private behaviour' is not inherently different from other sorts of behaviour. There are, however, some serious methodological or practical problems in trying to investigate it. Indeed, there are interesting questions about how we are able to even talk about these private events.

Let us consider an increasingly private series of events. A woman in late pregnancy can feel the baby (that is, the foetus) kicking. Another person will be able to feel it if they put a hand on her abdomen, and they may actually be able to see the distension of the mother's abdomen when the baby kicks. A person with a stomach ache following food poisoning feels a severe pain with a specific internal location. No one else can feel the pain, but they may able to tell from the first person's facial expression and posture that the problem is a stomach ache. A person who has recently been bereaved may feel a great sense of loss, they may feel unable to act except slowly and awkwardly; these changes in their behaviour may or may not be perceived by others. A person may remember a joke and then smile, but someone watching at the time will probably not know why they smiled.

There is thus a continuum. Sometimes we respond to stimuli that are immediately obvious to us and to other people, sometimes we respond to stimuli that are intense but located within our bodies and thus not readily observed by others, and sometimes we respond to less intense and more remote stimuli. Similarly, our responses themselves range from being intense and readily observed by others and by ourselves, to being faint and scarcely noticed, even by ourselves.

One of the issues addressed by Skinner (for example, in Skinner, 1957) has also been of interest to philosophers. In Skinner's term, how does the verbal behaviour of describing or 'tacting' (see Section 7.5) come about for private events? That is, how do we acquire the necessary language to talk about our pain etc.? Skinner suggested that there are a number of ways that this can happen. First of all, there may be a public accompaniment to the private stimulus. For example, when a child has a painful fall, the mother says, 'That must hurt!' A second method is where there is a collateral response. Perhaps the child fell earlier and is now limping (a collateral response). The mother says, 'Your leg must be hurting.' Again, the internal stimulus that is labelled as a pain will often have been accompanied by external stimuli such as damage to the leg, but will also elicit the same response on occasions when the child cannot see any external damage.

Private behaviour interacts less with the environment – it does not generally have consequences except in terms of other internal events – and thus it is harder to change. However, it can be made more conspicuous and thus more susceptible to the techniques of behaviour change that are applied to public behaviour. Suppose you have aggressive thoughts about someone (for example, 'I really want to hit him when he says that!'). This behaviour may never lead to an actual assault on the person, thankfully, but it may none the less be disturbing to you, and it can be changed through a self-monitoring exercise followed by 'positive practice'. You could carry out a form of behavioural assessment on yourself. Critically, this would involve recording all the negative thoughts of this kind that occurred over a period of time. You might discover, for example, that you typically had such a thought 20 to 30 times a day, with 10 to 15 of these happening after you had just seen the person. A positive practice routine might be to construct a list of 10 positive statements about the person, and to spend 3 minutes each day repeating this list to yourself. You would continue to monitor the total number of negative thoughts a day that you had. If an appreciable reduction in these thoughts occurred, you could proceed to complete an ABAB design (see Section 6.5) to confirm that it was the positive practice that produced the improvement. That is, you could repeat the sequence of baseline (A) and intervention (B) conditions. A small number of papers in the scientific literature have demonstrated the efficacy of this approach.

## 7.9 COGNITIONS

The predominant approach in contemporary accounts of psychology is a cognitive one. The prevailing view is that a behavioural approach, inspired initially by J.B. Watson and later influenced by Skinner and others, proved useful up until the 1950s. From the 1960s, however, it is said that shortcomings in that approach were overcome through the development of cognitive psychology. Throughout this book, this conventional modern view has been rejected in favour of an alternative. The alternative presented here is that the approach of behaviour analysis, linked to Skinner's radical behaviourism, is well able to account for the phenomena of psychology. In so doing, it produces a coherent account of psychology, strongly rooted in biology.

It has not been our purpose to spend time contrasting behavioural and cognitive accounts. Instead, we have sought to show how a behavioural approach can be used to deal effectively with increasingly complex aspects of human behaviour. In this final chapter, we have come as far as providing an account of verbal behaviour and discussing an approach to thoughts and feelings. In this chapter and earlier, we have developed an account of relational learning and shown how it is linked to simpler forms of operant conditioning. Throughout, we have emphasized the ideas outlined in Chapter 1: the most important process is one of selection through a life-long interaction between the behaviour of the individual and their environment. In that statement, it must be remembered that behaviour and environment are conceptualized as consisting of functionally defined response and stimulus classes respectively. Furthermore, these classes themselves change in membership through that process of interaction.

The perspective generated by these basic principles is very different from that of contemporary cognitive psychology, which tends to define itself only by rejecting a very simplistic version of behaviourism. Consequently, it is difficult to make point-for-point comparisons. None the less, a few issues will be reviewed to aid the reader.

First of all, we have dealt from time to time with animal cognition. That is, we have discussed the performance of non-human animals on relatively complex tasks. Throughout the history of psychology, there has been an interest in problem-solving in animals and a tendency to ascribe highly complex – and thus 'cognitive' – skills to animals when faced with evidence of success in relatively complex tasks. In the present book, we have to show how a small set of learning principles can explain animal behaviour even in relatively complex tasks. This parsimonious approach has thus explained types of learning that others have dealt with under the heading of 'animal cognition'.

Those aspects of human psychology that involve verbal behaviour are central to cognitive psychology. Our approach has been to show how extension of those behavioural principles that deal adequately with other types of behaviour enables us to begin to account for verbal behaviour as well. This includes an account of the origins of verbal behaviour in children, which draws on relational learning and the perhaps uniquely human ability to learn about arbitrary relations between events, as well as those that are based on physical similarities and differences. Arbitrary relational learning deals with many of the issues that also come up in cognitive psychology and thus can be said to deal with certain sorts of cognition. However, the approach outlined here is clearly an extension of a behavioural approach rather than proceeding from a rejection of aspects of a behavioural approach. On this behavioural approach, these types of relational learning are seen as the basis of verbal behaviour.

In cognitive psychology, cognitions are also invoked to explain behaviour. They have a mediational role, and come between environmental events and behavioural events. We have explained at various points that, from the perspective of behaviour analysis, this is a confusing and unnecessary idea. It is closely related to the traditional mentalistic view that explains what we do – our actions – as the product of what we thought. As these thoughts are usually not measured separately from our actions (instead, they are inferred from them), we are just inventing another language for describing rather less clearly what we have already observed. The view taken here is that when they can be measured, our thoughts are another interesting aspect of our behaviour, and that all types of behaviour may be understood with reference to the environment. Of course, all types of our behaviour have neural correlates, and exciting discoveries about these are currently being made. To understand brain processes, however, will not provide a complete account of behavioural processes; as we saw in Chapter 5, each affects the other. Furthermore, the elements of brain processes are not identical with cognitions or the elements of cognitive processes. Brain processes can be related to behavioural processes directly, so cognitions are not necessary or helpful in making those links.

Our conclusion, then, is that most of the subject matter of cognitive psychology can be approached from the perspective of behaviour analysis. The exception is those aspects of the subject matter that deal with unobservable entities presumed to exist independently of behaviour, the brain and the environment. Inventing this type of entity is a mistake and does not help to explain anything.

## 7.10 SUMMARY

This chapter has attempted to sketch in the links between the well-established principles of behaviour analysis and the complex phenomena of human psychology, including those usually described as language and cognition. The well-established principle of parsimony in scientific explanation should encourage us to attempt this, despite the countervailing tendency to assume that human psychology is not likely to be analysable with relatively simple scientific principles. The same type of dispute has occurred in evolutionary biology. Darwin anticipated objections by discussing, and repudiating, the idea that very complex organs could not evolve through the simple processes he posited. Much more recently, quantitative modelling techniques have provided strong support for his view that no further principles are required.

Concept formation is an example of complex human behaviour that can be explained by extending the simpler behavioural processes already discussed. In humans and other animals, responses can be controlled by the relations between stimuli, rather than only by specific stimuli as in the examples of discrimination learning described earlier. Where the antecedent stimulus class is relatively complex, we may refer to concept formation, or having a concept rather than a discrimination. Concepts can be polymorphous, where a stimulus must have some out of a larger number of features to be a member of the antecedent class. Many natural concepts (such as the visual stimulus class, tree) are of this type and non-human animals have been shown to have them.

Humans also show learning based on arbitrary relations between stimuli; the most investigated type of this is stimulus equivalence class formation, first discussed in Chapter 4. This capacity, apparently not shared with other animals, may be the basis of human language and the distinctive features of human cognition. In language acquisition, children have extensive exposure to bidirectional training with multiple exemplars. This means that on many occasions there is object-name training, in which the child is shown the object and reinforced for saying the name, or there is name-object training, where the object is named by the adult and the child is reinforced for picking out the object. Such training occurs in respect of many different object–name pairs, and many action–name pairs. After experience with many examples, the child will treat the name and the object, or the name and the action, as equivalent without any specific training with this pair. This generalized ability will be shown on stimulus equivalence tasks where, after training with 'given A1 pick B1' and 'given B1 pick C1', A1, B1 and C1 will be treated as equivalent.

This type of learning provides an account of word meanings, because it explains how the physical object, the written word, a picture of the object and the spoken word can all be treated as equivalent. Because of the transfer of functions between stimulus class members, many other behavioural effects are also explained. For example, fear of real snakes will transfer to symbols of snakes, without any other relevant experience.

Equivalence is one of many types of arbitrary relational learning that may underpin human language. Behaviour analysts use the term verbal behaviour, instead of language, because this clearly refers to human action. Skinner's initial attempt to analyse verbal behaviour extended the idea of functionally defined response and stimulus classes to this type of activity. There is usually a speaker and listener, and the behaviour of one person as speaker is often a significant stimulus, either an antecedent or consequence for the other person. Thus the two people repeatedly exchange the roles of speaker and listener. Functional response classes include the mand, which is reinforced through a change in the environment, and the tact, which describes the environment and is typically reinforced by social attention.

There is much evidence that the continual interaction between young children and adults plays an important role in language development. This evidence comes both from experimental studies showing immediate effects on verbal behaviour, and long-term correlational studies showing strong relationships between family environment, rate of vocabulary growth and subsequent educational achievement. These effects of family environment are so large that they suggest that any intervention to enhance vocabulary development, and thus optimize educational opportunity, should occur very early in a child's life.

Human behaviour, unlike that of other species, is rule-governed as well as contingency-shaped. Verbal behaviour in the form of a rule may be acquired through verbal instruction or other means, and the rule may then determine other behaviour. Verbal instruction is a powerful technique for altering the behavioural repertoire and introducing specified behaviour. Rule-following behaviour is often reinforced with short-term consequences, such as social approval, even though the contingencies specified by the rule many involve very long-term consequences. A person's history of reinforcement for rule following tends to lead to rules being followed even when the rules do not accurately reflect the prevailing contingencies. People also devise verbal rules for themselves and follow them. This occurs in problem-solving situations, such as schedules of reinforcement, where other behaviour might be expected and rule following may not be adaptive.

Thoughts and feelings are types of behaviour, but they may be internal responses or responses to internal stimuli. Even when the events are to some extent private, the same behavioural principles operate as with public behaviour. It may be more difficult to tact (that is, describe) internal events, but there are none the less a number of ways a person may learn to do this that are simple extensions of the ways tacting develops for public events. Because private behaviour, such as thoughts and feelings, interacts less with the environment it is harder to change. However, there are self-monitoring techniques that make such behaviour more conspicuous and then more susceptible to change through the same techniques that are used with other behaviour.

Various aspects of animal and human cognition have been dealt with in this volume. These include the capacity of non-human animals to solve relatively complex problems and to learn to respond to complex aspects of the environment. These capacities are sometimes described as involving animal cognition. We have dealt extensively with the nature and origins of human verbal behaviour, a central topic in cognitive psychology. Verbal behaviour is intimately involved with arbitrary relational learning, which in turn may be a uniquely human attribute. From the perspective of behaviour analysis, it is unhelpful and unnecessary to invent cognitions as mental events that are intended to explain behaviour, nor do the rapid developments in behavioural neuroscience make the invention of cognitions necessary. As neuroscience develops, it will be possible to relate behavioural processes to brain processes. We have already seen, in Chapter 5, that each affects the other.

## 7.11 CONCLUDING REMARKS

Chapters 1 and 2 set the scene for this brief study of behaviour analysis, by providing an account of the main aims of behaviour analysis and placing it in a scientific and historical context. Chapter 3 gave an account of the basic principles; Chapter 4 went somewhat further, seeking to provide enough understanding of behaviour analysis to consider its applications to behavioural neuroscience in Chapter 5, to applied behaviour analysis in Chapter 6, and its extension towards providing an account of human language and cognition in this final chapter.

Many of the details, and indeed whole areas of significant development, have been left out to ensure that this brief study none the less provides an account that embraces many areas of psychology. For the reader who wants to go further in one or more areas, some suggestions as to where to start to obtain more information are given in the 'Further reading' section. This book was written primarily for the reader whose main aim is to gain a perspective on contemporary behaviour analysis as it applies to the discipline of psychology. It is hoped that the needs of such a reader have been met.

# Further reading

This book is intended to provide a brief introduction rather than a full-scale review of behaviour analysis. More extended treatments from the same perspective are provided in a number of texts, including those listed below.

## BEHAVIOUR ANALYSIS IN GENERAL

Catania, A.C. (1998) *Learning* (fourth edn). Upper Saddle River, NJ: Prentice Hall.
Leslie, J.C. (1996) *Principles of Behavioral Analysis* (third edn). Amsterdam: Harwood Academic.

## APPLIED BEHAVIOUR ANALYSIS

Leslie, J.C. and O'Reilly, M.F. (1999) *Behavior Analysis: Foundations and Applications to Psychology.* Amsterdam: Harwood Academic.
Martin, G. and Pear, J. (1999) *Behavior Modification: What It Is and How To Do It* (sixth edn). Upper Saddle River, NJ: Prentice Hall.

## MORE SPECIFIC AREAS IN BEHAVIOUR ANALYSIS

Dougher, M.J. (ed.) (1999) *Clinical Behavior Analysis.* Reno, Nevada: Context Press.
Guerin, B. (1994) *Analyzing Social Behavior: Behavior Analysis and the Social Sciences.* Reno, Nevada: Context Press.
Hayes, S.C., Barnes-Holmes, D. and Roche, B. (eds) (2001) *Relational Frame Theory: A Post-Skinnerian Account of Human Language and Cognition.* New York: Plenum.
Hayes, S.C, Hayes, L.J., Sato, M. and Ono, K. (eds) (1994) *Behavior Analysis of Language and Cognition.* Reno, Nevada: Context Press.

Novak, G. (1996) *Developmental Psychology: Dynamical Systems and Behavior Analysis*. Reno, Nevada: Context Press.

Sturmey, P. (1996) *Functional Analysis in Clinical Psychology*. Chichester, Sussex: Wiley.

## INTRODUCTION TO BEHAVIOURAL NEUROSCIENCE

Kandel, E.R., Schwartz, J.H. and Jessell, T.M. (1995) *Essentials of Neural Science and Behavior*. New York: Appleton and Lange.

McKim, W.A. (2000) *Drugs and Behavior: An Introduction to Behavioral Pharmacology* (fourth edn). Upper Saddle River, NJ: Prentice Hall.

It is better to read any area of science in the original, rather than in the second-hand version provided in textbooks. Following a reading of the present volume, and perhaps one or more of the other texts listed here, it should be possible to understand original behaviour analysis research in journal articles.

Basic research on behaviour analysis appears in:

- *Journal of the Experimental Analysis of Behavior*
- *The Psychological Record*

as well as in many experimental psychology journals.

Specialist journals for applied behaviour analysis include:

- *Journal of Applied Behavior Analysis*
- *Behavior Modification*
- *Behavior Therapy and Experimental Psychiatry*.

# References

Allison, J. and Timberlake, W. (1974) Instrumental and contingent saccharin licking in rats: response deprivation and reinforcement, *Learning and Motivation 5*, 231–47.

Anrep, G.V. (1920) Pitch discrimination in the dog, *Journal of Physiology 53*, 367–85.

Antonitis, J.J. (1951) Response variability in the white rat during conditioning, extinction and reconditioning, *Journal of Experimental Psychology 42*, 273–81.

Ayllon, T. and Azrin, N.H. (1965) The measurement and reinforcement of behavior of psychotics, *Journal of the Experimental Analysis of Behavior 8*, 357–83.

Ayllon, T. and Azrin, N.H. (1968) *The Token Economy*. New York: Appleton-Century-Crofts.

Azrin, N.H. and Holz, W.C. (1966) Punishment, in W.K. Honig (ed.), *Operant Behavior: Areas of Research and Application*. New York: Appleton-Century-Crofts.

Azrin, N.H., Hutchinson, R.R. and Hake, D.F. (1966) Extinction-induced aggression, *Journal of the Experimental Analysis of Behavior 9*, 191–204.

Baer, D.M., Peterson, R. and Sherman, J. (1967) The development of imitation by reinforcing behavioral similarity to a model, *Journal of the Experimental Analysis of Behavior 10*, 405–16.

Bandura, A. (1965) influence of model's reinforcement contingencies on the acquisition of imitative responses, *Journal of Personality and Social Psychology 1*, 589–95.

Baum, W.M. (1994) *Understanding Behaviorism: Science, Behavior and Culture*. New York: HarperCollins.

Catania, A.C. (1999) Ten points every behavior analyst needs to remember about reinforcement, in J.C. Leslie and D. Blackman (eds), *Experimental and Applied Analyses of Human Behavior*. Reno: Context Press.

Chen, Y.C., Chen, Q.S., Lei, J.L. and Wang, S.L. (1998) Physical training modifies the age-related decrease of GAP-43 and synaptophysin in the hippocampal formation in C57BL/6J mouse, *Brain Research 806*, 238–45.

Chomsky, N. (1959) A review of Skinner's *Verbal Behavior, Language 35*, 26–58.

Darwin, C. (1859) *The Origin of Species*. London: John Murray (published 1968, Harmondsworth, Middlesex: Penguin Books).

Dawkins, R. (1996) *Climbing Mount Improbable*. Harmondsworth, Middlesex: Penguin Books.

Deitz, S.M., Repp, A.C. and Deitz, D.E.D. (1976) Reducing inappropriate classroom behavior of retarded students through three procedures of differential reinforcement, *Journal of Mental Deficiency Research* 20, 155–70.

Dennis, I., Hampton, J.A. and Lea, S.E.G. (1973) New problems in concept formation, *Nature* (London) 243, 101–2.

Dugdale, N. and Lowe, C.F. (2000) Testing for symmetry in the conditional discriminations of language-trained chimpanzees, *Journal of the Experimental Analysis of Behavior* 73, 5–22.

Fantino, E. (1977) Conditioned reinforcement: choice and information, in W.K. Honig and J.E.R. Staddon (eds), *Handbook of Operant Behavior*. Englewood Cliffs, New Jersey: Prentice Hall.

Ferster, C.B. and Skinner, B.F. (1957) *Schedules of Reinforcement*. New York: Appleton-Century-Crofts.

Foxx, R.M. and Azrin, N.H. (1972) Restitution: a method for eliminating aggressive-disruptive behavior of retarded and brain damaged patients, *Behaviour Research and Therapy* 10, 15–27.

Foxx, R.M. and Bechtel, D.R. (1983) Overcorrection: a review and analysis, in S. Axelrod and J. Apsche (eds), *The Effects of Punishment on Human Behavior*. New York: Academic Press, 133–220.

France, K.G. and Hudson, S.M. (1990) Behavior management of infant sleep disturbance, *Journal of Applied Behavior Analysis* 23, 91–8.

Garcia, J. and Koelling, R.A. (1966) Relation of cue to consequence in avoidance learning, *Psychonomic Science* 4, 123–4.

Gladstone, E.W. and Cooley, J. (1975) Behavioral similarity as a reinforcer for preschool children, *Journal of the Experimental Analysis of Behavior* 23, 357–68.

Goh, H. and Iwata, B.A. (1994) Behavioral persistence and variability during extinction of self-injury maintained by escape, *Journal of Applied Behavior Analysis* 27, 173–4.

Gormezano, I., Schneiderman, N., Deaux, E.B. and Fuentes, I. (1962) Nictitating membrane: classical conditioning and extinction in the albino rabbit, *Science* 138, 33–4.

Gray, J.A. (1975) *Elements of a Two-process Theory of Learning*. London: Academic Press.

Guthrie, E.R. (1940) Association and the law of effect, *Psychological Review* 47, 127–48.

Guttman, N. and Kalish, H.I. (1956) Discriminability and stimulus generalisation, *Journal of Experimental Psychology* 51, 79–88.

Hart, B. and Risley, T.R. (1995) *Meaningful Differences in the Everyday*

*Experience of Young American Children.* Baltimore: P.H. Brookes.

Hayes, S.C., Barnes-Holmes, D. and Roche, B. (eds) (2001) *Relational Frame Theory: A Post-Skinnerian Account of Human Language and Cognition.* New York: Plenum.

Hayes, S.C. and Hayes, L.J. (1992) Verbal relations and the evolution of behavioral analysis, *American Psychologist* 47, 1385–92.

Herrnstein, R.J. and Loveland, D.H. (1964) Complex visual concept in the pigeon, *Science* 146, 549–51.

Hsiao, K., Chapman, P., Nilsen, S., Eckman, C., Harigaya, Y., Younkin, S., Yang, F.S. and Cole, G. (1996) Correlative memory deficits, A beta elevation and amyloid plaques in transgenic mice, *Science* 274, 99–102.

Hull, C.L. (1943) *Principles of Behavior.* New York: Appleton-Century-Crofts.

Hunt, H.F. and Brady, J.V. (1951) Some effects of electroconvulsive shock on a conditioned emotional response ('anxiety'), *Journal of Comparative and Physiological Psychology* 44, 88–98.

Iwata, B.A., Dorsey, M.F., Slifer, K.J., Bauman, K.E. and Richman, G.S. (1982) Toward a functional analysis of self-injury, *Analysis and Intervention in Developmental Disabilities* 2, 3–20 (reprinted in *Journal of Applied Behavior Analysis* 27, 197–209).

Iwata, B.A., Pace, G.M., Dorsey, M.F., Zarcone, J.R., Vollmer, T.R., Smith, R.G., Rodgers, T.A., Lerman, D.C., Shore, B.A., Mazaleski, J.L., Goh, H., Cowdery, G.E., Kalsher, M.J., McCosh, K.C. and Willis, K.D. (1994) The functions of self-injurious behavior: an experimental-epidemiological analysis, *Journal of Applied Behavior Analysis* 27, 215–40.

Kamin, L.J. (1968) Attention-like processes in classical conditioning, in M.R. Jones (ed.), *Miami Symposium on the Prediction of Behavior: Aversive Stimuli.* Coral Gables, Florida: University of Miami Press.

Leslie, J.C. (1996) *Principles of Behavioral Analysis* (third edn). Amsterdam: Harwood Academic.

Leslie, J.C. and O'Reilly, M.F. (1999) *Behavior Analysis: Foundations and Applications to Psychology.* Amsterdam: Harwood Academic.

McAuley, F. and Leslie, J.C. (1986) Molecular analyses of the effects of *d*-amphetamine on fixed-interval schedule performances of rats, *Journal of the Experimental Analysis of Behavior* 45, 207–19.

McGee, J.J., Menolascino, F.J., Hobbs, D.C. and Menousek, P.E. (1987) *Gentle Teaching: A Nonaversive Approach for Helping Persons with Mental Retardation.* New York: Human Sciences Press.

Maricq, A.V. and Church, R.M. (1983) The differential effects of haloperidol and methamphetamine on time estimation in the rat, *Psychopharmacology* 79, 10–15.

Mineka, S., Davidson, M., Cook, M. and Keir, R. (1984) Observational conditioning of snake fear in rhesus-monkeys, *Journal of Abnormal Psychology* 93, 355–72.

Morgan, C.L. (1894) *Introduction to Comparative Psychology*. New York: Scribner.

Morris, R. (1984) Developments of a water-maze procedure for studying spatial-learning in the rat, *Journal of Neuroscience Methods* 11, 47–60.

Neisworth, J.T. and Moore, F. (1972) Operant treatment of asthmatic responding with the parent as therapist, *Behavior Therapy* 3, 95–9.

NIH (National Institutes of Health Consensus Development Conference Statement) (1989) *Treatment of Destructive Behaviors in Persons with Developmental Disabilities*. Bethesda, MD: NICHD.

Northup, J., Wacker, D., Sasso, G., Steege, M., Cigrand, K., Cook, J. and DeRaad, A. (1991) A brief functional analysis of aggressive and alternative behavior in an outclinic setting, *Journal of Applied Behavior Analysis* 24, 509–22.

O'Hare, E., Weldon, D.T., Mantyh, P.W., Ghilardi, J.R., Finke, M.P., Kuskowski, M.A., Maggio, J.E., Shephard, R.A. and Cleary, J. (1999) Delayed behavioral effects following intrahippocampal injection of aggregated A beta (1–42), *Brain Research* 815, 1–10.

O'Reilly, M.F., O'Kane, N., Byrne, P. and Lancioni, G. (1996) Increasing the predictability of therapeutic interactions for a client with acquired brain injury: an analysis of the effect on verbal abuse, *Irish Journal of Psychology* 17, 258–68.

Pavlov, I.P. (1927) *Conditioned Reflexes*. London: Oxford University Press.

Pennypacker, H.S. (2001) Discussant, Symposium 350. Private events: data on thoughts and feelings, 27th Annual Convention of Association for Behavior Analysis, New Orleans, La., May.

Premack, D. (1965) Reinforcement theory, in D. Levine (ed.), *Nebraska Symposium on Motivation*. Lincoln, Nebraska: University of Nebraska Press.

Rescorla, R.A. (1968) Probability of shock in the presence and absence of CS in fear conditioning, *Journal of Comparative and Physiological Psychology* 66, 1–5.

Rescorla, R.A. (1988) Pavlovian conditioning: it's not what you think it is, *American Psychologist* 43, 151–60.

Richardson, L., O'Hare, E., Cleary, J., Shephard, R.A. and Kim, E.-M. (2000) Protective effects of NSAID treatment in LPS and Ab-induced inflammation in the brain. Annual Convention of Society for Neuroscience, New Orleans, La., November.

Robertson, I.H. (1999) Setting goals for cognitive rehabilitation, *Current Opinion in Neurology* 12, 703–8.

Rosenzweig, M.R. (1984) Experience, memory and the brain, *American Psychologist* 39, 365–76.

Rosenzweig, M.R. and Bennett, E.L. (1996) Psychobiology of plasticity: effects of training and experience on brain and behavior, *Behavioural Brain Research* 78, 57–65.

Seligman, M.E.P. (1970) On the generality of the laws of learning, *Psychological Review* 77, 406–18.

Sidman, M. (1960) *Tactics of Scientific Research*. New York: Basic Books.

Sidman, M. (1971) Reading and auditory-visual equivalences, *Journal of Speech and Hearing Research* 14, 5–13.

Sidman, M. (1990) Equivalence relations: where do they come from?, in D.E. Blackman and H. Lejeune (eds), *Behaviour Analysis in Theory and Practice: Contributions and Controversies*. Hove, Sussex: Lawrence Erlbaum.

Sidman, M. (1994) *Equivalence Relations and Behavior: A Research Story*. Boston, MA: Authors Cooperative.

Skinner, B.F. (1938) *The Behavior of Organisms*. New York: Appleton-Century-Crofts.

Skinner, B.F. (1950) Are theories of learning necessary?, *Psychological Review* 57, 193–216.

Skinner, B.F. (1953) *Science and Human Behavior*. New York: Macmillan.

Skinner, B.F. (1956) A case history in scientific method, *American Psychologist* 11, 221–33.

Skinner, B.F. (1957) *Verbal Behavior*. New York: Appleton-Century-Crofts.

Skinner, B.F. (1969) *Contingencies of Reinforcement: A Theoretical Analysis*. Englewood Cliffs, New Jersey: Prentice Hall.

Skinner, B.F. (1972) *Beyond Freedom and Dignity*. New York: Bantam.

Skinner, B.F. (1974) *About Behaviorism*. New York: Knopf.

Sturmey, P. (1996) *Functional Analysis in Clinical Psychology*. Chichester, Sussex: Wiley.

Thorndike, E.L. (1898) Animal intelligence, *Psychological Review Monograph Supplement* No. 8.

van Dellen, A., Blakemore, C., Deacon, R., York, D. and Hannan, A.J. (2000) Delaying the onset of Huntington's in mice, *Nature* 404, 721–2.

Van Houten, R., Axelrod, S., Bailey, J.S., Favell, J.E., Foxx, R.M., Iwata, B.A. and Lovaas, O.I. (1988) The right to effective behavioral treatment, *Journal of Applied Behavior Analysis* 21, 381–4.

Vollmer, T.R., Iwata, B.A., Zarcone, J.R., Smith, R.G. and Mazaleski, J.L. (1993) The role of attention in the treatment of attention-maintained self-injurious behavior: noncontingent reinforcement (NCR) and differential reinforcement of other behavior (DRO), *Journal of Applied Behavior Analysis* 26, 9–26.

Watson, J.B. (1913) Psychology as the behaviorist views it, *Psychological Review* 20, 158–77.

Williams, J.H., Gray, J.A., Sinden, J., Buckland, C., Rawlins, J.N.P. (1990) Effects of GABAergic drugs, fornicotomy, hippocampectomy and septal-lesions on the extinction of a discrete-trial fixed ratio-5 lever-press response, *Behavioural Brain Research* 41, 129–50.

# Possible answers to study questions

## Chapter 1

1. Can our thoughts be changed by environmental consequences? One difference between thoughts and other behaviour is they do not usually have consequences in the external environment. However, we can arrange for consequences to occur. One approach to this has been called 'thought stopping'. A person may have compulsive negative thoughts such as 'I am a bad person' or 'I am always a failure'. They can be trained to administer a negative consequence when they engage in one of these thoughts. For example, they might keep a thick elastic band around one wrist, and stretch and release it, causing a slightly painful effect, whenever one of these thoughts occurs. This has been used quite extensively as a self-monitoring technique that can be effective in reducing the frequency of such thoughts. In order for the technique to be carried out properly, the person concerned would also have to be trained to keep accurate records of their thoughts. Techniques for this type of behavioural record-keeping will be discussed in Chapter 6.

2. A possible answer to this question was offered by Pennypacker (2001). We are aware of the thoughts we have and the actions we take. However, the thought does not usually take as long as the action. This means that we routinely observe that the thought occurs before the action. Given that we normally attribute 'causal agency' to the first of two events in a sequence – we say, for example, that the second billiard ball moves *because* it was struck by the first one – we then believe that our thought caused our action. According to behaviour analysis, however, both thought and action are happening because of interaction between our environment and us. We will return to this issue in Chapter 7.

# Chapter 2

The three terms – antecedent, behaviour and consequence – are defined in terms of each other. There is no escape from this because they are all aspects of the same phenomenon. The phenomenon is that interaction between a person's behaviour and their environment produces changes in the behaviour. If someone learns to hide (a young child in a game of 'hide and seek', for example), then over a period of time an observer will be able to monitor changes in their behaviour. The child might spend less time out in the garden and more in places where she is hard to see. A more detailed analysis of how the child's behaviour has changed will involve finding out what the functional classes of 'hiding place' and 'hiding' currently are for that child. These are questions that can be addressed with the methods of behavioural assessment and functional analysis, which will be outlined in Chapter 6.

# Chapter 3

Later (in Chapters 4 and 7), the so-called principle of parsimony will be discussed. Parsimony means 'few-ness' and the essential idea is that explanations should always be as simple as possible. In this example, we can be parsimonious by explaining the change in the rat's behaviour in terms of the law of effect, itself a very simple principle. Any other explanation is likely to be unnecessarily complex by comparison. If we attribute mental states to the rat (for which we have no evidence except the changes in behaviour) we are probably also implying some verbal reasoning ability. Is that plausible? Would it be plausible if we repeated the experiment or an equivalent one with a mouse, or a bee?

The attribution of mental states to the rat can also be seen as an example of anthropomorphism (see Chapter 2). This is assuming that other animals have our human capacities. While a common assumption, this is assumed to be false from the perspective of behaviour analysis until evidence is obtained that directly supports the presence of any particular capacity in a non-human species. Again, the main point here is that we can provide an account of the rat's behaviour using only very simple principles.

# Chapter 4

1. False. Reinforcement has only occurred when the reinforced response is selectively increased. In this example, another unreinforced response has increased in frequency.
2. False. Operant response classes are functionally defined.
3. False. As we noted in Chapter 3, a reinforcement contingency is effective when it results in presentation of an opportunity to engage in a response of which the participant is currently deprived! That is rather a mouthful, but it is not the same as a criterion of making the participant 'feel good' or of 'liking' the reinforcer.
4. False. This issue will be further discussed in Chapter 6. We have noted in the present chapter that extinction can have unpleasant side-effects (the extinction burst and extinction-induced aggression). Functional analysis (introduced in Chapter 2 and further developed in Chapter 6) provides us with much better ways of changing behaviour.
5. False. This is the 'trickiest' statement in the list, and the reasons why it is false will become clearer in Chapter 6. The problem is that delivery of a reinforcer affects not just the behaviour immediately before it, but also the behaviour that occurs a little before that. There is a risk that, in the example, given 'errors' will be reinforced, as well as 'correct' responses. This makes it difficult to decide what to do once a series of errors has occurred. A possible solution will be to reinforce a correct response only if it does not immediately follow an error.

The answers were all 'false', because these statements were taken from a list, constructed by Catania (1999), of common mistakes about reinforcement.

# Chapter 5

There are a number of possible examples embedded in the text of Chapter 5. Further familiar examples are that depression is on many occasions said to be caused by traumatic life events, such as bereavement, but that the recommended treatment is none the less usually drug therapy. This is thus a common example of environmental 'cause' followed by biological 'cure'. Depression can, of course, also provide examples of the opposite type because endogenous ('internal') depression is said to be 'caused' by biological changes but may yet by 'cured' by environmental changes, such as a positive major life event.

The quotation marks are employed in the above paragraph to indicate that it is not appropriate to write as if a single causal factor can be identified for a psychological phenomenon. Indeed, the way the word is generally used means that it would be better not used at all – at least in scientific discourse.

# Chapter 6

Here are some examples of behavioural problems that could be addressed in this way:

- smoking
- unhealthy eating habits
- excessive drinking
- untidiness
- teeth cleaning
- contributions to house cleaning
- gardening.

Remember, you want to know why they do it, or do not do it, before proposing an intervention. This means that there was a 'catch' in the proposed protocol in the question. You will not be fully able to 'give an indication of what intervention might be appropriate' until the results of a behavioural assessment are available. Otherwise, you will be falling into the trap of assuming that you know what the critical reinforcement contingency maintaining the behaviour is, prior to doing an assessment.

# Author Index

Hutchinson, R. R. 88

Iwata, B. A. 35, 149, 150, 176, 181, 174

Kalish, H. I. 95
Kalsher, M. J. 35
Kamin, L.J. 65
Keir, R. 109
Kim, E.-M. 133
Koelling, R. A. 66
Kuskowski, M. A. 134

Lancioni, G. 152
Lea, S. E. G. 191
Lei, J. L. 137
Lerman, D. C. 35
Leslie, J. C. 60, 78, 121, 131, 145
Lovaas, O. I. 181
Loveland, D. H. 191
Lowe, C. F. 103

Maggio, J. E. 134
Mantyh, P. W. 134
Maricq, A. V. 131
Mazaleski, J. L. 35, 174
McCosh, K. C. 35
McAuley, F. 131
McGee, J. J. 181
Menolascino, F. J. 181
Menousek, P. E. 181
Mineka, S. 109
Moore, F. 172, 173
Morgan, C. L. 187
Morris, R. 135

Neisworth, J. T. 172, 173
NIH 177, 178
Northup, J. 152
Nilsen, S. 134

O'Hare, E. 133, 134
O'Kane, N. 152
O'Reilly, M. F. 145, 152

Pace, G. M. 35
Pavlov, I. P. 10, 17, 21, 42, 43, 44, 45,
    61, 66, 85, 90, 97
Pennypacker, H. S. 219
Peterson, R. 110

Premack, D. 59

Rawlins, J. N. P. 126
Repp, A. C. 163
Rescorla, R. A. 67
Richardson, L. 133
Richman, G. S. 35
Risley, T. R. 199, 200, 201
Robertson, I. H. 137
Roche, B. 195
Rodgers, T. A. 35
Rosenzweig, M. R. 137

Sasso, G. 152
Schneiderman, N. 90
Seligman, M. E. P. 54
Shephard R. A. 133, 134
Sherman, J. 110
Shore, B. A. 35
Sidman, M. 102, 103, 153, 202
Sinden, J. 126
Skinner, B. F. 14, 21, 22, 23, 24, 25, 27,
    32–33, 35, 38, 46, 47, 48, 49, 54,
    56, 81, 121, 196, 202, 205, 206

Slifer, K. J. 35
Smith, R. G. 35, 174
Steege, M. 152
Sturmey, P. 149

Thorndike, E. L. 18, 19, 21, 22, 37, 59
Timberlake, W. 60

van Dellen, A. 138
Van Houten, R. 181
Vollmer, T. R. 35, 174

Wacker, D. 152
Wang, S. L. 137
Watson, J. B. 14, 20, 21, 37, 206
Weldon, D. T. 134
Williams, J. H. 126, 129
Willis, K. D. 35

Yang, F. S. 134
Younkin, S. 134
York, D. 138

Zarcone, J. R. 35, 174

# Subject Index